EDUCATION AND THE STATE

EDUCATION
AND THE
STATE

edited by JOHN F. HUGHES

AMERICAN COUNCIL ON EDUCATION · *Washington, D.C.*

© 1975 by American Council on Education
One Dupont Circle, Washington, D.C. 20036

379.73
Am35e

Library of Congress Cataloging in Publication Data
American Council on Education.
  Education and the state.
  Papers presented at the 56th annual meeting of the American Council on Education, held in the fall of 1973.
  Includes bibliographical references.
  1. Education and state—United States—Congresses.
I. Hughes, John F., ed. II. Title.
LC89.A77   1975   379   74-34083
ISBN 0-8268-1259-1

PRINTED IN THE UNITED STATES OF AMERICA

Contributors

STEPHEN K. BAILEY, Vice-President, American Council on Education
ELIAS BLAKE, JR., President, Institute for Services to Education
LAURA BORNHOLDT, Program Executive, Lilly Endowment
HOWARD R. BOWEN, Chancellor, Claremont Colleges
ERNEST BOYER, Chancellor, State University of New York
ALLAN M. CARTTER, Professor in Residence, University of California, Los Angeles
EARL F. CHEIT, Program Officer in Charge, Division of Education and Research, The Ford Foundation
JOSEPH P. COSAND, Professor of Education, and Director, Center for the Study of Higher Education, University of Michigan
HAROLD L. ENARSON, President, Ohio State University
DAVID FROHNMAYER, Associate Professor of Law and Special Assistant to the President, University of Oregon
DEXTER L. HANLEY, S.J., President, University of Scranton
ROBERT W. HARTMAN, Senior Fellow, Economic Studies, The Brookings Institution
THEODORE M. HESBURGH, C.S.C., President, University of Notre Dame
ANITA HUGHES, Chairman, Human Ecological Services and Systems, Federal City College
BENNETT KATZ, Senator, State of Maine
CARL KAYSEN, Director, The Institute for Advanced Study
JAMES F. KELLY, Vice-Chancellor, State University of New York
CLARK KERR, Chairman, Carnegie Commission on Higher Education
RUBY G. MARTIN, Counsel, Committee on the District of Columbia, U.S. House of Representatives
S. V. MARTORANA, Professor of Higher Education and Research Associate, Center for Study of Higher Education, Pennsylvania State University
PETER MASIKO, JR., President, Miami-Dade Community College
ROBERT B. MAUTZ, Chancellor, State University of Florida
RICHARD M. MILLARD, Director, Higher Education Services, Education Commission of the States
STEVEN MULLER, President, Johns Hopkins University

JAMES A. PERKINS, Chairman, International Council for Educational Development

CYRENA N. PONDROM, Professor of English and Assistant Chancellor, University of Wisconsin—Madison

PAUL C. REINERT, S.J., President, Saint Louis University

VIRGINIA B. SMITH, Director, Fund for the Improvement of Postsecondary Education, U.S. Department of Health, Education, and Welfare

VERNE E. STADTMAN, Associate Director and Editor, Carnegie Commission on Higher Education

DAVID E. SWEET, President, Minnesota Metropolitan State College

KENNETH S. TOLLETT, Distinguished Professor of Higher Education, Howard University

WILLIAM VAN ALSTYNE, Professor, Duke University School of Law

JOHN VASCONCELLOS, Assemblyman, State of California

CASPAR WEINBERGER, Secretary, U.S. Department of Health, Education, and Welfare

CHARLES Z. WILSON, Vice-Chancellor for Academic Programs, University of California, Los Angeles

Contents

xi   Foreword, by Roger W. Heyns

xiii   Preface

1   Education and the State
Stephen K. Bailey

EDUCATION GOALS AND THEIR FINANCING

15   Setting National Goals for Higher Education: What Is College For?
Carl Kaysen

28   Setting National Goals and Objectives: Postsecondary Education
Joseph P. Cosand

    COMMENTARIES

40   National Goals in an Untidy World
Laura Bornholdt

44   Resources for Setting State Goals
Bennett Katz

48   A National Education Allowance
Steven Muller

51   The Future Financing of Postsecondary Education
Allan M. Cartter

    COMMENTARIES

70   Academic Freedom and the Financing of Higher Education
Howard R. Bowen

74   Some Doubtful Assumptions Examined
Harold L. Enarson

77   On Closer Examination
Robert W. Hartman

86   The Federal Stimulus in Postsecondary Education
Caspar W. Weinberger

Equalizing Educational Justice

95 Governmental Strategies for Educational Reform and Innovation
Verne A. Stadtman

COMMENTARIES

113   Procedural Reform: A Strategy
John Vasconcellos

116   Equity through Change
Elias Blake, Jr.

120 The City and the Campus
Virginia B. Smith

COMMENTARIES

133   The City as Campus
David E. Sweet

137   The Dynamics of a Metropolitan Community College
Peter Masiko, Jr.

140   City and Campus: Scrutinizing the Alternatives
Charles Z. Wilson

Management and Governance in Higher Education

147 The Management Systems Challenge: How to be Academic Though Systematic
Earl F. Cheit

COMMENTARIES

173   A Proper Role for Management Systems
Robert B. Mautz

176   The Challenge to Academic Managers
Paul C. Reinert, S.J.

179   Management Systems: An Aid, Not an Answer
James F. Kelly

184 Coordinating Federal, State, and Institutional Decisions
James A. Perkins

COMMENTARIES

197   New Imperatives in Institutional Decision Making
Ernest Boyer

200   Decisions *Will* Be Made
S. V. Martorana

204   Coordination, a Necessity
Richard M. Millard

EDUCATIONAL REFORM AND INNOVATION

211 The Faculty and the Government
Kenneth S. Tollett

COMMENTARIES

232 Affirmative Action for Excellence
Cyrena N. Pondrom

238 Effects of Collective Bargaining Laws on Institutional Processes
Dexter L. Hanley, S.J.

242 The Hazards of Legal Perspectives
William W. Van Alstyne

246 Legislating Attitudes
Theodore M. Hesburgh, C.S.C.

COMMENTARIES

252 Legislating Attitudes: A Response
David B. Frohnmayer

259 The Social Influence of Legislative Acts
Ruby G. Martin

262 The Time Is Now for Women's Equity
Anita Hughes

267 The Moods of Academia
Clark Kerr

Foreword

IN THE FALL OF 1973, the American Council on Education focused its Fifty-sixth Annual Meeting on the public policy issue confronting postsecondary education. Clearly recognizing that public policies have moved inexorably toward assuring greater equality of opportunity for all citizens to benefit from continuing education, the Council set as its theme for the meeting "Education and the State." Indeed, the need for a national forum to discuss issues concerning the content and thrust of public policy had already been highlighted by the United States Congress in its enactment of the Education Amendments of 1972, which redefined the federal role in supporting postsecondary education.

While public policy issues affecting education have been a continuing topic of debate and discussion over the decades of our national existence, too often these discussions have been fragmentary and groups of participants isolated from one another. Historically, educators and legislators have been living in separate worlds, despite their common pursuit of goals aimed at improving education beyond the high school. Public administrators, on their part, have often been given legislative mandates for execution without the advantage of full public discussion of alternatives and priorities. Educators, on their part, have often declined to take part in what they regard as the nitty-gritty of the political arena. A forum for public debate of main intellectual and political issues has been lacking. The result is a lack of understanding rather than a meeting of minds and a merging of efforts toward common goals of constructive legislation.

The American Council believes that the discussion and papers presented at the Fifty-sixth Annual Meeting represented a major step in the direction of providing an active forum for educators, legislators, and administrators to work together in advancing the cause of education.

The meeting was planned and organized by John F. Hughes. The Council is indebted to him for conceptualizing and directing its execution, and to Helen Gioia, administrative secretary for the meeting.

ROGER W. HEYNS, *President*
American Council on Education

Preface

BY THE BREADTH OF ITS THEME, "Education and the State," the Fifty-sixth Annual Meeting endeavored to cover a wide range of public policy issues. Just the task of selecting eleven of the most prominent issues was in itself a test of priority setting. Evidently the test was passed, judging by the intensity of interest and the high quality of the contributions at the eleven panel sessions. This impression was borne out by overall comments and corridor discussions. And if everything else at the meeting had gone sour, the address by Art Buchwald at the final general session would have more than compensated for the failure. Fortunately, Art merely iced the cake with a brilliant performance on the evolution of the Watergate scandals.

Among the principal speakers was Stephen K. Bailey, who gave a keynote speech which echoed the theme of the meeting, stressing the role of academe in the realm of public interest. Clark Kerr and Caspar Weinberger, as well as Art Buchwald already noted, made significant contributions to the general sessions with remarks which are included in this volume.

An address by the Honorable Walter F. Mondale made more memorable a dinner given by the Council to the members of the Carnegie Commission on Higher Education, whose work provided much of the substance for the panel discussion.

The papers were edited by Olive Mills of the Council staff, whose skill and understanding were immeasurably helpful in organizing this book as well as in polishing the manuscript.

JOHN F. HUGHES

Education and the State

STEPHEN K. BAILEY

THE UNDERLYING THEME of the Council's 1973 Annual Meeting is a persistent human paradox: the simultaneous need for structure and for antistructure, for dependence and for autonomy, for involvement and for privacy, for community and for identity. Today, as we perceive this elemental paradox in the tensions between the academy and the state, it is useful to keep in mind its generic quality. For at heart we are dealing, I submit, with a dilemma we cannot rationally wish to resolve. The public interest would not, in my estimation, be served if the academy were to enjoy an untroubled immunity. Nor could the public interest be served by the academy's being subjected to an intimate surveillance. Whatever our current discomforts because of a sense that the state is crowding us a bit, the underlying tension is benign. Like most paradoxes, this one is a great humbler. It chastens intellectual arrogance. It induces bargains and compromises and makes politicians and brokers of us all. And it reminds us of the ultimate paradox of freedom: the absolute belief that only tentative beliefs may safely be permitted.

All this simply says that the precise border between the state and the academy is, and must be kept, fuzzy. For if a precise delineation is sought, I think that the state has more than the academy has of what it takes to draw the line. Citizens of this century need no reminder that soldiers and officials can grab and hold territory more effectively than scholars—at least in a very long short-run.

In the stunning Sakharov Dialogue reprinted in part in the *New York Times* in late August 1973, First Deputy Prosecutor General Malyarov says to the physicist Sakharov, "We assumed that you would express your opinions as a Soviet citizen about certain shortcomings and errors, as you see them, without attacking the Soviet social and political system as such... [Your attacks] cannot be overlooked by the Prosecutor's Office, which is charged with enforcing the law and protecting the interests of society." Throughout the dialogue, the prosecutor keeps repeating this theme. "Any state," he reiterates, "has a right to defend itself." The incident that really troubled the prosecutor was a Sakharov interview on Swedish radio. "In that interview," Malyarov bitterly complains, "you denounced the Soviet system in our country, calling it a system of maximum non-freedom, a system that is undemocratic, closed, deprived of economic initiative, and falling to pieces."

Sakharov responds very simply, "I did not say 'falling to pieces.'"[1]

And it is well that he did not. For it is not. Many of us are old enough to remember the claims made by some Western intellectuals a generation ago that tyranny was an interim necessity—a prelude to the "withering away of the state." Since then we have learned painfully that states do not wither. They metastasize, they elongate, they crystallize, they harden, they become transmogrified by conquest and by revolution, but they do not wither. Soviet leadership is more humane today; the massive bloodletting seems to have stopped, although external deviousness seems to continue. Three years of jail has replaced the firing squad. But the Soviet oligarchy still draws a hard line which gives a frangible license for Soviet intellectuals to discuss, promulgate, and publish anything that is not deemed threatening to those in power.

There is still a distance, I believe, between the Soviet polity and ours. It would be fatuous to reduce the tragic and saddening events of recent months in this country to White House pique at acts of lèse majesté. To paraphrase Herbert Agar, to blame Watergate on presidential paranoia would be to rewrite Hamlet and make the Prince die in the last act by slipping on a banana peel.[2] The root causes of Watergate are complex and diffuse. But the proximate causes were surely related to an inconsolable political itch—an itch produced by the hair shirt of institutionalized self-criticism: an opposition party, a free press, morally provoked clergy, and protected academics.

Has the state no right to defend itself? States surely do have such a right. The paradox of democracy is that if, in exercising that right, the guardians of the state mute the state's critics, they have simultaneously destroyed the democratic state itself. Miscreants in the current administration threatened the underlying civility and the sacred immunities of our political traditions. It is for that reason the state has had to chastise them. If this view seems too Hegelian, the chastisement may be attributed to the Congress, the courts, the press, and Gallup—I am not concerned with a metaphysical point. I am suggesting that the ultimate

1. *New York Times*, Aug. 29, 1973, p. 33.
2. "The Truth Is Good News," *Harper's Magazine*, May 1942, p. 561.

protectors of the academy are those instruments and consciences of the polity—of the state as democratic system—that stop heavily mandated power from pressing its advantage. Relationships between rulers and their critics are thereby kept fuzzy, flexible, and in part ineffable. There is fostered in the citizenry just that degree of political irreverence needed to ensure a fragile tenure for those exercising even transient authority.

In short, viewed from one perspective, the state is the adversary of the academy—and vice versa. Viewed from a more elevated perspective, the academy is for the state a benign antibody, and the state is the academy's legitimator, benefactor, and protector. Both perspectives are valid. May they remain in tension.

THE STATE AS BENEFACTOR: SOME FACETS

The academy is frequently less than gracious in admitting its dependence on the state. But that dependence is both real and essential. Some of you may remember Thomas Carlyle's only partly fanciful version of the origin of universities. He pointed out that in a world without books, when a man had something he wished to communicate, he could do so only by gathering the learners around him. As many as thirty thousand went to hear Abelard. Then, of course, other would-be teachers figured that Abelard's intellectual "rock festival" was a ready-made audience, so they went where Abelard was. After that bit of historical conjecture, Carlyle continues: "It only needed now that the king took notice of this new phenomenon; combined or agglomerated the various schools into one school; gave it edifices, privileges, and encouragements; and named it *Universitas,* or school of all sciences."[3]

County councils are not kings, to be sure, but what is it that they and their state authorities give a local community college but "edifices, privileges, and encouragement"? What is Harvard's tax-exempt status but a "privilege and encouragement" conferred by King Demos?

Recently we on the American Council staff have been creating a new Policy Analysis Service and preparing a policy agenda for FY '75. Part of my learning has been the scope and essentiality of the "edifices, privileges, and encouragements" currently made available to institutions of postsecondary education by the national government and all other public authorities in our federal system. The protections and dispensations range all the way from tax exemptions and direct appropriations to

---

3. *On Heroes, Hero-Worship and the Heroic in History,* Lecture 5 (1841).

student loans, risk guarantees, contract enforcement, campus security, fair personnel practices, support for basic and applied research—where does one begin or end? And all this is in addition to the state's underlying acts of legitimation through chartering and licensing. It took me some time as a regent in New York to understand what is really a fairly simple proposition. The license to do academic business enjoyed by the State University of New York is granted by the University of the State of New York—that emanating ectoplasm of the Board of Regents, that pale reminder of the once majestic royal prerogative.

To pretend that education is a coordinate power, like the church in medieval church-state relations when the Pope had troops in this world as well as in the next, is to misinterpret contemporary as well as historical reality. The fact is that the academy exists and prospers by public sufferance. In a fundamental sense, this has always been true. Those in the academic community have reason to recognize this truth today with considerable poignancy. The actual amounts, proportions, and concomitant guidelines of direct public support have grown astonishingly in the past two decades. The figures alone are familiar: Public spending for higher education two decades ago was $2 billion; today it is $16 billion. In 1953, almost half of all college students were attending private institutions; today that function has dropped to one-quarter. The sense of public suzerainty is today infinitely greater than it was. We once could relish as a part of academic folklore the story of President Taft on his way to a state visit at Harvard. A reporter asked A. Lawrence Lowell's secretary, in the Harvard Yard, when the President would arrive. The secretary replied, "We're not quite sure; he's in Boston meeting Mr. Taft."

Harlan Cleveland has recently identified what he calls "Seven Everyday Collisions in American Higher Education."[4] At least six of these collisions directly involve relations with the state, and the seventh does so indirectly. As I read his paper, I reflected on the academic world enjoyed by my late uncle, Ernest Hatch Wilkins, when he was president of Oberlin in the 1930s—and I use the word *enjoyed* advisedly. Here was a lovely, land-locked Athens, presided over by a distinguished specialist in Dante, protected by a deep spiritual moat that, as I remember it, began a few miles east of Elyria and extended halfway to the then marginally desolate fiefdom of Toledo.

"Affirmative action?" Uncle Ernest never heard of it.

4. Unpublished paper presented at the 1973 meeting of the Asian–U.S. Educators Conference, Chiengmai, Thailand, July 15–20, 1973.

"Accountability?" Of course! To the trustees on matters profane; to God on matters sacred.

"Open enrollment?" Most certainly! For Jefferson's "natural aristocracy."

"Equal opportunity?" Remember Oberlin's distinguished place in the history of American coeducation, and its early liberalism in admitting a few highly qualified sons and daughters of former slaves?

"Disruption?" Panty raids are unseemly and really cannot be countenanced.

"Fiscal crisis?" Fortunately, the leadership of the aluminum industry is composed of education statesmen.

How distant that world really is. Even the "land-grants," with a few unhappy exceptions, seemed then to buy an enormous amount of support and autonomy with no greater risk to man's eternal soul than the surreptitious dispensing of a few choice seats on the fifty-yard line.

THE ACADEMY IN A POLITICAL WORLD

Today, we scarcely know who we are, let alone who's in charge. We no longer are "higher," we are simply—or perhaps, less grandly—postsecondary. The more expensive we become, the more suspicious our protectors and providers become about the value of our humanistic pretensions. Even some of our best friends in Congress doubt that we should receive general federal subsidies just to keep us going. The administration has made it perfectly clear that graduate research and training in the pure and applied sciences are not high national priorities, and has thus put our national science enterprise, in the words of Daniel S. Greenberg, in a position "not unlike that of a baseball team with a superb line-up of starters, a sparsely filled bench, and a decaying farm system."[5] The "1202 Commissions" will presumably be benign, but there is concern that they might impose another (and this time federally mandated) meddlesome layer in the already complex machinery of state planning and control. Title VI funds for foreign language and area studies are rescued annually, like Pauline hanging from the edge of the cliff. NLRB zigzags its way through the murk of collective bargaining rules, most of which were written with never a thought to college and university types.

To top it all off, we exist in this ambiguous and dangerous jungle doubting that we are armed with the skills and attitudes appropriate to

---

5. "Science and Richard Nixon," *New York Times Magazine*, June 17, 1973, p. 24.

survival. Whether we believe it to be fair or just, we have a reputation—at least in some important quarters in the nation's capital—for being exclusive, self-indulgent, patronizing, and sloppy. In an increasingly egalitarian world, our own generally accepted, if slightly droll, status displacements (the pecking order from Harvard to Cornell to Syracuse to Oswego State to Onondaga Community College to Ajax Business School) are no longer amusing. Eight thousand tax-paying proprietary schools want to know why training a historian for unemployment at the taxpayers' expense is better than training an accountant for useful employment at the learner's expense. And parents and legislators are listening for our answer or at least for an intelligible and defensible rephrasing of the question.

Rephrasings and answers, of course, there are. Surely we need both historians and accountants. The underlying reality is that if the academy is dependent on the larger society, the larger society—most especially the state—is as dependent on the academy as it is on institutions that concentrate on precise skill training. It is the academy that educates for the essential professions and for the preservation and extension of the arts and sciences. Furthermore, although it is true that there are unemployed or underemployed historians, it is also true that on occasion the discipline of history exercises an enormous force on events. If we can successfully negotiate the raging white water of the present Middle East conflict, we as a nation may be close to a long and stable peace partly because of Professor Kissinger's acute understanding of Prince Metternich and the Congress of Vienna. The academy keeps the minutes of previous meetings and frets over their meaning. This process gives society whatever sense of continuity and community it has. Humans are basically small-town animals. When our effective environment transcends the ward and the hamlet and becomes urban, continental, and global, it is the academy that describes and transmits the historical symbols that permit us to identify with strangers and to form a mega-polity. TV, radio, and the press help; but essentially their reporters and pundits repair for insight to what Lord Keynes called "some academic scribblers of a few years back."

If much of our social science at the moment seems to occupy an analytic dead-air space between an informing public philosophy on the one hand and practical management hints on the other, there are signs that a new generation of scholars is restive with the aridity and scientific scholasticism of the recent past. The federal government, through applied-research programs like RANN (Research Applied to National Needs) of NSF and the mission-oriented programs of the National Institute of Education, is nudging the academic world that way. And where discipline-bound universities find it difficult to respond adequately, the knowledge industry conjures "profits" and "nonprofits" that fuse the products of disciplinary specialization into a useful amalgam. Even so, where does the knowledge industry get its analytic and synthetic brain power if not from the academy—perhaps especially from the stunning irrelevancies of pure research? Norbert Wiener was a professor at MIT, but the control systems of the mind-blowing apparatus of NASA were largely his shadow.

Looking ahead, it is preposterous to assume that this nation alone or in concert with other nations will solve such recalcitrant problems of the political economy as inflation, the gut-rending trade-offs of the energy and environmental crises, international money, international development, and the benign exploitation of ocean resources, without superbly educated human beings. Technicians and practical geniuses are needed in abundance. But there is also a need for apostles of new paradigms, preachers of new prophecies. A bright geneticist stationed in one of the various grain institutes of philanthropy can help to fashion a green revolution in Asia. But it takes a Clifford Wharton to suggest that the problems caused by the green revolution may be more complex and more attenuated than the problems that stimulated it. In the next few years and decades, whether the human race is searching for ways to tame the Promethean fire of fusion, produce an antiaphrodisiacal protean additive, wrestle with the ethics of cloning, or illuminate the chemical base of mental illness, the academy is the root producer of requisite talent. Whatever caricatures are sketched by our detractors (sometimes, alas, by ourselves), the academy remains very nearly the state's most precious resource. We in ACE must help our political leaders to understand this essential truth. Postsecondary education has many friends in the nation's capital and in the various state capitals—in the legislatures, in executive departments, in the judiciary, in the media. The simple fact is that educators have not been adequately helpful to those who are trying to be helpful to them.

It is not that academicians lack political skills. Woodrow Wilson once commented to some Democratic cronies in the State House in Trenton, after listening to some backroom political plotting, "You guys are amateurs!"

We in the academy somehow lack that combination of humility and self-assurance that commends us to those with whom we must now do political business. We work inadequately at explaining ourselves. In spite of the prodigious efforts of the Carnegie Commission, our ignorance about ourselves is an abyss. Our data base is shockingly inadequate. Responses to responsible political questions tend to emerge too late and in too pretentious and inutile a form; and we are contemptuous of irresponsible political questions at considerable peril to ourselves. ACE is trying to improve its capacity at the interface between public and educational policy through new structures and new staff; but improvement will take time, and improvement will take time and understanding and help from other associations and from our member institutions. Without their prompt and considered response to our questions, we cannot be of much help to them.

We in postsecondary education are not well organized to do political battle effectively, whether in Washington, or at the state level, or on individual campuses. We are hampered by all kinds of misconceptions about the assumed constraints of our tax exemptions. Lobby laws written for the amusement of oil companies tend to unnerve us or to make us guilt-ridden. Instead of proceeding on the assumption that, in any head-on clash, the First Amendment would prevail over Section 501(c)(3) of the Internal Revenue Code, we duck and weave. Some of us would be happier if all educational associations took the bifurcated route of the National Education Association, or shifted to 501(c)(6); or, better still, if Section 501(c)(3) were rewritten in such a way as to permit the beneficiaries of tax-exempt foundations to petition legislators unashamedly. But until those or other desirable changes take place, many of us will look to the "right of petition" clause of the First Amendment as our shield and defender.

POSTSECONDARY EDUCATION: SOME PRACTICALITIES

If we are to survive in any meaningful sense in the cluttered political world that surrounds us, there are certain things we must do.

First, we must learn to extend our understanding and sense of interdependence to the larger educative world of which we are a part: elementary, secondary, postsecondary; public and private; traditional and nontraditional. Our unloveliest collective attribute, I think, is our tendency to look down our noses at each other and at other types and levels of education. Our attitudes toward both proprietary schools and union apprenticeships have been particularly supercilious—and we have paid a political price for our preciousness. I commend to you the remark of E. B. White that he would "rather watch a really gifted plumber than listen to a bad poet"; that he would "rather watch someone build a good boat than attend the launching of a poorly constructed play."[6] In short, we need the understanding and support of our sister educators, just as they need ours.

Second, we must learn to appreciate the functions and the contributions of politicians, to emulate their most persuasive arts, and to be both critical of, and charitable about, their failings. We have been generous in our criticisms of President Nixon. Have we been equally generous in our praise for his efforts to ensure world peace and for his unstinting support of the National Endowment for the Humanities? Have we confessed our own sins? Politicians grow understandably angry, and then faintly weary, when they hear strident campus squatters criticize politicians for playing loose with the law or for confusing ends and means. Those of us who knew and loved Courtney Smith can never totally reconcile ourselves to the student and faculty bullying that literally broke the heart of that delicately gentle man of reason. In the long haul, our only lasting claim to public support is that colleges and universities are homes for reasonable beings who find their delights and settle their disputes through discourse. Whatever the provocations (and they were many), whatever the positive distillates (there were some), we lost our soul a bit in the 1960s. Part of our present anguish is the pain of enforced penance.

Third, we must develop the capacity to inform ourselves and others about ourselves; and we must learn to defend ourselves in concert with allies. We must put our own houses in administrative order and solve, to the public's satisfaction as well as our own, our internal problems of governance. We must collect timely and pertinent information about the impact of public policies and regulations, including information about the practical limits and spiritual costs of certain kinds of accountability systems. We must learn to work comfortably with others who find us faintly fey: the working press, friendly officials, and preoccupied legislators.

Finally, and most difficult of all, we must learn to get our own heads on straight: know what to press for, know what to defend, know what we ourselves value. ACE and its sister associations cannot do this

---

6. *New York Times*, July 11, 1969, p. 43.

alone. The questions of essential purpose must be sweated out on each campus, in each school. We here in Washington hope we can help identify issues and catalyze a consensus for resolving them. But the task of defining what we are seeking to accomplish on behalf of education is basically a responsibility of the institutions.

I can only share with you a personal hope: that in trying to be true to ourselves, through the variable gusts of these troubled years, we do not settle for other people's definitions of our function. We live at the sufferance of a political and highly utilitarian society. But we cannot afford to be simply the mirror image of that society, nor can that society afford to let us be. Whatever catering we must do to the career utilities of the market and to the egos of the hustings, we have a central task to perform that comes close to our ultimate reason for being.

Preposterous as it sounds in the present manpower-oriented, cost-benefit context, we must affirm that it makes a difference that Virgil took Dante on a guided tour; that Gilgamesh feared death; that Job found his way through undeserved pain; that Michelangelo created the Creator; that Beethoven composed his Ninth Symphony; that Tycho Brahe counted stars; that Buddha made friends with snails; that Langston Hughes noticed raisins in the sun and that Lorraine Hansberry noticed Langston Hughes; that Kant found a categorical imperative; that Maslow observed promise in the growing-tips of human personality; that the Grand Inquisitor chastised Jesus; that Einstein pondered arcs; that William Butler Yeats found Innisfreedom. For these are the glories and the extensions of our common humanity.

It is argued that such things make no difference—that the Mona Lisa is no better than the Marilyn Monroe calendar. If God is dead, then anything goes. But what if He is not dead? What if He is only seriously indisposed? And what if our quintessential task is to bring Him back to health, not necessarily as a metaphysical wraith or as a deistic watchmaker, but as the symbol (and perhaps the reality) of the struggle of persons for self-conquest, for the equities of justice and universal community, for the delights and wonders of exploration and creative diversity, for the purity of truth, and in both an ecological and spiritual sense, for what Steinbeck called "a sense of oneness with the whole shebang"?

Surely it is here that the academy and the democratic state find an essential identity of purpose. Ultimately, we are about the same job: the civilizing and refining of human attitudes and behaviors—most especially our own, for the light of example blinds all rhetoric. Sometimes the task seems hopeless. We learn to admire Confucius; but we still bark at strangers and snarl at our children. We prate equality and tolerance, and denigrate the useful work of a neighboring community college or of a doddering but patient Mr. Chips down the hall. The work of civilizing, hardly begun, is never ending, for it has to be repeated each generation. A part of the patiently acquired wisdom is indiscriminately ridiculed by each new generation, or like the water lily simply closes up with the coming of the evening. As we look around, we know that without an adequate number of centers of periodic synthesis (which we do not have), we cannot prune back our intellectual fecundity. As a result, as the inheritance proliferates, generational transfer becomes at best attenuated and at worst strangulating.

But with all of these hurdles (no one said it would be easy), the task must continue. Our capacity to continue will depend upon some key understandings:

- Our understanding that the state is our legitimator, benefactor, and protector;
- The state's understanding that the academy is important to the polity, the economy, the culture, in short, to the public interest, as transmitter and producer of knowledge, as preparer for work and leisure, as social critic;
- Our mutual understanding that the tough problems ahead, for the nation and for the world, cannot be solved without superbly educated minds;
- Our own understanding that we need to improve our policy-analysis skills, our data base, and our capacity to make political friends if we are to help those who wish to help us;
- Our renewed understanding that our most essential task is to increase the society's capacity for civility and for civilization.

What civility and civilization mean was stated with great eloquence some years ago by one of America's towering intellectual figures, the late Carl Becker of Cornell:

> To have faith in the dignity and worth of the individual . . . as an end in himself; to believe that it is better to be governed by persuasion than by coercion; to believe that fraternal goodwill is more worthy than a selfish and contentious spirit; to believe that in the long run all values are inseparable from the love of truth and the disinterested search for it; to believe that knowledge and the power it confers should be used to

promote the welfare and happiness of all [persons] rather than to serve the interests of those individuals and classes whom fortune and intelligence endow with temporary advantage—these are the values which are affirmed by the traditional democratic ideology. . . . They are the values which since the time of Buddha and Confucius, Solomon and Zoroaster, Plato and Aristotle, Socrates and Jesus, men have commonly employed to measure the advance or decline of civilization, the values they have celebrated in the saints and sages whom they have agreed to canonize. They are the values that readily lend themselves to rational justification, yet need no justification.[7]

If we can recapture this sense of values and this sense of mission, all else, in a political sense, will be added unto us. If so, then it is possible that in some future time a few admirers will look with gratitude at what endures of our collective endeavors and say, as Matthew Arnold said more than a century ago about Oxford,

What is our puny warfare against the Philistines compared with the warfare which this queen of romance has been waging against them for centuries, and will wage after we are gone?[8]

7. *Freedom and Responsibility* (New York: Knopf, 1949), pp. xl–xli.
8. *Essays in Criticism,* 1st series (1865).

EDUCATION GOALS
AND THEIR FINANCING

Setting National Goals for Higher Education: What Is College For?

CARL KAYSEN

IN ADDRESSING THE QUESTION "What Is College For?", I look at higher education from a variety of perspectives, all of which, however, reveal the same conclusions. First, I was a member of the Carnegie Commission on Higher Education who has participated for six years in its review of the American higher educational enterprise. In this capacity, I shall summarize our conclusions about purposes. Second, and perhaps more fundamentally, I am an economist interested in research and in higher education who has tried to understand the social processes that shape their magnitude and character. Finally, like other academicians-turned-administrators, I have reflected on the enterprise I direct—the Institute for Advanced Study—and tried to interpret its experience in general terms. Since that institution is dedicated to the cultivation of science and learning at their purest and most unworldly levels (some would say in their most extreme and irrelevant forms), responsibility for relating it to the rest of the academy and to the world offers a continuing lesson on the values of learning vis-à-vis the other values and purposes of our society.

PLURALISM IN AMERICAN HIGHER EDUCATION

In *The Purposes and the Performance of Higher Education in the United States,* the commission presented its answers to the title question, What is college for?, by distinguishing five main purposes:

[1] The provision of opportunities for the intellectual, aesthetic, ethical, and skill development of individual students, and the provision of campus environments which can constructively assist students in their more general developmental growth
[2] The advancement of human capability in society at large
[3] The enlargement of educational justice for the postsecondary age group
[4] The transmission and advancement of learning and wisdom

[5] The critical evaluation of society—through individual thought and persuasion—for the sake of society's self-renewal[1]

The five purposes are those of the whole enterprise of higher education; individual institutions do not necessarily attempt to serve them all, and differ in the relative weight they give to those which they do serve. The first, fourth, and fifth purposes are concerned with education as such and particularly with undergraduate education. The second encompasses research, the dissemination of the fruits of research, including problem solving in behalf of other social instrumentalities, the training of highly skilled professionals to meet society's needs, as well as a perhaps less-clearly defined general enhancement of "the information, the understanding, and the cultural appreciation and opportunities of the public at large."[2] This mission corresponds partly to what is sometimes defined as "public service" by higher education. It is primarily the function of the universities, especially those which lead in research and graduate and professional training, and concerns other kinds of institutions much less. The third purpose—enlargement of educational justice—involves the whole of higher education, of course, but is instrumental, rather than substantive. Not even the strongest critics of our present educational enterprise contend that it does *nothing* but hand out credentials, and therefore the only useful question to be asked of it is the equity of the distribution.

Higher education's performance in respect to these purposes draws mixed grades from the Carnegie Commission: two A's; one B; one Incomplete, with hope for a satisfactory final performance; one C-minus with uncertain prospects for improvement. Performance in both the advancement of human capability in society at large and the transmission and advancement of learning and wisdom were rated as superior. The only changes the commission recommended concerned the funding needed to maintain superior performance. Performance in broadening access to higher education and adapting education to broader access is deficient, but improving, and with good prospects for further improvement. The recommendations address the means for realizing those prospects.

On the evaluative, or critical, function—defined as "performing the role of social critic or evaluator by individual faculty members and

1. Carnegie Commission on Higher Education, *The Purposes and the Performance of Higher Education in the United States: Approaching the Year 2000* (New York: McGraw-Hill, 1973), p. 1.
2. Ibid., p. 24.

students"[3] and seen as an indispensable contribution to society's capacity for renewal and growth—the commission viewed performance as at best uneven, and was not hopeful of improvement. The public in general and legislators and public officials in particular have long had a mixed record in understanding the need for such criticism and supporting the restraints on the behavior of administrators, trustees, and funding agencies that make critical appraisal possible. They have tended for the most part to view academic freedom as a special privilege given to the professoriate and, more lately, to students, to be "irresponsible," rather than as an institution with a vital social purpose. Inasmuch as officials and politicians are the immediate objects of much of the criticism, their attitude is hardly surprising. More recently, however, attacks from within the academy have been more threatening than those from without. To be tolerable to the larger society, freedom for social criticism and prescription must remain the privilege of the *individual* teacher and student (or the like-minded group), while academic institutions as such refrain from expressing views or acting politically. But the last half-dozen years have seen the growth of a demand on the part of substantial minorities of both faculty and students for institutional commitment and for expression of commitment by direct action as well as persuasion through speech and writing.[4] If such views persist and are translated into action even occasionally, the prospects for protecting the freedom to criticize from self-preservative reactions from both outside and within the academy are dim. The commission's recommendations are directed equally to the society at large and the academic community, speaking to both the internal and external dangers.

With respect to the first of the five purposes—the one that is most closely identifiable with traditional notions of "college education"—the commission found the performance of the system "generally adequate" but requiring improvement. In more detail, we say:

> In terms of providing opportunity for academic and technical competence, higher education . . . is generally adequate and sometimes superb. For meeting standards of academic conduct, it is generally adequate. For exploring cultural interests and enhancing cultural skills, it is improving but the adequacy of programs varies from campus to campus. And for

3. Ibid., p. 43.
4. Ibid., p. 48; table 4 shows data from the commission's survey of faculty and student opinion. From a fifth to a third of the faculty and a higher proportion of students believed that violence on and off the campus might be both justified and necessary to achieve "meaningful social change."

obtaining a good general understanding of society, it is often poor and may be deteriorating. We accept the developmental view of youth and the expectations of many students that the campus will be helpful to their total developmental growth, but we share with others an uncertainty as to how this continuing development can best be assured, and what role the campus should play in it.[5]

Crudely summarized, the grade sheet on college education reads: academic and technical training, good to excellent; sophistication and training in the arts, fair to good; general education for citizenship, poor; personal development, variable but often inadequate, needs improvement.

It is striking that these comments are almost the only ones in the commission's reports (as opposed to the studies it has sponsored and financed) that deal with the substance of education as opposed to its organization, governance, financing, distribution, and so on.[6] Further, remedies for the deficiencies enumerated are suggested only in the most general terms, whereas in areas of finance, governance, and the like we have made many highly specific recommendations. Indeed some critics of our work have made a similar observation the focus of their complaints. An article entitled "A Six Million Dollar Misunderstanding," by Donald McDonald, which appeared in the September/October 1973 issue of the *Center Magazine* of the Center for the Study of Democratic Institutions, is representative. According to its claims, the commission has failed to say anything of significance about the substance of higher education, and thus the commission's emphasis on pluralism, "any person, any study," is essentially an avoidance of responsibility, a tacit and unsupported acceptance of the educational status quo.

These observations are essentially correct. The commission members accepted the de facto pluralism of American higher education. Further, we may well have failed to articulate our acceptance sufficiently to justify it to others. I cannot agree, however, that in so doing we avoided our responsibilities, and that we have ratified the status quo out of some mixture of inattentiveness, ignorance, cowardice, and subservience to views expressed in the past by our chairman. Since we did not articulate a commission position on educational pluralism, I can speak only for myself in saying that the commission ratified or even endorsed it because we thought there was no other sensible and useful position for us

---

5. Ibid., pp. 1, 20–21.
6. The substance of the curriculum is examined in a series of essays prepared for the Carnegie Commission on Higher Education: Cary Kaysen, ed., *Content and Context: Essays on College Education* (New York: McGraw-Hill, 1973).

to take. Our task is well described in the title here addressed, "National Goals...," and the general theme: setting national goals in the context of the developing relationship between higher education and the state. We had thus to deal at every turn with the question, What will society pay for?, and to examine that question in the light of what society was currently paying for, and why. In higher education, the context was the great growth in enrollments both absolutely and relative to the cohorts of high school graduates. Much of the growth has been concentrated in institutions becoming newly important on the educational scene: publicly supported junior colleges, state colleges, and quasi-independent "branches" of the traditional state universities with a different range of activities from those of the parent centers. A large proportion of these students differed substantially in social background, educational attainments, and life plans from the typical students in the more traditional liberal arts colleges and universities, which continue to be thought of as embodying "higher education," both by many of their faculty members and by the public.

In 1968, when the commission started its work, 60 percent of all undergraduate enrollments were in these newer types of institutions, most of them publicly supported and controlled. Only 10 percent were in the great research universities, both public and private, and 8 percent were in liberal arts colleges, overwhelmingly private. Growth in the ensuing decade was expected to be much greater in the first than the latter two.[7] Further, we had to ask what students wanted and could be led to want, as well as what institutions could and would do. Ignoring these questions would have ensured that we talked only to ourselves; asking them seriously made our recognition and acceptance of educational pluralism the inevitable starting point of our work.

THE EVOLUTION OF "LIBERAL EDUCATION"

Much of the criticism of an easy pluralism originates from humanists on the faculties of the great universities and the older, more selective liberal arts colleges. Often their attitudes reflect some combination of guild interest and nostalgia for a golden age—whether of prescribed courses or genuine demand for liberal culture in the humanist tradition is less clear. Economists should be the last to sneer at guild interests;

---

7. See Carnegie Commission on Higher Education, *New Students and New Places: Policies for the Future Growth and Development of American Higher Education* (New York: McGraw-Hill, 1971), Appendixes A, B.

ideally we should affirm their vitality with as much vigor as we question their beneficence in any particular set of concrete circumstances. As for the nostalgia, we all share it to a degree. Who does not wish to believe that every "educated" man should have a nontrivial grasp of the various modes of knowing and of the variety of products which they yield? If traditional humanists are stubbornly—and properly—unwilling to yield to the sciences a monopoly on claims to valid knowledge and, in particular, to the social sciences' claim to valid knowledge of mankind, they usually refrain from asserting publicly that they alone represent what every educated man should know. Natural and social scientists are for the most part closer to the concerns of the everyday world, are less embattled, and perhaps for this reason are more willing to concede the claims that literary and artistic culture is indispensable to liberal education. Further, tradition persists in the academy and, even after a century, the "new" fields are still deferential to the classical and humanistic learning which dominated American higher education—such as it was—for the first two and a half centuries after the founding of Harvard College. Music, drama, dance, film, and the visual arts are barely beginning to reach academic respectability as disciplines to be practiced, as well as types of cultural activities to be studied historically.

The concept of liberal education described above—a serious involvement with the various kinds of intellectual experience represented by the humanities, the natural sciences, the social sciences, and more recently the (nonverbal) arts combined with some degree of deeper entry into one of them—is itself relatively new. It arose as the older classical and humanistic learning adapted to the evolving experimental sciences (as opposed to the older "natural philosophy") and, slightly later, to the emerging social sciences (as distinct from history and moral philosophy). These developments unfolded in the last quarter of the nineteenth century; the consequent changes in undergraduate curricula were largely achieved by the beginning of World War I and have persisted till well after World War II.[8]

The modified view of what constituted a liberal education succeeded a quite different curriculum, one which combined classical learning, mathematics, and Christian culture as its central elements. This

---

8. See Laurence R. Veysey, *The Emergence of the American University* (Chicago: University of Chicago Press, 1965), an excellent study, and his introductory essay, "Stability and Experiment in the American Undergraduate Curriculum," in Kaysen, *Content and Context*, pp. 1–63.

predecessor had a much longer history, especially in the English-speaking world. The dominance of the earlier tradition coincided with the rise of the university or college as the characteristic training institution for most of society's elites. In its earliest history, of course, the university was more clearly devoted to professional training, in theology, law, and medicine, but nostalgia has not typically reached back so far for its objects. But even after the rise of science, the break-up of Christian culture, and the decline of classical learning and its partial supersession by the study of "modern" literatures and history, especially English literature and European and American history, the central function of the college as the characteristic institution for training or at least socializing most of society's elites persisted.

THE PROFESSIONALIZATION OF SCIENCE AND LEARNING

The last three to four decades have seen two sets of profound changes, one in the academy's relation to society, the other within the academy itself. Both were initiated or crystallized by the events of World War II. Together, they call into question the viability of any shared notion of liberal education and, in particular, today's orthodox notion of breadth plus depth defined in terms of the three or four grand divisions of knowledge and calculated in units of courses.

I have already remarked the first of these changes: a college education is no longer the training of an elite. Somewhat more than half of an age cohort currently enters the process; between a quarter and a third achieves a degree. An elite-in-training acknowledges the authority of "official" values even when they personally do not participate in them. The same cannot be said for a half or a third of an age cohort in so diverse a society as ours. This difference is currently intensified by an unusually rapid period of cultural change, so that young people in general differ more sharply from their elders in fundamental matters of value than has been usual. Thus it is less and less likely that students want, or can be led to want, an education defined according to the traditional combination of the traditional divisions of knowledge served up in the traditional mode. So I interpret the cry for "relevance," as well as the level of enrollments in "professional" as opposed to "liberal" subjects, on which I shall comment below.

Also within the last three or four decades, the academic world itself changed from one in which the characteristic activity was the teaching of undergraduates and the representative faculty member was a teacher. He might or might not also have been a scholar or scientist contributing to the advancement of science and learning as well. If he was, research was in a sense incidental to his main activity and he was almost certain to be on the faculty of one of the dozen or fewer universities where most of the country's research activity took place. Among this small group, a still smaller number of scholars and scientists were men of international standing in their fields. Now, however, it is the scientist or scholar who is the representative faculty member. His characteristic activities are research and scholarship and the training of graduate students who will in turn carry on these tasks. The number of universities where serious work is done has multiplied at least fivefold, and a substantial proportion of it stands at the highest level in the international world of learning.

Statistically, of course, the picture has changed much less drastically: undergraduate teaching still bulks large in the total activity of the professoriate, and the proportion of the group that contributes significantly to the advance of science and scholarship remains small. But from the standpoint of academic values, the change is overwhelming; it has been strikingly portrayed by Jencks and Riesman in *The Academic Revolution*.[9] This representative professor typically has neither the time nor the inclination to teach those who are not on the way to becoming professionals of his subject, whether as committed graduate students or undergraduate majors from among whom the graduate students will be recruited. This tendency is stronger in the sciences and the "harder" social sciences, but it is certainly not absent in the humanities, especially in the form of unwillingness to deal with literature or history in translation. The more a man is successful and celebrated as a scholar, the less willing and able is his institution or even his department to press him to teach what he is not inclined to. At the same time specialties multiply, the materials and techniques to be mastered in each grow in volume and complexity, and the standards of specialist training advance accordingly. Thus a dilemma develops. It is precisely the teaching of nonspecialists which constitutes the core of liberal education in the orthodox view. Yet as long as the demand for specialist training exists to any degree, it is precisely the teaching of nonspecialists that will be given second place.

All this of course is most characteristically true of the great universities devoted to research and graduate training, and less so of other

---

9. Christopher Jencks and David Riesman, *The Academic Revolution: An Analysis of American Higher Education* (Garden City, N.Y.: Doubleday, 1968).

institutions with different clienteles. But the great influence of the universities as models, as centers of ideas, and especially as training grounds for the faculties of the major part of the whole academic enterprise means that the dominant attitudes and values of university faculties are widely diffused throughout the system.

The focus on specialized scholarship has also undermined the consensus on what constitutes a liberal education. The three (or four) division formula has at least as much vitality as a political accommodation among competing interests claiming the resources of the university as it has as an intellectually coherent formulation that commands wide assent. The shallowness of agreement is revealed by any faculty discussion on changing requirements. Indeed, I think it no exaggeration to say that if the faculty of any of our great universities had to determine anew the requirements for the B.A., its members could not now agree on what they should be.

PROFESSIONAL TRAINING AS LIBERAL LEARNING

So far, I have defended the Carnegie Commission's endorsement of pluralism, its implicit acceptance of the view that the content of college education will be determined by the millions of choices that students make among the tens of thousands of offerings that the thousands of different institutions provide, and rightly so. In sum, my defense is: For these students, these faculties, these institutions, these sources of support, how else?

I now go beyond the commission's wise abstinence and offer my own substantive notions of what a college education might be for. In so doing, I pause to acknowledge the deep tension between the analytical and predictive mode of dealing with social phenomena on the one hand, and the prescriptive mode on the other. Anyone trained in the social sciences is usually inhibited in prescription by his respect for the difficulty of understanding enough about any social system of even moderate complexity to provide a sufficient basis for useful prediction. Yet the same training teaches me that it is only by taking thought that man can add a cubit to his stature. Policy choices do matter, and the prophet too is part of the social process. But only that prophet whose insights into the nature of the process are accurate enough to reveal to him the bounds of the possible can hope to be heard and perhaps attended.

In this spirit, I respond to the title question, What is college for?, by answering: Primarily training in a profession. This should become the norm; it need not be the universal practice any more than liberal education is now. Such a goal appears to me to be more consistent with the constraints discussed above than the liberal education we presently proclaim.

First, and perhaps most important, some kind of professional training is likely to engage the serious efforts and interests of the majority of students in a way that the present conventional requirements for the B.A. do not. Economic and vocational motives are strong among those that lead students to college, especially so among the newer streams of students in the more rapidly growing institutions, but not only there. An examination of the distribution by fields of study of bachelors and other first degrees granted in recent years shows that slightly fewer than half were in the traditional fields of the arts and sciences: 18 percent in the arts and humanities, 20 percent in the social sciences, 10 percent in natural sciences and mathematics. Fields classifiable as falling within the "traditional" professions of architecture, engineering, law, medicine, theology, and arms account for 7 percent; those in such "newer" professions as business, education, agriculture and forestry, the newer health professions, home economics, library science, and a half a dozen smaller fields accounted for over 40 percent. The remainder were unclassifiable. If we recognize that at least some of those studying under the rubric of the arts and sciences were pursuing "professional" training in teaching, the academic profession, or in some of the scientific fields, we see that professional training in one or another sense engages as much as 50–60 percent of the present undergraduate body.[10]

Many of us who teach or have taught in both undergraduate and professional programs (including those graduate programs that train for the academic profession) have, I am sure, shared my own experience of finding that the same students who were operating far below their capacities in college became fully engaged (as in my own experience) in law school. College was for "fun"; law school was "serious." This experience was complemented, of course, by that of teaching the bright, committed undergraduate who, by the end of his sophomore year if not before, was headed for a Ph.D. and as a graduating senior surpassed all but a handful of graduate students ready for their preliminary examinations for the doctorate.

I have already argued that what is true of the students is even more

---

10. See U.S. Office of Education, *Digest of Educational Statistics, 1971*, tables 117, 120; *1972*, tables 114, 117 (Washington: Government Printing Office).

so of their teachers. The best teaching efforts are most likely to be evoked in just the context of serious commitment which I have been ascribing as more characteristic of professional than of liberal education.

Finally, such a definition of the primary purpose of a college education would do much to restore the connection between the culture of the academy and the culture of the larger community that it looks to for support, and increasingly through the processes of popular politics. Earlier, I assigned part of the responsibility for the present malaise of liberal education to the breaking of the connection between elite culture and mass higher education. But the matter goes deeper, for the values of liberal humanism and traditional "high culture" find increasingly little sustenance as the culture of any elite outside the academy. However, there is an elite culture in our society, one shared by the leaders of most of the institutions of business, government, the professions, and, for that matter, a good part of academe. It is the culture of rational problem solving by the application of organized knowledge. In some cases the organized knowledge is that of natural science, as in the practice of medicine or the design of aircraft, and the problem solving itself is a recognized field of applied science. In others—for example, law and many branches of public administration—the relevant knowledge cannot be said to correspond directly to any specific branch of science, but rather consists of a mixture of more or less applied social science and the traditional modes and procedures of the profession itself. But all embody the same spirit, which in turn is close to the spirit of experimental science itself. Is it unwarranted optimism to discern that, in the demand for more relevance, there is an appeal to this same spirit, among other things?

To suggest that professional education become the central purpose of college is not to say that it should be the only one and that nothing should be offered as learning for its own sake. To begin with, the pursuit of learning and science as ends in themselves has also been institutionalized as a profession, the academic profession. So the potential scholar and scientist would, like other potential professionals, pursue his chosen path from the first, as he now so frequently does. More important, the taste for knowledge and understanding for their own sakes is more likely to follow than to precede an appreciation of their instrumental power. Our present sequence, which puts liberal education before professional training, is more likely to be just wrong than right. A real engagement with the intellectual effort that professional training demands is surer to stimulate the taste for learning in those in whom it has not developed than is a set of prescribed courses taken to meet the requirements for a degree. In concrete terms, the exponents of pure science and scholarship, especially the less instrumentally applicable parts of it, would continue to have the opportunity to appeal to the nonspecialist, but without the protective effects of a quota of requirements. What survives as general education, that is, what the nonspecialist chooses to learn out of curiosity and interest in these circumstances, is likely to be of more permanent value.

Two objections to the scheme here proposed deserve anticipatory answers. First, American institutions of higher education are indeed diverse, and no one prescription is likely to fit them all, even a plan so broadly drawn as the present one. In particular, there are elite institutions—selective liberal arts colleges and the undergraduate divisions of the great universities—which continue to recruit enough students with both the intellectual training and the cultural background to give vitality to the orthodox picture of liberal education. My own narrow experience leads me to doubt this probability, but, in any event, there is no reason why such institutions cannot continue to offer the traditional program, though I would urge them to provide the professional option as well.

Second, and more important, if by any happy or unhappy accident this change in the fundamental orientation of college education were to take place, how would the pursuit of knowledge as an end in itself, which constitutes the inner core of the academic enterpirse, be sustained and supported? Where would the next generation of scholars and scientists be recruited? How would their labors be paid for? The broadest answer to both these questions is that European and most British universities have long operated on a model similar to the one here proposed, and have still maintained the academic enterprise. True, they have dealt with a much smaller fraction of the age cohort, who have undergone a more rigorous and usually a longer process of secondary education than ours. Further, they have maintained a much narrower view of what constitutes a "profession," and a comparatively large fraction of their students have specialized in the more traditional branches of humanistic learning. Nonetheless, the fact that the enterprise abroad can be vital under such circumstances makes at least a prima facie case for its viability here.

But more specific answers can be given. As far as recruitment goes, I venture the guess that the number of potential historians of literature and translators of Greek texts who will be lost because they were not required to take freshman World Literature will be counterbalanced by the number of budding lawyers who will be seduced from law to letters after they have learned as lawyers what it means to read a text with care. At least one American Nobel laureate in physics began his academic life as an electrical engineer; and John von Neumann, whose extraordinary academic career reached from Budapest via Berlin to Princeton and included work of genius in mathematics, theoretical physics, and half-a-dozen more applied fields, received his first degree in chemical engineering.

What I have called "the spirit of rational problem solving" is close to the spirit of science in some ways. In other ways perhaps more fundamental, it is quite different. It lacks the concern with the aesthetic elements of logical symmetry and generality of ideas at high levels of abstraction that characterize the deepest elements of science. Further, problem solving is outwardly oriented, whereas the more fundamental part of the scientific enterprise shares with humanistic and other kinds of learning an inward orientation toward knowledge and ideas in themselves. Would, then, a frank appeal to the common culture of rational problem solving as the basis for the support of higher education not endanger the deeper spirit of learning? I have argued elsewhere that we have already crossed that line, and dangerously so.[11] Our society has supported science on utilitarian grounds, and now appears to be moving to support the humanities for purposes of cultural consumption. In both cases, there are wide gaps between the rationalizations directed toward legislators and their publics, and the choice of specific work to receive support, a choice still made largely on the criteria of the academy. Both enterprises would be more safely supported if they were seen as necessary inputs to an output more comprehensible to the paying public and its legislators—an output of professional competence and applied knowledge, for which there was a visible market demand.

Such a change would not be without costs. One obvious cost is a shrinkage in the scale of the activities now described and supported as research and scholarship. This cost might in any event be unavoidable, and the academic enterprise would do well to initiate the change. By so doing, it may be better able to ensure that what remains is the best work.

11. See Carl Kaysen, *The Higher Learning, the Universities, and the Public* (Princeton, N.J.: Princeton University Press, 1969).

Setting National Goals and Objectives: Postsecondary Education

JOSEPH P. COSAND

WHO PLANS AND WHO DECIDES the national goals and objectives for postsecondary education? The complexity of the answer becomes apparent from the magnitude of the enterprise: enrollments of over nine million in higher education; the instructional staff of roughly a half-million plus supporting personnel in institutions; and the proportion of the gross national product (2.7 percent) that goes to education expenditures in institutions of higher education, more than double the proportion a decade ago. The importance of educational services and the sheer size of the enterprise dictate that interest in, and concern for, goals and objectives reach beyond the education community to become a matter of public policy, federal and state.

The growth of the investment in higher education relates in large part to the explosive increase in enrollments during the 1960s and the early 1970s and the corresponding necessity to increase the number and size of institutions. In addition, the institutions were asked to assume both expanded and new responsibilities for research and service to their communities, their states, and the nation, including enrolling an ever-expanding heterogeneous student population. Too often and for too long, institutional response to these demands has been a crisis reaction to pressure, with little or no long-range planning on an institutional, consortium, state, or regional basis—let alone on a national basis. In turn, these pressures have led the education community to a preoccupation with numbers—numbers of institutions and branch campuses, numbers of full- and part-time students, numbers of dollars in budgets, numbers of government and foundation grants, numbers of new curricula and new graduate schools, numbers of faculty, faculty salaries, teaching loads and tenure, and numbers of graduates from two- and four-year colleges and from universities.

Few of us in the profession managed to think, to plan, to evaluate, to look beyond the present. We reacted or overreacted to one crisis after another through surprise, unpreparedness, and expediency. But now postsecondary educational needs for the rest of this century and beyond must be examined in the light of changing social needs and the growing demands for new approaches to learning being voiced by a heterogeneous clientele.

A NEED FOR CONFIDENCE

The shift from continuous rapid growth and response to a climate of concern and fear has caused both a loss in self-confidence within the education community and a decrease in public confidence. Moynihan has noted:

> All of the surveys made of American public opinion in the last five or six years have shown an astonishingly precipitous decline in confidence in our institutions. . . . American higher education has had a grand time explaining that nobody trusts the President, nobody trusts the Congress, nobody trusts big business, nobody trusts big labor. The best poll taken on confidence in higher education showed that in 1966 about 61 percent of the American people would express a great deal of confidence in higher education; last year it was down to 33 percent.[1]

However, other recent polls have shown the American people to have even less confidence in Congress (21 percent), newspapers (18 percent), and advertising (a mere 12 percent).[2] Moynihan states further,

> We are none of us particularly proud of ourselves just now. We aren't particularly confident about our situation. And yet the basic ecology that ultimately shapes our sense of national well-being is once again moving in a good direction.[3]

The decline in public confidence perhaps reflects a national concern that the education community has failed to exert a strong sense of direction and confidence, notably seen in its lack of cooperative effort over the past decade. Too many individuals, institutions, and organizations, whether in higher education or in government, have been self-serving and short-sighted. However, there are evidences today of growing cooperation among institutions of higher education, among organizations repre-

---

1. Daniel P. Moynihan, " 'Peace'—Some Thoughts on the 1960's and 1970's," *Public Interest*, Summer 1973, pp. 10–11.
2. *Washington Post Outlook*, July 29, 1973.
3. Moynihan, "Peace," p. 11.

senting higher education, and among the states through the Education Commission for the States. The new vigor may have prompted Moynihan's brief statement of optimism.

The strengthening sentiment for cooperation may stem from survival instincts and the visceral concern of individual faculty members, departments, graduate schools, and institutions themselves. It appears that the traditional solo flights by faculty members, administrators, boards, and by higher education institutions and organizations are changing in favor of group activity organized on a collegial or geographic basis. These changes are to be applauded, and the foundations and governmental agencies stimulating such activity are to be encouraged. Interaction among institutions will foster an improved understanding of the totality of postsecondary education and, in so doing, assist the process of setting national goals and objectives.

Contributors to National Policy Formulation

It is important that those concerned with postsecondary education be aware of the variety of contending forces that have an interest in, and influence on, our national goals and objectives. These forces have tended to move in strength and thus power, from institutional administrators, faculties, and boards to the national organizations, to the states, and to the federal government. A review of their inputs will be useful.

The *federal government* heavily influences national goals and objectives through financial assistance to students and to institutions, through affirmative action decisions as interpreted and administered by the Office for Civil Rights of the U.S. Department of Health, Education, and Welfare, through the vacillation between categorical and noncategorical aid, through the changing philosophies—year by year—about what is important or not so important, through the individual biases of persons and groups of persons.

In the *executive branch*, the input comes from (1) the bureaucracy of the U.S. Office of Education (USOE); (2) the assistant secretaries of HEW and their staffs—primarily those in administration, planning, legislation, and finance, along with the Assistant Secretary of HEW for Education and the Secretary of HEW; (3) the Office of Management and Budget (OMB) staff members in the area of higher education and the Director of OMB; (4) other agencies such as the Treasury Department, the Department of Labor, the Department of Defense; and (5) the White House. This hierarchical apparatus too often produces top-level decisions based on budgetary expediencies that have ignored the information inputs of the postsecondary education community.

In the *Congress* the input to decisions affecting postsecondary education goals and objectives comes primarily from the education and appropriations committees of the House and Senate. Staff aides to the senators and representatives, along with the committee counsels, play an important role in the decision-making process of the Congress. The postsecondary education community must develop a capability to inform senators and representatives and their aides factually and frequently concerning higher and postsecondary education as a totality. In fact, they have an obligation to help write the legislation affecting their institutions.[4]

National organizations such as those headquartered at One Dupont Circle are deeply involved in the setting of goals and objectives, but have tended to reflect the narrow views of their special constituencies rather than the totality of postsecondary education. However, evidence is increasing that these units do wish to cooperate and to regard the American Council on Education as their coordinating unit. Their location in the National Center for Higher Education permits ready exchange and should encourage a united effort among the "establishment" forces.

Various *foundations* have participated by funding commissions and study groups concerned with all segments of postsecondary education. Certainly the most far-reaching effort came through the Carnegie Corporation grant which funded the Carnegie Commission on Higher Education. The commission reports, presented over the period 1967 to 1973, are well known and have had a major influence on the postsecondary education community as well as on the state and federal governments. Reform measures for postsecondary education have been stimulated by the Commission on Non-Traditional Study, the Commission on Academic Tenure, and the task force chaired by Frank Newman. This impressive array of information is now before us as we analyze, evaluate, and decide upon the national goals and objectives for higher education and for postsecondary education.

A great change in the involvement of *the states* in establishing state goals and objectives has taken place in the last fifteen years. Perhaps the

---

4. See Robert C. Andringa, "Why Won't Educators Help Congress Write Education Laws?" *Chronicle of Higher Education,* July 30, 1973, p. 12. The author is minority staff director of the Committee on Education and Labor of the House of Representatives.

best-known early example of intensified state interest is the legislatively created California Coordinating Council on Higher Education, established in 1960, to plan an educational continuum consisting of the community colleges, the state colleges, and the University of California. The council's early decision to become, not an administrative superboard, but rather an advisory body to the executive and legislative branches of government has been a significant factor in higher education planning in California. Now practically all states have a central spokesman for higher education—a council, a commission, a board, a chancellor, or a secretary, or some combination of these. State planning received a boost by the congressional creation of "State Planning Commissions" in section 1202 of the Education Amendments of 1972, but was set back by the executive branch decision in 1973 to delay creation of the commissions. In spite of this momentum—and also because of it—a degree of anxiety exists among established institutions that somehow state planning will lead to state control. In any event, state planning will have an increasing influence on national goals.

A ROLE FOR THE INSTITUTION

The individual institution, for its part in the process of setting national goals, must develop a set of objectives focused on its mission, student clientele, and service responsibilities. This endeavor can profit from cooperative efforts among several institutions (consortia and councils) to share information and resources. The coordinating devices also help offset needless duplication and competition, which may produce, not symbolic parity, but undesirable homogeneity and weakness. To meet the diverse needs of the nation's diverse student clientele, we must maintain a diversity of institutions with well-stated, attainable, and adhered-to objectives. The move toward cooperation and sharing will strengthen our institutions and thus materially affect our national goals and objectives.

The universities, the state colleges, the liberal arts colleges, the community colleges and four-year urban institutions, the technical institutes, and the nontraditional institutions all have their individual and collective roles. Each must serve its particular function with distinction, and through this service each will have its own status. In view of the diversity among students, with their great differences in interests, motivation, and abilities, there is no place for a hierarchy of academic snobbery or prestige. Each institution that fulfills its goals and objectives with excellence is in itself prestigious and worthy of the highest recognition. The institution that negates its objectives and tries to be a poorer quality something else cannot achieve respect within the community of postsecondary education.

BLENDING THE INPUTS

Setting national goals and objectives requires the best input and thinking of all segments of the postsecondary community. Strong, knowledgeable people are needed at the institutions—among faculty, students, administrators, and boards. In addition, strong, knowledgeable people are needed in the executive and legislative branches of our state and federal governments, and the same kind of strength and leadership is needed from our national organizations and commissions, from our state organizations and commissions, from business, industry, labor, the professions, and the foundations. A merging of views from all these sources will tend to eliminate ignorance, bias, and arrogance, and develop, instead, an understanding of the problems to be faced and of the solutions to be reached through the formulation of national goals and objectives for postsecondary education to serve the nation's people. The education community must face these questions: Is it possible, in the survivalist climate that exists, to achieve a collegial attack on a series of highly complex problems? Can the education community, through such a cooperative effort, eliminate its tunnel vision and thus strengthen the total effort to better the services to our student population? If the answer is "no," then solutions will be sought by an impatient public through legislative and executive action at both the state and the federal levels.

In approaching the task of formulating national goals and objectives, the education community must be aware not only that the concept is novel but also that there are forces which would guide such an effort. In particular, we must not allow the self-interest of an individual or of a group in a position of influence and power, especially at the level of the federal government or an influential national organization, to dominate the process. The opportunity for a powerful force to influence or to determine national goals and objectives is enormous and frightening. If such power bases are permitted to function unilaterally without challenge or question by those affected, cooperative effort will have little chance to determine national goals. This must not be permitted to happen. No person, no small group of persons—some isolated from the realities of postsecondary education—can be allowed in isolated ignorance to make decisions concerning the major problems facing the nation today.

Unfortunately, the individual components of postsecondary education can also blindly engage in narrowly conceived power struggles.

IDENTIFYING NATIONAL GOALS

I have now reviewed the setting and analyzed some forces, active and potential, most likely to influence the process of a national formulation of acceptable goals for postsecondary education. I shall look next at recent major efforts launched in this direction, and then turn to the question of consensus on a set of goals and the means for achieving them. In particular, I shall address those goals related to nontraditional postsecondary education. A useful start is with the recommendations of the Carnegie Commission on Higher Education and the legislative process that occurred at the federal level in enacting the Education Amendments of 1972, which were in part influenced by the Carnegie reports.

The 1968 Carnegie Commission report *Quality and Equality* emphasized two urgent national priorities: (1) "to achieve greater equality of opportunity for all able young people, both for their own benefit and for the benefit of the nation"; (2) to achieve "a substantial expansion of health service personnel." To meet these priorities, the commission proposed that start-up grants be provided to establish five hundred new community colleges so that postsecondary education would be within commuting reach of 95 percent of the population.[5] The five hundred figure has since been lowered in keeping with lower enrollment projections, but the Carnegie proposal is still valid and also still unfulfilled.

In recognition of the Carnegie Commission priorities, the Congress, in writing the Education Amendments of 1972, incorporated its own goals, including: (1) provision of student aid in sufficient sums to assure that no qualified student will lack the resources to complete his or her education, (2) federal funds to expand facilities to be within reach of all students seeking postsecondary education, and (3) cost-of-instruction allowances for institutions to defray expenses incident to the federally aided students. However, the appropriations to accomplish these goals have not been recommended by the President nor enacted by the Congress. Consequently the far-reaching national goals recommended in 1968 have not been approached, much less realized. Instead, the administration and the Congress have locked horns over which parts of the student aid measures are to be partially funded. The funding issue must

5. *Quality and Equality: New Levels of Federal Responsibility for Higher Education* (New York: McGraw-Hill), p. 49.

be resolved if the national needs for postsecondary education are to be served.

In its 1970 report *A Chance to Learn*, the Carnegie Commission stated bluntly that "Today, the denial of equal opportunity for higher education is also the denial of equal access to full partnership in American society." It then formulated specific policy goals for education which linked the concept of equal opportunity to the achievement of measurable, scheduled progress beginning with the year 1976, when, it proposed, national policy would provide that:

- All economic barriers to educational opportunity be eliminated.
- The curriculum and the environment of the college campus not remain a source of educational disadvantage or inequity.
- Substantial progress be made toward improvement of educational quality at levels prior to higher education, and toward provision of universal access to higher education where it is not now available.[6]

By the year 2000 the Carnegie Commission believes:

- Opportunities can and must be totally free of the last vestiges of limitations [for postsecondary education] imposed by ethnic grouping, or geographic location, or age, or quality of prior schooling. . . . By the year 2000, [colleges should not have] to provide compensatory education.
- There should be no barriers to any individual achieving the occupational level which his talent warrants and which his interest leads him to seek.
- The cost of social services needed to cope with the consequences of educational disadvantages far outruns the economic support necessary to confront the sources of deprivation. Inequality of opportunity must not continue to sap the strength of our nation.[7]

The Carnegie Commission report *The Open-Door Colleges* includes an epigraph by James B. Conant, in which he notes: "The extension of the years of free education through the establishment of local two-year colleges has been the expression of a new social policy of the nation. Or perhaps I should say a further thrust of an old policy."[8] Although Conant refers to "free" education in the local community college, this has been realized only in California and other isolated instances. The open-door college—the comprehensive community college—came into being after

6. *A Chance to Learn: An Action Agenda for Equal Opportunity in Higher Education* (New York: McGraw-Hill, 1970), p. 27.
7. Ibid., pp. 27–28.
8. *The Open-Door Colleges: Policies for Community Colleges* (New York: McGraw-Hill, 1970), p. iii.

World War II and has since experienced a phenomenal growth in both numbers of colleges and students. It is truly an American innovation and has been the one institution to give credence to "equality of opportunity" at the postsecondary education level, with its low cost, commuter orientation, and open admissions policy. It has provided a depth and breadth of lower division and occupational curricula designed to serve the interests, abilities, and the occupational-cultural and social needs of the entire community.

The following national goals were postulated by the Carnegie Commission for these two-year community colleges:

By 1976
- Open access to all public community colleges.
- The removal of financial barriers to enrollment.
- A state plan for the development of community colleges in every state.
- Comprehensive programs which provide meaningful learning options in all public two-year institutions of higher education.
- Achievement of the goal of a community college within commuting distance of every potential student, except in sparsely populated areas where residential colleges are needed.
- Plans for 230 to 280 community colleges initiated in 1976. [This number has now been substantially reduced in line with projected enrollments.]
- Low tuition or no tuition in community colleges.
- Adaptation of occupational programs to changing manpower requirements and full opportunities for continuing adult education.

By 1980
- 35 to 40 percent of all undergraduate students enrolled in community colleges. [This has already been exceeded in some states—notably California and Florida.]

By 2000
- 40 to 45 percent of all undergraduate students enrolled in community colleges.
- Continuing adaptation of the community colleges to the changing educational and occupational needs of our society as we approach the twenty-first century.[9]

The above goals of national significance were reemphasized and expanded in the Carnegie Commission report *Less Time, More Options,*

9. Ibid., pp. 51–52.

and again stressed the importance of equal opportunity. Additional national goals included:

By 1980
- Associate in Arts degrees generally available in all colleges [to provide certified achievement for those who do not complete the baccalaureate degree].
- State planning includes all postsecondary education.
- Federal support to students includes all postsecondary education.
- The average length of time [to an AA degree, 1½ years;] to a BA degree . . . 3 years.
- Tests fully developed and accepted in lieu of formal course work and in lieu of college credit.
- Experiments undertaken with "open universities."

By 2000
- "Open universities" well established.
- An "educational security" program in full operation.[10]

The commission stated that "these reforms, if accomplished, would be the most significant undertaken since the modern system of higher education emerged from the classical college beginning a century ago," by serving "better both the interests of the students and the needs of society."[11]

GOALS FOR NATIONAL PLANNING OF POSTSECONDARY EDUCATION

Another proposal linked to the attainment of a viable national policy was the Carnegie Commission recommendation for the creation of a Council of Advisers on Higher Education attached to the White House to undertake studies and recommend policy for postsecondary education.[12] This recommendation has not been adopted and thus there is no direct representation to the White House for postsecondary education nor has there been since the departure of Daniel P. Moynihan as Counsellor to the President. The goal is becoming more urgent as the problems become more complex and more demanding of solutions during the final quarter of the twentieth century. The need is for a council that is free from either governmental or institutional bias and therefore free to make its recommendations for the good of our present and potential

10. *Less Time, More Options: Education Beyond the High School* (New York: McGraw-Hill, 1971), pp. 31, 21.
11. Ibid., pp. 31–32.
12. *Quality and Equality*, p. 51.

students and the good of our society, rather than for the benefit of our government and the institutions and their respective empires. A council of this caliber is not only needed by society but is also essential to the very process of formulating viable goals.

Policy and goal formulations must be based on timely and reliable data on all aspects of the various fields of postsecondary education. This need was recognized by the Carnegie Commission, and it viewed filling that need as another priority. In *A Chance to Learn*, the commission makes the important point that a national policy for equal educational opportunity must be based on the most recent and significant information bearing on the issue. Specifically, the commission recommended the establishment of "a unit within the U.S. Office of Education, with an appropriate advisory committee reporting to the Commissioner of Education," "to study, recommend, and monitor policy and strategy; to devise measures of progress and issue annual evaluation reports; to serve as a clearinghouse for materials and consultation, to propose further means to articulate the efforts at all educational levels; and to coordinate and oversee the activities within each regional area."[13] This recommendation, like most others, has been ignored thus far by the administration.

The Congress, through the Education Amendments of 1972, adopted two Carnegie Commission recommendations aimed at including all types of institutions in postsecondary education planning: (1) statewide planning was legislated for *all* postsecondary education, and (2) federal support to students in *all* postsecondary education was legislated. This broadening of planning and support to all of postsecondary education was revolutionary, and now must be implemented if equality of opportunity for the individual student is to be realized. The amendments added some 4,500 accredited proprietary institutions to the prior community of 2,600 accredited two- and four-year colleges and universities. The financial implications of this major change in national policy are now being studied by the presidentially appointed National Commission on the Financing of Postsecondary Education, which will report to the Congress on December 31, 1973. Its findings and recommendations may well cause major shifts in public policy for higher education.

In one of the final Carnegie Commission reports, *The Purposes and the Performance of Higher Education in the United States*, the following conclusions and recommendations affecting national policy are of great

13. *A Chance to Learn*, p. 25.

importance to the extent that they cause present postsecondary legislation to be funded or new legislation to be enacted. The Carnegie report summarizes the main purposes of higher education in the United States today as follows:

- The provision of opportunities for the intellectual, aesthetic, ethical, and skill development of individual students, and the provision of campus environments which can constructively assist students in their more general developmental growth
- The advancement of human capability in society at large
- The enlargement of educational justice for the postsecondary age group
- The transmission and advancement of learning and wisdom
- The critical evaluation of society—through individual thought and persuasion—for the sake of society's self-renewal[14]

These purposes should be realized by individual institutions—whether public, private, or proprietary—in keeping with their respective objectives and capabilities in order to provide educational opportunities beyond the high school for all, regardless of race, background, age, or affluence. The Carnegie Commission, in this report, looks to the future and recommends priorities for action which, it is to be hoped, will enable us to cope with the major changes in the higher education enterprise occurring in the last quarter of this century.

The nation is faced with some direct questions: Education for whom? By which institution? For what purpose? For access by whom? To what end? To answer these questions, the nation must have policies that are acceptable to the states and to the individual institutions on the function, structure, and financing of postsecondary education, and they must be answered in that order: function, structure, and then finance.

The concluding statement in *A Chance to Learn* is appropriate when we think of setting national goals and objectives. "The Commission believes that a commitment to adequate support for better educational systems, to comprehensive student aid, and to removing the consequences of discrimination is truly basic to the nation's future."[15] Perhaps the best assurance of achieving this national goal is the proposed National Council of Advisers which could, with vision and integrity, advise the profession and the state and federal governments in providing postsecondary education to the people of the United States, so that all may enjoy the potential richness of this country, culturally, socially, and economically.

14. *The Purposes and the Performance of Higher Education in the United States: Approaching the Year 2000* (New York: McGraw-Hill, 1973), p. 1.
15. *A Chance to Learn*, p. 29.

National Goals in an Untidy World

LAURA BORNHOLDT

HISTORIANS ARE TRAINED to acknowledge and appreciate that we live in an untidy world in which the best laid plans of mice and men go agley and in which all blueprints for the future have built-in uncertainties, whether acts of God or acts of men. This awareness has never kept historians from participating in planning for a future or adopting policies to help shape the future, but it does carry a compulsion to look for uncertainties disguised as certainties, wherever they be found.

I realize that most educators would share the basic assumption of both the Kaysen and Cosand papers that no radical change in American society is likely soon. Yet John Rawls and Christopher Jencks would challenge the starting point of both papers and insist that setting goals for higher education should not be attempted without setting some intermeshing goals for changing society itself. Nothing short of a revolution in educational policy would follow. Clearly, if Jencks and Rawls represent a view that takes hold in our lifetime—and if the rest of us are the troglodytes—then all the valences shift and all talk of goals and objectives based on the old rhetoric will prove short-lived. *Could* it happen? Certainly. *Will* it happen? Unlikely.

Even though one shares the basic viewpoints of the two papers—and the Carnegie Commission, for that matter—and assumes change will be incremental rather than radical, discussing values-goals-objectives in brief is difficult. One needs to be able to move from a rhetoric of the ideal, general, and all-is-possible to the level of the existing, possible, and available strategies among the real options, including costs and their distribution. The significance of general principle becomes meaningful only with specific interpretations and applications. Thus, I shall sketch only three or four factors that will remain unruly in any plans for the future and then make two or three comments on Kaysen's prescription for tomorrow's liberal arts education.

Mr. Kaysen's paper properly reminds us of the diversity that *is* higher education in the United States—diversity of students and goals, diversity of institutions and degrees. In a salutary way it restates that a republic like ours can never *plan* its higher education as may be done in a socialist state with a planned economy and a manpower-needs table to fill. In the early 1960s when Ghana was establishing its national university system, its educational leaders and politicians shopped around among several national models. Two of us were spokesmen for "the American way," and both of us tried to speak for the American baccalaureate degree and its role in preprofessional training. We found no takers, however, for the idea of a liberal arts education in the American mode. "That's a luxury for a wealthy capitalist society," they said. They had a manpower-needs table and proposed to take the shortest route to filling it.

In this country such a direct approach to goals and objectives is not open to us. Although national manpower needs are routinely calculated in many fields, the projections are known to be fallible and rough in our mixed economy (consider the predictions made about the number of teachers to be needed in the 1970s versus the actuality), and their relationship to student career choices is highly erratic. Set quotas for different skills run at an angle, if not directly counter, to our national credo of individualism, for our people have maintained and do maintain that at least in time of peace every citizen shall have free choice in what he does with his life. (The past decade has concentrated on translating this rhetoric into something approaching reality for the disadvantaged groups who had found it a mockery, but that's another story of a general principle floating until it was pinned down with a specific policy with a real price tag.)

There is a paradox, then, in talking about "national needs for higher education": at one and the same time are meant a national system adequate to the full realization of the needs of the individuals who make up the society *and* the society's collective needs for specific skills and talents. The two are not the same; they are hard to keep separate; and almost everyone is too sloppy in references to them.

There is some experience in American higher education for influencing career choices by extending different kinds of carrot, but, even so, there are also cautionary warnings for policy-makers and goal-setters, counselors and students. Federal programs that are dependent on annual congressional appropriations are frequently subject to jerks and retrievals long before even one generation of students can test the program. The ultimate support for every goal in higher education is public opinion, which is not the most constant of lovers.

A system that is wide open to individual student choices—no sticks and few carrots—can in normal times rely on fairly constant student motivation. But these are not normal times, and the rapidity of social change defies attempts at projections of career choices, hence reliable projections of institutional enrollments. To give only two instances, we cannot now anticipate the effects that will stem from dissipation of the belief that more education leads directly to greater earning power. And we do not know how persons who find they are overtrained for their jobs will cope with this as a lifelong problem or what their experience will say to younger people coming into the world of higher education. India's experience is not likely to be ours because the line between our white- and blue-collar jobs is less significant than it is on the subcontinent. But given job projections and degree production at the present level, the United States will have its own version of career deflation.

In this posttechnological age, we may well be fated to solve one set of problems only to generate others of greater difficulty. We probably have already done so in developing our highly rationalized state and regional systems. Only a Luddite would call for their elimination: state and regional planning agencies have become economic and financial necessities. They ensure against indefensible duplication of facilities; they anticipate and call attention to human needs. But they also exact a price that is not widely admitted or discussed. Not only faculty but also many top administrators are coming to feel remote from their institution's decision-making apparatus in the new world of systems. The academic vice-chancellor of a major state university recently described himself as a frustrated, unfree, and overpaid man. Charged with responsibility for the educational welfare of his institution, he considered himself a go-between for his institution and his state system, defeated in advance in his efforts to bring about change in his university's program and curriculum. By the time cost-benefit analyses for a new program had been completed, a comparison made with what other institutions in the state were doing, and the job market analyzed, his faculty had lost interest. His conclusion: there is lip service to diversity among the institutions within a system, but, in practice, it is extremely difficult to realize the diversity. The pressure for equity becomes a pressure for homogenization rather than diversity. In his view, accountants and academic middlemen are determining educational policy under the flag of institutional cooperation, both voluntary and guided.

Faculty, as Kaysen points out, can be self-serving and cantankerous and they can be provincial about their corner of the enterprise. To block their creative effort by forcing them to live in a bureaucratic maze is to deprofessionalize the profession. The natural counterforce is the faculty union which promises only to match one bureaucracy with another.

I wish now to comment on Kaysen's "What is College For?" His recommendation is protected by its modesty: a new norm for liberal arts degrees but not a model for all institutions. He recommends, too, that institutions adopting his suggestion of concentrating on providing professional training should maintain two tracks: the main track to the professions and a second track for the undergraduate who wants to pursue such loose goals as the critically trained mind and the sensitive soul.

The two-track model, it seems to me, is already developing in some of the best liberal arts colleges where they are rethinking their missions and looking for programs to help students build toward careers without, however, turning the institution into a vocational school. But the sharp focus on problem solving through the application of organized knowledge, which Kaysen suggests, is not yet common, and I, for one, hope it will not be. Obviously, problem solving is important: it gives the student great satisfaction and provides the community with useful citizens. Yet problem solving is less significant than the ability to define problems in the first place and the ability to play with ideas before moving to choose among the solutions. And problem solving as such is of less significance than learning that not all problems are solvable.

The practical education which Kaysen proposes would deprive the student of a whole dimension in his development: the cultivation of the imaginative and the empathetic elements of his nature through exposure to the significance of the irrational as well as the rational. A future professional needs to develop imagination, empathy, ability to play with ideas, and appreciation of the irrational. The first exposure may not "take," but it should be offered. And certainly professionals need to look at values and value systems before becoming immersed in a lifetime career.

The question need not be whether to offer liberal education before or after professional training, but whether it might be possible and desirable to combine them in undergraduate and graduate work. (If I understand the program newly adopted at the University of Chicago, they are doing just that with law, the social sciences, and rhetoric.)

The liberal arts college is buried every month or so and still survives. But to limit its mission essentially to training problem-solvers would smother one of its essential components—the humanities—and develop half-educated professionals. Our society can do better.

Resources for Setting State Goals

BENNETT KATZ

SOMETIMES THE DISTANCE between the State House in Augusta, Maine, and the National Center for Higher Education at One Dupont Circle seems forbiddingly great. And sometimes the scholarly reports emanating from the national level seem remote to the problems faced by a state legislature. Yet, as the four-term chairman of Maine's Legislative Committee on Education, I have become increasingly comfortable with the world of academe and have begun to see that the establishment of national goals and objectives has a true relationship to what goes on in the Maine Senate. I have pondered with Dr. Cosand what the guidelines should be for the "1202 Commissions"; I have been involved in dialogues on the relative priorities of student assistance programs to be funded. And I have found the publications of the Carnegie Commission on higher education absorbing and thought-provoking.

From my perspective, which has been forged in politics and tempered by the legislative process, I have learned that equality is a goal, not a reality, and I have learned that good legislation may be attacked, compromised, and rewritten, but can turn out to be even better legislation.

STATE IMPLEMENTATION OF NATIONAL GOALS

Dr. Cosand's paper has immediately centered on the matter of public confidence. In Maine, not only the people but also the legislators have been expressing some disenchantment with the educational system, particularly with the baccalaureate institutions. With wavering public confidence, can public support be maintained?

In many ways, the University of Maine exemplifies what takes place in state-national relationships with respect to goals and objectives, and public reaction to them. Created as a land-grant institution in a rural setting, the university was transformed during the latter 1960s into a university system with nine campuses. Until recently, university education in Maine was a four-year residential experience leading to a baccalaureate degree. Institutional rigidity and institutional goals dominated the entire process: the university did a fine job of meeting the needs of those citizens whose objectives happened to coincide with those of the university. It was a beloved institution that had a popular president who never bothered the legislature very much and an alumni association that supported the football team, if not the alumni fund. To a painful extent, Maine appeared to be unaware of changing national goals and objectives.

Today, the university, under its lay board, has moved rapidly to identify unfilled public needs, with priority being given to courses of two years or less. Computer education has been discovered, and all campuses are doing a creditable job of attempting to identify local community needs. National goals and objectives, as we see them, have been identified and adapted to our local situation. The university might be expected to receive the plaudits of Maine's people and the happy support of the legislature. In fact, legislative support has been good but not happy. It appears that the more the institution departs from its traditional role, the greater are its public problems.

As for an affirmative action program, in a state with only a million people, recruitment under such a plan can only be a sham. For this national goal to be realized, there would have to be national recruitment. Yet I am not completely certain that there is public support for a widespread program of recruitment of out-of-state blacks, Chicanos, and other minorities.

Both the Cosand and Kaysen paper have incorporated the Carnegie objective "the critical evaluation of society—through individual thought and persuasion—for the sake of society's self-renewal."[1] I have a feeling that in the unsophisticated corners of Maine the people would not support this goal, at least not at the University of Maine. I sense that they have had an adequate dose of attack on establishment values and are not enthusiastic about the prospect of having university professors point out in continuing indictment—no matter how scholarly—what's wrong with society. And as Kaysen notes, and I agree, where research and scholarship are priority goals of a campus, most taxpayers are far more interested in the teaching potential of the institution.

1. Carnegie Commission on Higher Education, *The Purposes and the Performance of Higher Education in the United States: Approaching the Year 2000* (New York: McGraw-Hill, 1973), p. 1.

EXTRASTATE RESOURCES

Of great interest to me is the process by which national goals and objectives for higher education are established within a state, and some delineation of its elements may prove instructive. The setting of goals is not necessarily confronted within a state on a formal basis but, rather, proceeds through information evolution that is mostly dependent on the nature and personality of the advocates. Even as federal responses are colored by the personality of a John Brademas, so in the state of Maine they are influenced by the perceptions of a Bennett Katz. Dr. Cosand's analysis of roles in determining decisions at the national level leads me to conclude that the federal government and the states are very different and yet very much the same. The influence of a governor, a legislature, or a chancellor often seems to have a greater weight than does all the documented evidence at hand.

In education, as in government, we are—thank heavens—still an assemblage of individuals. If, indeed, individuals have this extraordinary influence in the establishment of goals and in the implementation of these goals, who influences the influencers?

To begin, the three regional boards have an increasing influence. The Western Interstate Commission for Higher Education, the Southern Regional Education Board, and the New England Board of Higher Education have assumed responsibilities for better utilization of resources. They have, with some success, crossed state lines, but I must conclude that one does not have to travel abroad to find an iron curtain for there is one at every state boundary. Regional cooperation can lead to regional policies which in turn can become national policies and objectives. For example, the regional student program of the New England Board permits thousands of students to pursue, at resident tuition rates, courses of study not offered in the home state but available in another New England state. Perhaps one day we shall learn how to establish for students, within the farmework of their ability to pay, freer access nationally to specialty programs not offered in the home state. Further, perhaps regional success can influence internal state policy to slow down the proliferation of state medical schools, state colleges of veterinary medicine, and state crime laboratories or police training academies.

Who else influences the key persons who have the ability to make policy decisions? Certainly the success of the Education Commission of the States is unquestioned. I have a feeling that ECS has made a lot of people nervous, especially so in its early years. But ECS has emerged into a maturity of purpose that increasingly causes it to be accepted as an ally to be used by the states, by One Dupont Circle, and by the federal establishment. ECS has become a significant alternative voice on the national scene, regarded as forceful and influential. But the real potential and value of ECS lie hundreds and sometimes thousands of miles away from either Denver or Washington: because ECS is a compact of the states, its real influence is and should be more and more in state capitals.

The Maine legislature in 1973 enacted sweeping legislation in the field of property tax reform and school finance. The U.S. Office of Education has called it "one of the most significant equalization reform acts ever to become law in this nation." A prime ingredient in our success was the activity of the Maine Education Council, the in-state component of our delegation to the Education Commission of the States. The materials, assistance, encouragement, and sense of urgency developed by ECS were instrumental in achieving the realization of one of my personal goals. Also in Maine, we have enacted a Bill of Rights for the exceptional child, which is as liberal and far-reaching as any in the nation. I think without doubt that the proximate cause of this Maine enactment was the help and sense of urgency created by the HACHE project administered by ECS—*H*andicapped *C*hildren's *E*ducation, federally funded, ECS-administered, and a catalyst that has borne exciting fruit in the state of Maine.

One of the greatest disappointments of our legislative session was the defeat of a comprehensive student assistance program, which would have tied in with our existing student loan programs and the Education Amendments of 1972. Here again we see the influence that ECS has had in building an awareness of the program, suggesting alternative courses of action, and giving a sense of urgency to those of us who attempted to make national policy come true at the local level. That we failed in this session in no way reduces our resolution to attempt success next time.

Who sets national goals and objectives? The answer is and must remain: a broad partnership between the federal government and the states. To a great extent, the likelihood that the states will become "more equal" partners is enhanced by the influence that lies with the regional boards and the Education Commission of the States. Continuing effort must be made within the states to ensure that the relationship between the academic world and the political leadership becomes closer. In a balanced society each participant must establish his own position in a flexible relationship with all others concerned. We must avoid the scourge that a vacuum might cause a national administration to overstep its proper relationships with the states or might encourage a state legislature to thrust itself to an ill-advised extent into the role of academe.

We are all optimists at heart. We believe in the system. We believe in our abilities to maintain flexibility in attitudes and in relationships. And we are, or should be, encouraged by the knowledge that our generation is attempting more than has any other generation in history. Our detractors to the contrary, our nation has done more than any other.

Finally, we must acknowledge that we can do better. Indeed, we must do better. When we pass on to new hands the trusteeship for higher education, the trust put into our custody must be found to have been advanced toward meeting the needs of the nation and of its individual citizens.

A National Education Allowance

STEVEN MULLER

THE PAPERS BY Drs. Cosand and Kaysen invite direct response, but I choose, rather, to address two points supplementary to their positions. Both points relate to the tension between plurality and diversity in postsecondary education on the one hand and, on the other hand, the desire and need for national goals and objectives.

My first point: I favor the setting of broad national goals and objectives but fear the consequences of excess, or overly detailed, national planning.

In concluding his paper, Dr. Cosand invokes the closing statement from *A Chance to Learn*, calling for "a commitment to adequate support for better educational systems, to comprehensive student aid, and to removing the consequences of discrimination."[1] To this I subscribe with enthusiasm, for I believe it to be a sound and valid brief statement of national goals and objectives. What troubles me is the preoccupation with formulation of more detailed national policy: note that the focus of my concern is far more on the national than on the state level.

---

1. Carnegie Commission on Higher Education, *A Chance to Learn: An Action Agenda for Equal Opportunity in Higher Education* (New York: McGraw-Hill, 1970), p. 29.

The genius and tradition of postsecondary education in the United States has been spontaneity and response to demand. In response to the needs of society and other needs of students, scores upon scores of institutions of postsecondary education have been created in this country over succeeding decades. Each new institution was created to meet a demand of one sort or another by offering particular kinds of instruction, by meeting the needs of particular students, by serving a particular area, and so on. Each of these institutions as it lived on became a source of creativity as a community, and the creativity of postsecondary education has rested much more with each of these many communities than with any general or national plan or policy. Thus, we can speak of, and pay tribute to, the plurality and diversity of postsecondary education. We should be aware that many of these separate institutions have tended to imitate one another and many of them are more alike than different, but to respect diversity does not require that it be perfect.

It is now fashionable to criticize these many institutions of postsecondary education for the institutional selfishness and competition that often mark their coexistence. Such criticism is not unfounded, nor are institutional selfishness and competition necessarily virtues. However, it is a wide-open question whether attempts to correct these flaws will in the long run produce a better or a worse complex of postsecondary education. The imperfections of a free marketplace of students and institutions are evident, but awareness of these imperfections does not lead me to conclude that a managed system would be superior. In my view the case has not yet been made that institutions of postsecondary education themselves cannot improve their performance and their mutual relationships; nor has it been demonstrated that a system of national management would not cause more problems than it solves.

For what it may be worth, the national policy I favor—the emphasis again is primarily on the national context—is comprehensive student aid. It should be national policy to equip every person in this country with the means to enter postsecondary education, at a suitable time and place, provided that individual is qualified for admission to a recognized institution. Such a policy should take into account that for many citizens there may be more than one suitable time and many suitable places. It is my belief that such a policy would enable all of our effective institutions of postsecondary education to supervise and prosper, and would penalize only those whose performance is less than effective. To carry the argument one step further, I would rather pay the price of no institutional support to any institution than to purchase such support at the cost of a national system of supervision, evaluation, and control of postsecondary education. I question the merit in the distinction many of us seek between national supervision or coordination and national control. Though there are few advocates for national control, it would, in likelihood, follow on the heels of national supervision and coordination. We have no experience with a national managed system, but we do have experience with the occasional impact that public national policy has had on postsecondary education. Such experience indicates that national public policy is changeable, and, on occasion, major changes in national public policy have done damage to postsecondary higher education far greater than any damage caused by the free operation of our institutions. It is fair to observe that the broad definitions contained in Dr. Kaysen's paper—be that right or wrong—are simply not applicable to all institutions of postsecondary education, as he explicitly recognizes. His argument is a well-considered and wholly constructed prod and food for thought and discussion, but I reject it as national policy regardless of the merits of the argument.

My second point is simple. I believe that at this time we are far less in search of national policy than we are in urgent need of the commitment and will to act.

In discussions about the purposes and circumstances of postsecondary education, there is ready agreement that at least part of the need is for open access with appropriate means to postsecondary education for all citizens qualified to benefit from it. Why, then, not begin at once to create a national educational allowance, which, though it may not be enough by itself, is both simpler and more universal than the basic opportunity grants? Surely the concept of requiring opportunities for students is easier to justify to taxpayers than are the varying merits either of institutions or of national management. An effort at this time to devise a fail-safe nationwide policy and system has a dubious chance of success and is already exacting a heavy toll of time and energy. We would do better to begin to act at the national level. I can think of no better goal, objective, or action than the creation of a national educational allowance.

The Future Financing of Postsecondary Education

ALLAN M. CARTTER

THE FINANCING OF HIGHER EDUCATION calls to mind the old professorial adage: the questions may remain the same year in and year out, but the answers change. Perhaps no other subject in the field of higher education has received so much attention over the years, and in few other areas has it been so difficult to adapt the prescriptions for the future to changing circumstances. The 1970s, however, present some new facts, some new perceptions, and—as the result of recent developments in public policy—some changes in the environment in which higher education exists. And it goes almost without saying, knowledgeable people both inside and outside higher education are questioning old assumptions and prescriptions more critically than ever before.

The economists in higher education, when viewing the world of business and commerce, have often said that in some ways a little depression is a good thing. It is not desirable as a steady state, but it may be useful as a time when enterprises are forced to reevaluate their objectives and accomplishments, cull the unproductive, and scrutinize budgets with a piercing eye and a red pencil. There is a natural tendency toward institutional obesity in times of affluence and rapid expansion, and, just as elections every few years instill a certain vigor into the political process by threatening to turn rascals out, so—it might be argued—a little belt tightening every now and then has some beneficial economic side effects. The denizens of higher education are understandably less objective when they are the central subjects—when it is their ox that may be gored.

Several external events have changed the circumstances in which we live:

1. The increase in the percentage of the 18–21 age group attending college has halted, and today the proportion is smaller than in 1970.[1]

---

[1]. U.S. Bureau of the Census, *Current Population Reports*, Series P-20, no. 241, 1973 (Washington: Government Printing Office).

It is hard to determine whether this is a temporary post-Vietnam phenomenon, or whether the saturation point for the age group has been almost reached.

2. The future size of the college-age group, which only five years ago looked as though it might pause only briefly in its continued growth to the end of the century, now looks stable over the last quarter of the century. Births in 1972 (and, thus, the 1990s' freshmen) were 20 percent fewer than 1954s' births (who were 1972s' freshmen). Census Series F projections predict that the 18–21 population in the year 2000 will be exactly the same size as in 1972.[2]

3. The possible overexpansion of graduate education, which seemed speculative in 1965, became a reality by 1970. While many scientific and technological fields, in which there is considerable industrial employment, have begun to recover from the initial impact of oversupply, in those fields of study where the demand is largely academic, the job market will be difficult for the next decade or two.

4. Tight budgetary constraints have become a relatively fixed part of the landscape, reflecting inflation, the emergence of other pressing social claims on the public fisc, and a relative decline in the (formerly excessive) confidence that the public has in education as a cure-all for the ills of modern society.

5. The new federal philosophy, expressed in the Education Amendments of 1972 (although not yet fully implemented), establishes as a federal responsibility the basic funding of a system of universal access to higher education, and selects direct student aid as the means of implementation.

These factors make the prospect for the next fifteen years quite different for colleges and universities from the experience of the fifteen years since Sputnik.

In *Higher Education: Who Pays? Who Benefits? Who Should Pay?*,[3] the Carnegie Commission on Higher Education reviewed financing trends over the past forty years and recommended a path for the future development of higher education. Although the recommendations will not be accepted uncritically in all quarters (some believing that the recommendations are too radical, and others that they do not go nearly far

---

2. U.S. Bureau of the Census, *Population Estimates and Projections*, Series P-25, no. 493, December 1972 (Washington: Government Printing Office).

3. New York: McGraw-Hill, June 1973. Hereafter referred to as *Who Pays? Who Benefits?* The material in this paper, except for the last section on financing recurrent education, is drawn primarily from that source.

enough), they are the result of several years of reflection by as dedicated and objective a group of knowledgeable observers as might be mustered. The recommendations were based on a careful review of recent trends, the recognition of changing circumstances within which higher education must live in the future, and a broad sense of priorities among social goals and objectives for the nation in the last quarter of this century.

THE RISING COSTS OF HIGHER EDUCATION

Over the last dozen years the number of full-time equivalent (FTE) students in higher education has risen by a factor of 2.5. Concurrently, the cost per student has risen by an almost equivalent factor, and the percentage of students in public institutions has increased from 59 percent to 74 percent.[4] This combination of factors has placed a heavy strain on the public purse. Total public (and, thus, taxpayer) subsidies for higher education have grown from $2,231 million in 1959–60 to an estimated $13,228 million in 1971–72. Table 1 shows the growth in public and philanthropic subsidies and net family outlays for higher education from 1929–30 to 1971–72 (*net family outlay* is defined as tuition and fees, plus basic subsistence costs, less student aid).[5]

Table 1: *Public and Philanthropic Subsidies and Net Family Outlays for Higher Education, 1929–30—1971–72*

(in millions of dollars)

Year	Subsidies			Net Family Outlay	Total
	Institutional, from Public Funds	Student Aid, from Public Funds	Gifts and Endowment Income		
1929–30	$ 171.4	$ 1.0	$ 100.6	$ 498.1	$ 771.0
1939–40	214.5	1.2	119.1	587.7	922.5
1949–50	957.7	998.0	234.3	899.3	3,089.3
1959–60	1,960.4	270.8	667.8	2,668.5	5,567.5
1969–70	8,657.5	1,736.1	1,783.3	7,724.8	19,901.7
1971–72[a]	10,425.0	2,803.0	2,040.0	8,683.0	23,951.0

Source: Carnegie Commission on Higher Education, *Higher Education: Who Pays? Who Benefits? Who Should Pay?* (New York: McGraw-Hill, 1973), Appendix A, and 1971–72 estimates by Cartter.

[a] Estimated.

The strain imposed on public funds is evident if one compares the 433 percent increase in public subsidies over the last twelve years with

4. Ibid., p. 66.
5. In all the figures that follow, 25 percent of federally sponsored research grants are included as a public subsidy of education, and veterans' and social security benefits for students enrolled in college are included as subsidies to students (an exception is noted in Table 2). See ibid., chap. 3 and Appendix A, for further descriptions and definitions of terms.

the increase of only 116 percent in GNP or of 243 percent in state and local tax receipts (two-thirds of educational subsidies come from state and local sources). The per student family outlay for higher education over this same twelve-year period increased only 35 percent and decreased in real terms (constant dollars) by 5 percent.[6]

This latter phenomenon needs comment, for it may seem at marked variance with how most parents perceive the costs of sending their sons or daughters to college. Between 1960–61 and 1972–73 the basic costs of attending college rose by 68 percent for the average in-state student in residence at a public institution and by 94 percent for the comparable student at a private college or university. In real terms the increases were 15 percent and 33 percent respectively.[7] However, the decline in the proportion of students in high-cost private institutions altered the mix in such a way that the overall average family outlay declined slightly in constant dollars.

Table 2 indicates subsidies and family outlays per capita and illustrates again the significant increases in public subsidy levels. Figure 1 casts the data in Table 2 in constant dollars, and shows that today public subsidies per student are about three times as high in real terms as in the prewar period and are nearly double the level of a dozen years ago.

The point of highlighting the historic increase in public subsidy levels is not to argue that they are too high today—one might as easily argue that they are too low—but, rather, to suggest that this upward trend is unlikely to continue. If the major social task still facing the nation is assuring access to higher education for capable potential students from low-income families who do not now attend, then some redistribution in the burden of costs may be necessary.

Over the past generation, the percentage share of cost borne by the average parent has declined from approximately two-thirds to nearly one-third, as indicated in Table 2. In constant dollars (see Figure 1) the average parent pays less today for sending a son or daughter to college than in 1929 or 1939.[8] While philanthropic giving has increased absolutely, the per student yield of gifts and endowment income has remained

---

6. See Table 2 and Fig. 1. For GNP and tax receipt data, see *Economic Report of the President*, January 1973 (Washington: Government Printing Office, 1973), Tables B-1, B-72.

7. U.S. Office of Education, *Projections of Educational Statistics to 1980–81* (Washington: Government Printing Office, 1972), Tables 44, 43.

8. *Who Pays? Who Benefits?*, p. 33.

Table 2: *Per Capita Student Subsidies from Public and Philanthropic Sources, and Net Family Outlays, 1929-30—1971-72*

Year	Subsidies						Outlay by Students and Parents		Total	
	Institutional, from Public Funds		Student Aid, from Public Funds		Gifts and Endowment Income					
	$	%	$	%	$	%	$	%	$	%
1929-30......	$ 194	22.2	$ 1	0.1	$114	13.0	$ 565	64.7	$ 874	100.0
1939-40......	185	23.4	1	0.1	103	12.9	507	63.7	796	100.0
1949-50......	444[a]	34.4	463[a]	35.9	109	8.4	275	21.3	1,291	100.0
1959-60......	706	35.2	98	4.9	240	12.0	961	47.9	2,005	100.0
1969-70......	1,444	43.5	289	8.7	297	9.0	1,288	38.8	3,318	100.0
1971-72[b].....	1,553	43.5	417	11.7	304	8.5	1,293	36.3	3,567	100.0

[a] Approximately one-third of GI bill expenditures were for tuition fees; they are classified here as institutional aid, but $143 per capita could be reclassified as student support. In 1949-50 about 55 percent of students were receiving veterans' benefits. By contrast, in 1969-70 only 9 percent were eligible for veterans' assistance.
[b] Estimated.

55

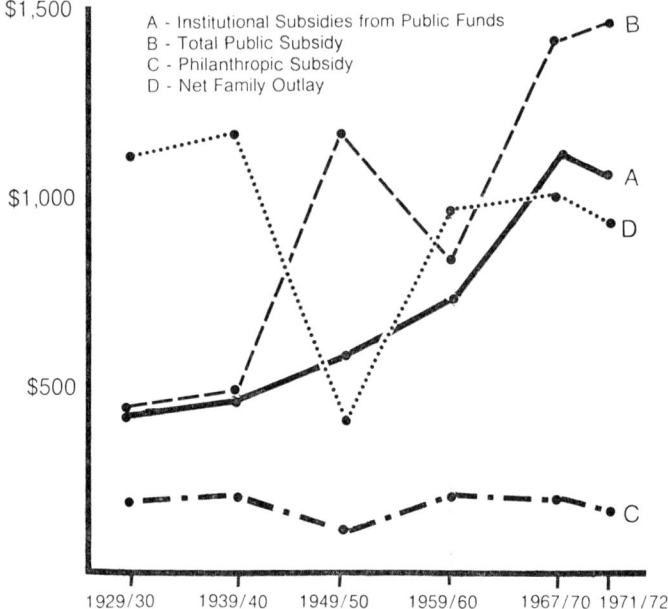

Fig. 1: Per capita student subsidies from public and philanthropic sources, and net family outlay, 1929–30—1971–72, in constant 1958 dollars. Note that 1949–50 was the peak in college attendance of World War II veterans.

nearly constant in real dollars. The major transformation in the postwar period has been the rising share of taxpayer costs.

THE WIDENING TUITION GAP

The rapid increase in public costs has come about partly, as noted, because an increasing proportion of students attend public rather than private colleges, and also because the lower tuition community colleges (and to some extent the four-year state colleges) have expanded more rapidly than the higher tuition state universities. The increase in the taxpayer share has been accentuated over the last two decades because tuition charges in the public sector have risen less rapidly than in the private sector. Private institutions have had not only to meet rising costs but also to compensate for the decline in endowment earnings and private gifts relative to total costs; in 1953–54 philanthropic funds accounted for one-third of total income, whereas today less than one-fourth comes from this source. In this same period the percentage increase in tuition fees has been smaller in the public institutions, and most markedly in the public universities, which account for about 40 percent of public enrollments.[9]

June O'Neill, in a study of educational sources of funds, published by the Carnegie Commission in 1973, provides a comparison of "net tuition income per student" for recent years. Net tuition income, after allowing for tuition remission and scholarships awarded out of current general funds, is a better measure of the real "price" of education than announced tuition levels. She notes that public institutions have been increasing student aid out of their own funds more rapidly than have private institutions, thus widening even further the effective tuition gap between the public and private sectors. Table 3 shows net tuition income for universities, four-year colleges, and two-year colleges over the past eighteen years. The ratio of private to public tuitions has risen steadily in this period from 2.9:1 to 4.7:1 for the university section, and from 4.1:1 to 5.5:1 for four-year colleges. The two-year colleges have about returned to their earlier relationship. Overall, however, the net tuition rate has gone from 3.5:1 to 5.3:1 since 1953–54.

In light of this widening tuition gap, it is not too surprising that the share of enrollment in private colleges and universities has been declining at an increasing rate over the last fifteen years. As Table 4 indicates, since 1955 enrollments in private institutions have declined from 44 percent to less than 27 percent of the total.

The new federal philosophy of aid to education appears to be moving toward direct student assistance rather than institutional aid. Eventually, if appropriations match authorizations, this "treatment" may assist in maintaining the health and vigor of public and private institutions; yet the first hesitant steps only partially support a new influx of students who require more institutional assistance and, often, more expensive educational service as well. At the state level, however, there are some encouraging signs that governors and legislatures are beginning to be concerned about the welfare of the state's total educational resources. The rapid expansion of state scholarship programs, totaling approximately $280 million in 1972–73, and the increased number of states assisting private institutions,[10] are evidences of this new concern.

9. Ibid., pp. 22, 144; *Projections of Educational Statistics*, Table 43.
10. Four states have direct formula grant programs: Pennsylvania has its long-established selective support program, and three other states have contractual arrangements with private colleges to enable them to enroll additional students. At least seven other states have contracts with one or more private institutions to support study in particular fields (predominantly medicine and dentistry).

Table 3: *Net Tuition Income per FTE Student, Public and Private Institutions, 1953-54—1971-72*

Year	Public Sector ($)			Private Sector ($)			Ratio, Private/Public			
	Univer-sities	Four-Year Colleges	Two-Year Colleges	Univer-sities	Four-Year Colleges	Two-Year Colleges	Univer-sities	Four-Year Colleges	Two-Year Colleges	Weighted Average
1953-54.........	$157	$ 94	$ 53	$ 459	$ 389	$ 302	2.9	4.1	5.7	3.5
1957-58.........	177	105	69	565	471	554	3.2	4.5	8.0	3.8
1961-62.........	207	135	80	776	634	672	3.7	4.7	8.4	4.3
1965-66.........	257	182	115	975	885	752	3.8	4.8	6.6	4.5
1969-70.........	279	211	156	1,246	1,111	938	4.5	5.3	6.0	5.1
1971-72 est.....	296	234	182	1,383	1,280	1,106	4.7	5.5	6.1	5.3
Percentage increase 1953-54— 1971-72........	89	149	243	201	229	266				

Source: June O'Neill, *Sources of Funds to Colleges and Universities* (Berkeley, Calif.: Carnegie Commission on Higher Education, 1973), p. 45, as updated by the commission staff.

Table 4: *Enrollment in Private Institutions, 1955–70*
(in thousands)

Year	Enrollment		Percentage in Private Institutions	Five-Year Change (Percentage Points)
	Total	Private Institutions		
1955	2,679	1,180	44.0	—
1960	3,583	1,467	41.0	−3.0
1965	5,526	1,902	34.4	−6.6
1970	7,920	2,120	26.8	−7.6

Source: *Who Pays? Who Benefits?*, p. 66.

PUBLIC AND PRIVATE SHARES OF TOTAL ECONOMIC COSTS

In debates on how the costs of higher education are borne, probably no subject is more controversial than inclusion or exclusion of foregone income. The economist, who is concerned with problems of overall resources allocation, views the lost income while an individual pursues full-time study as both a personal and a social cost of education. If there were no higher education, its seven million FTE occupants would be a part of the labor force, and—given time for market adjustments—most would find employment. However, by virtue of the millions of persons engaging in study, at any one moment in time those individuals are sacrificing potential earnings and the economy is yielding up some potential output. (In the long run both the individual and society may be better off as the result of such further education.)

For the student who must give up a job to return to college, foregone earnings are a real and visible cost. For students who continue to enjoy parental support, however, lost earnings are seldom part of a rational calculation about whether or not to attend college. And, for many parents, the alternative to sending their son or daughter to college is not that of capturing additional earnings for the family, but of seeing their offspring leave home as a separate economic unit. Thus foregone income has somewhat limited applicability to the individual situation, although it may be a useful concept in weighing the optimal social investment of resources in human capital development.

Even in the human capital approach, there are inherent problems in interpretation. In any calculation of rates of return, ideally all personal and social benefits should be part of the numerator, and all costs—including foregone income—should be part of the divisor. But nonpecuniary benefits are seldom quantifiable, and a significant part of personal expenditure on education is more appropriately classified as consumption rather than investment. Thus, to an individual (and perhaps to society at large) even a zero, or even negative, rate of return on expenditure may not be a rational reason for foregoing advanced education. If it were, few academicians would have pursued the Ph.D. or have entered academic employment, with its estimated 4 percent return.[11] Given these caveats, it may still be useful to observe the share of total economic costs of higher education borne by students and their families. Table 5 shows the Carnegie Commission estimates of these amounts from 1929–30 to 1970–71.

Table 5: *Estimated Foregone Income of College Students, 1929–30—1970–71*

Year	Per Student	Total (in millions)
1929–30	$ 562	$ 495
1939–40	521	604
1949–50	1,492	3,615
1959–60	2,347	6,517
1970–71	3,668	23,104

Source: *Who Pays? Who Benefits?*, p. 50.

Two significant points emerge from the inclusion of foregone income. First, when total economic costs are taken into account, the family share of the costs of higher education show a remarkable stability over the last forty years. Prior to World War II the family share was 70 percent, taxpayers provided 19 percent, and philanthropy 11 percent. Over the most recent decade these percentage shares have been 68 percent, 27 percent, and 5 percent. Second, as the family share of the direct cash outlay on education has declined since World War II, the foregone income costs have risen significantly. In 1940 approximately 25 percent of the economic cost for the family was in the form of tuition payments, 50 percent was for subsistence, and 25 percent was foregone income. In 1970, approximately only 15 percent was tuition cost, 20 percent was subsistence cost, and 65 percent was foregone income.[12] In earlier days when the wages of unskilled labor were relatively low, and in periods of depression when unemployment was high, the opportunity costs of attending college were much less than they are in today's relatively prosperous world.

    11. This figure is the most reliable estimate I have seen of the yield on investment in the Ph.D. See P. Taubman and T. Wales, "Education as an Investment and a Screening Device" (MS; New York: National Bureau of Economic Research, 1972).

    12. See *Who Pays? Who Benefits?*, chap. 7, for a discussion of foregone income and total economic costs.

EQUITY CONSIDERATIONS

In its 1971 report *New Approaches to Student Financial Aid*, the College Scholarship Service task force concluded that, "If it were possible to reconstitute the entire system of higher education, it could be done in such a way that all financial need of qualified students could be met today with existing resources."[13] The panel had in mind that the total subsidy for higher education, from all public and philanthropic sources, totaled slightly over $15 billion in 1971–72, or approximately $2,250 per student.

The CSS panel noted three ways in which the system functions less than ideally insofar as social equity is concerned: (1) It was mildly critical of institutional policies, noting that its studies indicated that high-need students tended to be excluded from entry, and that students with the greatest need frequently had a below-average share of grant funds in their total student aid package. (2) It expressed concern that a high proportion of student aid was beyond institutional control.[14] Similarly, the Carnegie Commission noted that, of an estimated $4 billion in student aid funds expended in 1971–72, less than 20 percent were funds at the discretion of the institutions themselves, and over 55 percent were in the form of veterans' benefits and social security dependents' benefits, not entirely based on need. And (3) it pointed out that by far the greatest sum of public monies were expended as institutional subsidies, with random benefits to all students regardless of need. On this point, the Carnegie Commission also noted: "More than two-thirds of all support funds function to subsidize the 'price' of higher education. Because many students from upper-income group families attend institutions with tuitions which are far below costs (true in the case of many private colleges and universities as well as public institutions), these educational subsidies are not distributed as effectively as might be the case if minimizing the financial barrier to attendance were the primary goal."[15]

There was a time several decades ago when, in many states, public colleges and universities attracted a student population composed largely of those who could not afford to attend a private college. Thus it was easier to defend a policy of zero or low tuition as a means of targeting benefits to a relatively homogeneous socioeconomic group. This is no

---

13. Panel on Student Financial Need Analysis, Allan M. Cartter, chairman (New York: College Entrance Examination Board, 1971), p. 7.
14. Ibid., p. 9.
15. *Who Pays? Who Benefits?*, p. 39; see also pp. 57–58.

longer true. The 1972 Bureau of the Census survey of undergraduates showed the following percentages of students in public institutions, by family income group:[16]

	Percentage
Under $3,000	81
$3,000–$5,000	82
$5,000–$7,500	86
$7,500–$10,000	84
$10,000–$15,000	80
Over $15,000	77

From a strictly equity standpoint, therefore, tuition subsidies are a relatively ineffective way of aiding students from low-income families.

The comprehensive survey conducted in 1972 by the California State Scholarship and Loan Commission of how students and families meet college costs is illuminating in this respect, inasmuch as California traditionally has offered a wide variety of relatively low tuition public education but has not been among the leading states in providing financial assistance to students.[17] The California survey found that family contributions to the cost of education (from parents, student resources, and loans) for students attending the University of California averaged $1,930 for families with incomes below $6,000 and up to $2,530 for families with incomes above $18,000. The family contribution for students from the lowest- and highest-income groups averaged respectively $1,320 and $1,860 in the state colleges, $970 and $1,450 in the public community colleges, and $1,920 and $3,310 in the private colleges.

When one estimates the total monetary outlay on education (including subsidies from public and philanthropic sources), it appears that students and their parents in the under-$6,000 family income group contributed about 40 percent of the total cost of education, while students and their parents in the over-$18,000 income group contributed 55 percent.[18] Even allowing for the College Scholarship Service standard as-

---

16. See ibid., p. 92; based on U.S. Bureau of the Census, *Current Population Reports*, Series P-20, no. 236, 1972 (Washington: Government Printing Office), Table 8.

17. In the mid-1960s, California was first in the nation in the percentage of high school graduates entering college, but last in the nation in the amount of institutional student aid available per student. This situation has been significantly altered over the past five years by the development of the state scholarship program. For recent data, see California State Scholarship and Loan Commission, *Student Resources Survey* (Sacramento: The Commission, 1972).

18. *Who Pays? Who Benefits?*, Appendix C.

sumption that all students should be expected to contribute at least $600 from summer earnings toward their college costs, one might have concluded that a system with real social equity would have resulted in only a 15–20 percent range for the lowest-income group, up to perhaps 70–75 percent for the highest-income group. Obviously, if the cost to students and their parents is still a minimum of $1,300–$1,900 a year to attend a four-year college, there is still a long way to go to remove effectively the financial barrier to college attendance.

THE FINANCING TASK FOR THE DECADE AHEAD

Between 1973 and 1978 there will be an 8 percent growth in the size of the 18–21 age group; in the succeeding ten years there will be a 17 percent decline, followed by a gradual return to the 1973 level by the year 2000. If the proportion of 18-year-olds completing high school rises by about 0.5 percent per year (it rose nearly 1 percent a year in the 1960s, but has not increased for the past two years), higher education would have to expand by 12–15 percent during the remainder of the 1970s just to maintain the present attendance rate. However, achievement of the goal of universal access and the elimination of financial barriers to college attendance in this decade will probably mean increasing the number of young people in college by 30–40 percent. Almost all of this increment in enrollment, however, will come from low socioeconomic groups, and substantial financial assistance will be required. And, as noted above, there is considerable room for improvement in assistance to low-income students already in college. It seems reasonable to conclude, therefore, that, even if educational costs were to remain at their 1973 level, a 50 percent or greater increase in funds would be required.

As most studies of educational costs have emphasized, education—as a labor-intensive industry—does not benefit substantially from productivity improvements, as most American industry does. Thus, it seems likely that the cost per student will continue to rise in this decade as it has in past decades, at about the rate of increase in disposable income. This assumption produces an approximate 5 percent annual increase in costs—somewhat greater if inflation continues at its recent rate.

Even these relatively conservative assumptions lead to a projected increase in required educational funds of about 110 percent between 1973 and 1980. In the same period the national income, under the same inflation assumptions, would be likely to increase by less than 50 percent. Facing these prospects, the Carnegie Commission concluded that if the nation is serious about the objective of equality of educational opportunity and wishes to make universal access to postsecondary education a reality in this decade, there must be some redistribution in the burden of education costs.

The commission has recommended basically: (1) a gradual increase in tuition charges at public institutions from the current level, equal to approximately 17 percent of educational costs, to a new level approximating one-third of costs (this increase would release some funds for expanded state scholarship programs, partly to relieve the states of rapidly escalating expenditures for higher education through this decade, and to help redress the growing imbalance between public and private tuition levels), and (2) a gradual increase in federal funds for higher education, primarily through direct student assistance, raising the federal share of public funding to a 50:50 status with the states (from the current ratio of about 42:58).[19]

The logic for the significant increase in federal assistance is that this will be necessary to provide for the equalization of opportunities among states and regions, that the progressive federal tax structure is a more equitable base of funding, and that the progressive income tax now appropriates the greatest portion of the income advantage resulting from education to federal, rather than to state and local, tax revenues. Hartman has shown that, even under current attendance patterns, nearly two-thirds of the state and local taxes that support education are paid by taxpayers who have not attended a public college or university.[20] Based on Hartman's data, I have estimated that the average public college graduate, who can be expected at age fifty to enjoy an approximate $4,500 income advantage over his high school graduate neighbor, is likely to pay only an additional $210 in state taxes annually. That would be insufficient to pay one-half of the interest charges on the amount of state subsidy to his education, had the state borrowed the funds. By contrast, the same individual would pay an approximate additional $1,500 in federal income tax annually.

The commission has recommended that the federal government, through an enlarged Basic Opportunity Grants program, provide up to 75 percent of educational costs in the first two years of college (with a

19. Ibid., pp. 105–9. This ratio includes all federally funded research expenditures. If only one-fourth of such funds is included as education-related, the federal share would increase to 44.

20. Robert W. Hartman, "Equity Implications of State Tuition Policy and Student Loans," *Journal of Political Economy*, May–June 1972, p. 161.

somewhat higher ceiling than the present $1,400), and up to 50 percent in succeeding years, based on need. It is also recommended that federal funds match state scholarship funds on a 1:3 basis, rather than merely matching incremental state funds.[21] Thus a student with 100 percent need would have approximately full funding in the first two years of college and about three-fourths funding in upper division years.

The commission also strongly urged again the creation of a National Student Loan Bank, with income-contingent repayments over a period of thirty to forty years. It felt that ground is being lost in the creation of an adequate loan program, just when loans may become an even more important part of the financing picture. The elimination of forgiveness features and the deferral, rather than the complete subsidization, of interest charges while a student is still in college would permit such a loan program to be self-financing over the long run and obviate the need for strict eligibility requirements. By making the federal government first creditor and arranging repayments through the federal income tax mechanism, collection and monitoring procedures could be greatly simplified.[22]

ARE THE CARNEGIE COMMISSION RECOMMENDATIONS ADEQUATE?

The recommendations of the commission will not be met by unmixed praise. At the one extreme, those who support the principle of full-cost pricing and a voucher or an educational opportunity bank program may feel that the proposals are hardly more than a token move in the right direction. At the other extreme, those who are wedded to the principle of free tuition in public institutions will undoubtedly feel that they represent a giant step in the wrong direction. Among the commission membership the same variety of viewpoints was present, and only by grappling with the issues over the period of several years did a consensus position emerge that seemed capable of resolving (or at least mitigating) many of the emerging financial problems and of achieving the objective of universal access to higher education for those who have both the ability and the motivation. The recommended evolutionary approach toward a new condition where students would have greater latitude of choice, and where diversity would be preserved, is not simply a working compromise but the attempt to work out a realistic blueprint for higher education that could be implemented over the next ten years. Clearly, in this observer's opinion, if the trends of the last few years continue un-

21. *Who Pays? Who Benefits?*, p. 112.
22. Ibid., p. 121.

changed, the incipient financial crises of the early 1970s will become permanent features of the landscape. I believe that many deep-rooted problems—particularly with respect to the coexistence of public and private higher education—have been unrecognized or ignored during the 1955–70 period of sustained growth and relative academic affluence. As institutions now approach conditions more akin to a steady state in enrollments and face continued budgetary constraints, this vessel which sailed so nicely in calm water before the wind may fare less well in sailing more turbulent seas.

For some institutions, these recommendations may provide assistance too little and too late. In some states it may take many years to overcome the traditional allegiances built up toward a particular point of view. There is an inherent danger that state action, which the commission believes must follow federal initiative, may adopt only the tuition increase half of the recommendations and actually take the situation a step or two backward from achieving universal access. And yet, to do nothing because there may be dangers in any new course is to lack the courage to attempt to solve our own problems. At the least, the commission has tried to take a comprehensive view of the total higher educational system; at the best, it has presented a practical, coherent program that will harmonize the diverse interests within higher education and society at large.

Beyond the Next Decade

The Carnegie Commission, in *Who Pays? Who Benefits?*, concluded: "We recognize that, at some point in the future, the United States may need a more drastic overhaul of the financing of postsecondary education than we suggest here. . . . Consequently, the financing of higher education will and should remain on the agenda for continuing examination for the foreseeable future" (pp. 17–18).

As one views the broad outlines of postsecondary education in this country, it seems apparent that pressures are growing to expand its boundaries to include areas of training and education that have not traditionally been—and may not be properly—part of "higher education" and to serve adult audiences in various forms of recurrent education. Recent federal legislation has encouraged further development of vocational and technical education, and proprietary schools are receiving new recognition. The reports of the Commission on Non-Traditional Study (Samuel B. Gould, chairman) and the Commission on Continuing

Education (the Reverend Theodore M. Hesburgh, chairman of the steering committee of the task force), and a report by the Carnegie Commission on alternative channels to life and work, all lend greater visibility to both the needs and the opportunities in these areas.[23]

Stephen Dresch has argued that public policy has precluded "adaptive evolution of the postsecondary educational system," stressing that "effectively, the function of public policy has been to so heavily subsidize the dominant mode of educational delivery as to render alternatives non-viable." He believes that by supporting institutions, which have been primarily concerned with traditional forms of education of young persons just out of high school, we have tended to homogenize and freeze postsecondary education into a single mold. In his view, adult "recurrent education represents a [potential] fracturing of the lockstep imposed by the traditional educational structure."[24]

One need not subscribe fully to Dresch's view to agree that had the American tradition been to provide subsidies to students rather than to institutions, the course of educational development might have been somewhat different. Experience under the GI bills is evidence that diverse types of education and training might be sought if students were given freer choice of how, where, and when to use their educational support.

I believe that the long-run trend in the United States—partly evident now in the expanding state and federal student aid programs, supported by the Carnegie Commission recommendations, and reinforced by the political and legal moves to recognize "youth" as adults at age eighteen—is to ensure that persons have sufficient resources to pursue meaningful education throughout their lives and to provide them choice among a variety of options.

I do not believe that the present system of institutional support in public systems of higher education will be displaced; rather, I do believe that the major portion of incremental public funds over the remainder of this century will be channeled to and through students.

23. Respectively, *Diversity by Design* (San Francisco: Jossey-Bass, 1973), 178 pp.; *The Learning Society: A Report of the Study on Continuing Education and the Future* (Notre Dame, Ind.: University of Notre Dame, Center for Continuing Education, 1973); Carnegie Commission on Higher Education, *Toward a Learning Society: Alternative Channels to Life, Work, and Service* (New York: McGraw-Hill, 1973).

24. "U.S. Public Policy and the Evolutionary Adaptability of Post-Secondary Education," Higher Education Research Project Report no. 2, Yale University, March 1973.

If the nation *is* moving in this direction, then I believe that new forms and procedures of funding must be devised that will make adult recurrent education a reality. At present, most student aid programs are geared to parental income, leaving the adult students (and often the young "emancipated" students) to fend for themselves. To add to the anomaly, our tradition of public education is to subsidize heavily undergraduate degree credit instruction and, to a lesser extent, graduate and professional instruction, but to charge adults full cost in continuing education programs.

In an insightful background paper for an international meeting in the fall of 1972, Gösta Rehn, director of Manpower and Social Affairs, Organization for Economic Cooperation and Development, proposed that member countries consider an integrated plan for all periods of "nonwork"—a plan that would provide "a high degree of interchangeability, to be established instead of the present systems for youth education, adult studies, vacations . . . and retirement."[25] Under such a plan educational costs, paid leaves of absence (sabbaticals), annual vacations of varying length, and retirement pensions would all become part of a single social insurance plan supported by employer and employee contributions.

In a recent paper, I proposed an adaptation of Rehn's proposal designed to fit the American scene.[26] I summarize that proposal only to indicate the kind of development that may be both feasible and desirable before this century is out.

Under this plan collegiate education would continue much as it is today except that each person would have a "drawing right" from the federal government equal to one-half of tuition costs (perhaps up to $1,500 annually) for four years. Funds so drawn could be used at any time for traditional higher education or for training experiences such as those provided by proprietary schools, trade union programs, on-the-job or apprenticeship training, civic organizations, as well as degree-credit work in traditional colleges and universities. Students to age twenty-two would also be eligible for supplementary financial aid from federal, state, and institutional sources depending on need, as at present.

After one entered the work force, there would be a 4 percent surtax

---

25. "Prospective View on Patterns of Working Time" (Paper prepared for an International Conference on New Patterns for Working Time, September 1972, Report no. 1 B, OECD [Paris]).

26. Allan M. Cartter, "The Need for a New Approach to Financing Recurrent Education" (Paper delivered at the Princeton Conference on Continuing Education, May 16–17, 1973).

on earnings until age sixty, with collections credited to an individual's social insurance account. After five years in the work force, an individual would be eligible for paid education leave, receiving income from the fund at 50 percent of current salary for a period equal to one month for each year of contribution. Up to age forty-five, paid leaves could be used only for approved educational purposes (although not necessarily of a vocational or professional nature); after age forty-five such accumulated rights could be used for any educational or noneducational leave purpose. At, or after, age sixty any unexpended balance in one's account could be used for terminal employment leave or be credited to one's pension account for higher retirement benefits. A spouse who has had no work experience could draw on the partner's eligibility at a one-half benefit level; this scheme is designed to ease the problem for wives entering or reentering the labor force.

The income maintenance portion of this plan would be self-financing; the costs of the tuition grant portion would be offset by savings in other current federal programs.[27]

The greatest barrier to continuing formal education in our society is financial: few persons can afford to take the time away from a job and make substantial income sacrifices in their adult years. Unless some means can be found to finance paid education leaves, the Hutchins dream of a "learning society," providing for adult education to everyone at all stages of grown-up life, will remain largely a dream. Those in the academic community have long appreciated the value of sabbatical leaves; in an increasingly technological age the potential personal and societal benefits of intermittent education throughout one's life are high and constantly rising. Skill obsolescence, labor force reentry problems, career advancement, and the continued broadening of one's intellectual and cultural horizons are all compelling reasons for devising arrangements which will both permit and encourage the individual pursuit of further education.

27. According to the proposal, income tax exemptions for dependents over eighteen and deductions for education expenses would be eliminated from the federal income tax provisions; social security dependents' allowances would be treated similarly; unemployment compensation would be limited to a maximum of ten weeks until educational benefits were exhausted; similar rules would be applied to public assistance eligibility; federal manpower training expenditures would be reduced by 50 percent; and veterans' benefits would be discontinued, although a double contribution credit might be granted for public service in the military, job corps, or other special programs. For 1972–73, it was estimated, the savings on existing programs would be slightly more than $10 billion, while tuition grants would have been approximately $8.5 billion.

As one looks ahead for higher education, the 1980s will be a time when the real costs to society of extending educational opportunities will be minimal. With the decline in the size of the 18–21 age group, the faculty and facilities necessary to begin to truly serve adult audiences will be more readily available.

Meantime, there is still some distance to go in this decade to serve the young and to bring equality of educational opportunity closer to reality. The Carnegie Commission, in its endeavors over the last five years, has kept that goal in the forefront of its priorities and has attempted to chart a course that would aid in that considerable achievement.

Academic Freedom and the Financing of Higher Education

HOWARD R. BOWEN

THE ISSUES IN FINANCING HIGHER EDUCATION are overwhelmingly matters of value rather than technique. The system of higher education finance is complex and untidy because the values to be taken into account are numerous, not all of them are mutually compatible, and not everyone agrees on their relative priority. Among the values often considered are: access for persons of all social classes, equity in the distribution of costs and benefits, responsiveness of institutions to their clienteles and to broad social objectives, efficiency of institutional operation, adequacy of total revenues, and so on. I shall consider the financing in relation to yet another value, one omitted from most current discussions—academic freedom.

ACADEMIC FREEDOM DEFINED

Academic freedom is usually thought of as the right and duty of individual professors to seek and to speak the truth, but this concept is only part of academic freedom. It also includes such matters as a latitude for institutions to decide whom to admit, what to teach, how to teach, what academic standards to maintain, what lines of research and scholarship to pursue, what to publish, and whom to employ as professors. Academic freedom implies wide scope for internal decision making based on professional judgment. It does not justify social irresponsibility.

Indeed, a major task of institutional boards and administrators is to ensure both that the academic community serves the society and that the society does not take over the university.

This kind of academic freedom has always been fragile. Historically, bishops, princes, major benefactors, and democratic government have often exerted undue pressures on colleges and universities. Nevertheless, the tradition of academic independence has survived. Such independence is valued for several reasons. It enables members of the academic community to seek and to speak the truth. It gives professional people, who are better qualified than most lay groups, a decisive influence over the advancement of knowledge. It frees the university to fill an indispensable role in social and artistic criticism. It creates incentives for institutional excellence by placing initiative in the institutions and by encouraging faculty and students to participate in matters affecting them. And it places responsibility for institutional success squarely on boards and administrators.

This kind of academic freedom enables the campus to be one of the few places in our society where ideas can be freely explored and where few restrictions are imposed by official ideologies or the need for early practical results. Institutions where these conditions have prevailed and which have maintained linkages with the social interest, have proved to be immensely productive for the long-run advancement of society and seldom subversive of the true social interest.

Academe needs independence for the same reasons that the law courts and the communications media, which also have responsibilities for the truth, need it.

THE ASSAULT ON ACADEMIC FREEDOM

In recent years, wholesale encroachments on academic freedom have occurred. Most of them have not been intended to curb academic freedom and not all of them have been undesirable. Yet their gross effect has been a major assault on academic freedom. Examples are the imposition on state colleges and universities of such controls as line-item budgets, civil service regulations, central purchasing, central architectural controls, state control of tuition rates, seizure of tuition income, regulation of teaching loads and tenure, arbitrary formulas for setting appropriations, central decision making by multicampus system offices and coordinating commissions. Other threats to academic freedom have included a multiplicity of federal categorical grant programs, the proposed

1202 commissions, judicial review of academic decisions, and affirmative action. To these must be added the recent barrage of criticism of higher education from public officials and others, indiscriminate demands for "innovation," the insistence on "accountability" without regard to the inherent difficulties of evaluating educational performance, the numerous proposals for reform of "governance," the attacks on voluntary accreditation, and the intrusion of partisan politics into academic affairs.

Not all of these outside influences, taken singly, are bad, and no one proposes that higher education be exempt from all social control. Taken together, however, these pressures have impaired the inner-direction of colleges and universities that we associate with academic freedom.

The outcome of these influences in combination has been to create two models of the university. One is the bureaucratic model, in which the university would become, for practical purposes, an agency of government, with basic decisions made by state or federal bureaucracies. The other is the full-cost pricing model, in which each service of the university would be financed by a user charge: instruction paid by tuitions; student aid, by long-term loans; auxiliary services, by fees; research, by grants and contracts; and public services, by fees.

In both models, the institution would be largely or totally other-directed. In the bureaucratic model, it would be controlled by government. In the full-cost pricing model, it would be market-oriented and would supply whatever services could be sold at a price sufficient to cover cost. These models are not just figments of my imagination. They are being advocated by most of those who would reform higher education. The bureaucratic model is advocated by those who emphasize the need for "planning and coordination"; the full-cost pricing model is advocated by economists who believe that the market can solve all problems and by government officials who would like to get higher education off the public budget. Both models are consistent with the "jam factory approach"; higher education should be valued, like a jam factory, according to its contribution to the gross national product.[1]

FINANCIAL FOUNDATIONS OF ACADEMIC FREEDOM

The method of financing has important bearing on academic freedom. Academic freedom will be strengthened to the extent that institu-

---

[1]. C. F. Carter, "Costs and Benefits of Mass Higher Education," mimeographed (University of Lancaster, 1972).

tions are financed by (1) unrestricted funds and (2) funds from diverse sources. The mode of financing is not the only determinant of academic freedom, but it is a factor. If an institution were to receive chiefly funds earmarked by a bureaucracy or a legislature or were to be financed mainly through the sale of its products in the market, its inner-direction would be negligible. Similarly, if it received all of its income from a single source, even though the funds were unrestricted, the freedom of the institution would in fact be narrowly circumscribed. Substantial unrestricted funds and diverse sources of support are what give a college or university its soul.

If, then, academic freedom is a goal of high priority, a system of finance along present lines is desirable: some of the funds come from tuitions, some from the states and municipalities with varying degrees of restriction, some from agencies of the federal government, and some from private donors such as foundations, corporations, and individuals. The system is diversified and can produce considerable amounts of unrestricted monies if bureaucratic tendencies are held in check. One can argue for various incremental changes in the system, for example, that tuitions should be a bit higher or lower, that the federal government should or should not make institutional grants, that the federal government should increase or decrease tax incentives for private giving, and the like. Of course, such incremental changes are not trivial, but they are of second-order importance as compared with the basic principle that institutions should have substantial unrestricted funds and should be financed from diverse sources.

I am in accord with Cartter's paper, and with the report of the Carnegie Commission on Higher Education on which it is based,[2] because it suggests that the present financial framework be preserved and that only certain modest incremental changes be made. I am somewhat relieved because I had feared that the commission might make a more extreme recommendation (for example, full-cost pricing) that would be destructive of institutional integrity and academic freedom.

I am not enthusiastic about some details of the Carnegie report. I would prefer that tuitions rise less than the commission recommends. In the interest of easy access I especially favor holding tuitions very low in both community colleges and state colleges. I am not enthusiastic about the suggestion that tuitions be higher for upper division and

2. *Higher Education: Who Pays? Who Benefits? Who Should Pay?* (New York: McGraw-Hill, 1973).

graduate study than for lower division study. On the other hand, I recognize that higher education must somehow be financed and that increased tuitions may have to make up for deficiencies in other sources. But I regard these matters as details. The basic principles of unrestricted funds and diverse sources are preserved.

PRIVATE HIGHER EDUCATION

My main quarrel with this Carnegie Commission report, as well as earlier ones, concerns the treatment of private higher education. It is not so much that I disagree with what it has said as that I feel that it has not given the private sector the emphasis it deserves. Again I emphasize the goal of academic freedom. I believe the private sector is a bastion of academic freedom in this country. I realize that the distinction between private and public institutions is not a sharp one. Yet, private institutions are largely exempt from bureaucratic control, and they are financially less dependent on government than most public institutions. They are, therefore, in a position—if adequately financed—to exercise considerable academic freedom and to use that freedom in the pursuit of academic excellence. The private sector must be preserved and strengthened in ways that will enable it to be independent, flexible, diversified, and pace setting. Yet, today its vital tax exemption is under threat, and the tuition gap between private and public institutions is steadily widening. Barring an early change in national policy, many private institutions are headed for oblivion. The recommendations of the Carnegie Commission are manifestly weak. For example, they suggest "gradual narrowing of the tuition differential" and "experimentation with different patterns" of aid which "would provide a diversity of experience that will be useful in developing guidelines for effective educational policy in the future."[3] Such recommendations strike me as fiddling while Rome burns.

Some Doubtful Assumptions Examined

HAROLD L. ENARSON

RALPH WALDO EMERSON, brooding on a troubled America, once said, "Who can remember when the times were not hard and money scarce?" And so it is with colleges and universities. The archives of almost any

---

3. *Who Pays? Who Benefits?*, pp. 114–16.

of the institutions will contain useful reminders that the money crunch, supposed to be so distinctive in the 1970s, is as old as higher education itself—tax-financed higher education at least. Such evidence abounds in the archives and is as fresh in memory as yesterday's legislative session. As Cartter notes in his paper, the financing of higher education has always been among our most difficult and enduring problems. It forces the search for ingenious, no-pain solutions even as it invites dealing with family rivalries between the public and private sectors of the higher learning.

What are we to make of the Carnegie Commission on Higher Education "package," offered in *Higher Education: Who Pays? Who Benefits? Who Should Pay?* and covered in brief compass in the Cartter paper? I have no quarrel with increasing the volume of our appeals for federal dollars, in this instance for full funding of the Basic Opportunity Grants provisions. But neither have I any illusions that a program neglected by the ninety-third Congress in its first session is likely to become a firm, long-term commitment undergirding a more stable, more equitable funding base. Nor have I any quarrel with very substantial increases in state assistance to low-income persons now deprived of "equal access." But I do quarrel with the central thesis that the path to salvation and solvency, equity and equality, lies in the substantial and continuing increase in tuition charges each year of the next decade for the great majority of our students, who look to the public colleges and universities to redeem the American promise of educational opportunity.

The Carnegie study purports to be an analysis of public policy whose logic derives from the pile-up of economic analyses. In fact, the study is simply an expression of conviction and preference on a battleground of policy making scarred by the march of contesting armies.

It is not that the statistics employed are loaded or inaccurate. But honest persons do read the same data differently. This is why men in bars quarrel over whether the glass is half full or half empty and why the incautious drown in lakes only four feet deep, on the average, that is. And if "the facts" per se do not have, cannot have unequivocal meaning, we should also note that the flow of argument is as revealing and eloquent in its silence as in its substantive content. In my reading the Carnegie report has more than its share of calculated silence.

It is asserted that a continued shift in the share of enrollment to the advantage of the public sector is somehow *bad*. But nowhere is the argument explicitly developed, as it must be if it is to be persuasive.

It is asserted that, by virtue of substantially increased tuition charges imposed on students in our public colleges and universities, new monies in substantial amount will be made available for financial assistance to the low-income population. But this is surely a very large and dubious assumption and is nowhere documented with evidence of how state legislatures typically behave.

It is asserted that steady, substantial increases in tuition year-in and year-out for the next decade in our state-supported institutions will not deter students from seeking access to the expanded opportunity we set as institutional and national goals. But surely that too is a very large and doubtful assumption. Have the Carnegie Commission members actually talked, as many of us have, with married students holding two jobs? with students who save and stint to start college again? with parents who have large families heading for college? with wives who work in order to put hubby through graduate school?

I reflect on the Carnegie report with growing puzzlement. Perhaps Ohio is atypical, but in the last session of the Ohio General Assembly, the voice of students rang out loud and clear and was heard by legislators, who then imposed a two-year freeze on tuitions even as they appropriated substantially increased amounts (not enough, of course) for the operations of postsecondary institutions. Our customers *believe* that higher tuition will drive them away from our colleges and universities. I find this pocketbook testimony more persuasive than aggregate economic analysis.

One may speculate whether the tools of economic analysis provide sufficient answers in an area where human choice and preference dictate precarious balance. For myself, I share the concern of students and parents, of alumni and legislators and the folks at the PTA, the Grange, and the labor union that higher education is—right now—being priced beyond the reach of many people. No amount of talk about universal access should obscure this clear and present danger.

I cannot believe that fifty state legislatures are ready to embrace a "sock it to the students" formula in the vague hope that narrowing the tuition differentials between the public and private institutions will somehow solve, or significantly ameliorate, the plight of the private schools. Do we purposefully contract opportunity in the good cause of expanding opportunity? In today's slang: No way!

And if *that* doesn't join the issue, I shall be surprised. After all, it is a domestic quarrel of long standing.

On Closer Examination

ROBERT W. HARTMAN

THE PAPER BY Allan Cartter and the longer Carnegie Commission report which it summarizes represent the most lucid and comprehensive game plan for higher education that we have.[1] They demand serious attention and, especially if one is inclined to agree with the conclusions, criticism. The following is a friendly criticism.

The thrust of Cartter's proposals is summarized by Table 1, which is derived from the Carnegie Commission report. The broad thrusts of the recommendations for public support of higher education are: (1) Support from all levels of government would grow 77 percent (in constant dollars) over the 1970–83 period, about the same as the rate of growth of the costs of higher education. (2) Federal outlays would grow twice as fast as state-local funds, and would constitute 60 percent of the increase in taxpayer support over the period. Federal aid expansion would be concentrated on student aid, although federal research and institutional support would grow somewhat faster than the real gross national product. (3) State and local general subsidies—primarily institutional aid to the public sector—is programmed to grow at about the same rate as enrollments in public institutions. In other words, the per student subsidy deriving from low tuition would be frozen at 1970–71 levels. Student aid at the state and local level is slated to be, far and away, the fastest growing form of assistance under the Carnegie proposals. With federal matching funds included, they might grow to as much as $2 billion in 1983.[2]

I believe that the broad goals which the proposals are designed to meet and the overall composition of the package of public instruments selected to meet the objectives are the right ones. My criticism deals only with the details of the proposal and with some of the rhetoric used to justify the plans.

---

1. Carnegie Commission on Higher Education, *Higher Education: Who Pays? Who Benefits? Who Should Pay?* (New York: McGraw-Hill, 1973).

The views expressed are solely those of the author, and should not be attributed to the trustees, officers, or other staff members of the Brookings Institution.

2. The commission proposes that the federal share of state scholarship programs be set at 25 percent (ibid., p. 123); thus in Table 1 the $1.5 billion shown for state and local student aid should be supplemented by $500 million from the federal student aid total of $5.7 billion.

Table 1: *Carnegie Commission Proposal for Taxpayer Support for Higher Education, 1970–83*

(in billions of 1970–71 dollars)

Source of Taxpayer Support	1970–71	1983	Percentage Change	Percentage Distribution of Change
Federal				
Institutional.............		$ 6.5		
Research................	$ 2.460			
Other institutional and graduate.............	1.330		71.5	25.5
Student aid..............		5.7	178.5	34.4
Veterans................	1.117			
Social security...........	.455			
Other...................	.475			
Total federal..........	$ 5.837	$12.2	109.0	59.9
State and local				
General..................	$ 7.604	$10.7	40.7	29.1
Student aid..............	.336	1.5	346.4	11.0
Total state and local....	$ 7.940	$12.2	53.7	40.1
All government.............	$13.777	$24.4	77.1	100.0

Source: *Higher Education: Who Pays? Who Benefits? Who Should Pay?* (New York: McGraw-Hill, 1973), pp. 24, 106, 162, 179–81.

The Federal Share and Student Aid

Cartter and the commission advocate raising the federal share of taxpayer support from its present 42 percent to 50 percent by the early 1980s,[3] with most of the expansion taking place in federal student grants and matching funds for state student grant programs.

The implicit level of student aid in these proposals seems to me to be out of line. Combined federal and state student aid would be $7.2 billion (in 1970–71 dollars) in 1983, when enrollments might total nine million full-time equivalent students.[4] If one-third of the students were to receive state and federal grants, the implied average benefit per student is $2,400 (in 1970–71 dollars) or $3,300 in current dollars. An average student grant of this magnitude, combined with the commission's advocacy of continued low tuition for lower division students, must mean that the commission is advocating that the federal government replace a fraction of the foregone earnings of low-income students as well as reimbursing them for the direct costs of education. Alternatively, the commission

---

3. Cartter's paper states that the increase would be from 33 percent to 50 percent, but I believe the former excludes research expenditures whereas the latter includes them. The percentages given in my text include research in both years.

4. *Who Pays? Who Benefits?*, p. 179.

may be advocating that eligibility for student grants extend to a very large fraction—say two-thirds—of all undergraduates at a smaller average grant.[5] In this case, for example, six million students might receive an average grant of $1,200.

Whatever the commission means, it is too much. Replacing foregone earnings—or paying students to attend college—is a premature proposal at best. If low-income students were given grants to cover direct costs (including subsistence) and were allowed to borrow funds to supplement such grants, their enrollment rates might rise into a range where even the most enthusiastic advocate of equal opportunity would be satisfied. Surely, with the present unwillingness of the Congress to attain even this goal, it is folly to plead for even more. Alternatively, if a grant program covers well over half of the student body in the 1980s, it is clear that such aid will extend to the children of families who are well above the median income in the nation. Although such a proposal is far superior to present financing arrangements—where large subsidies extend even to the very wealthy—it is hard, given competing public needs, to make a good case for such subsidies. In short, it seems to me that a program covering about one-third of the students in 1983, paying an average grant about equal to the authorized level of Basic Opportunity Grants (corrected for tuition increases), would result in a federal student aid budget of less than $4 billion in 1970–71 dollars.[6] If the Carnegie proposal of 80:20 sharing between the federal and state government were adopted, total student aid in 1983 would be about $4.7 billion, well under the $7.2 billion proposed by the commission.

I get the feeling from Cartter's paper and the Carnegie report that a fatal flaw of the modest proposal just outlined is that the federal share of taxpayer support does not come out to be 50 percent. Great emphasis is given to this magic number, and its defense seems to me to cloud issues more than illuminate them.

---

5. The commission report argues that "preferably one-half" of all students must be no worse off under its proposals than under the present system (ibid., p. 128). Since the average student paid tuition and fees of about $500 in 1970–71, and the commission recommends that such tuitions grow by about 6 percent per year to 1983, the median student would suffer a tuition increase of about $565 in 1970–71 dollars. To design a grant program that furnishes the median student with a grant of $565 would probably require giving small grants to about two-thirds of the students, so that the grants can taper off gradually.

6. Three million full-time equivalent students at a $1,260 average grant is $3.78 billion. The $1,260 is derived from an estimated average Basic Opportunity Grant of $700 in 1973–74 increased at 6 percent per annum. Perplexingly, the Carnegie Commission reaches a similar result in one footnote (ibid., p. 122).

For example, Cartter places great emphasis on the fact that, under present tax arrangements, the higher personal incomes produced through postsecondary education will yield small amounts of additional tax revenue to states and localities, but large revenue increases to the federal government. To Cartter, and to many others, this consideration seems to suggest that greater support should be provided at the federal level. This argument is misleading for a number of reasons.

First, if this reasoning implies that a state government will not undertake an educational investment unless it has a reasonable prospect of recovering its costs through enhanced future tax revenues, the argument is plainly false. Higher education at all levels has received magnificent support from states and localities in the past, despite the fact that state legislators knew they were "investing" in highly mobile forms of capital.

On the other hand, if Cartter is not telling us that governments behave so as to maximize tax yields but that they should so act, his case is even worse. Governments acting on behalf of the people should be interested in the real benefits accruing to their citizens singly or collectively; these benefits may accrue in enhanced money income to the educated individual, or in nonpecuniary form to him, or in money income or nonmoney gains to all of society. Incremental tax yields and their distribution among levels of government at best measure only the first—private, individual monetary gain—benefit and there is no reason to believe that they reflect the other benefits of higher education.[7]

To get the "proper" federal share, *particular programs* have to be evaluated, one at a time, with the best evidence brought to bear on the proper shares under each such proposal. Cartter makes a good case for a major federal role in providing access to higher education—arguing that federal involvement would enhance "equalization of opportunities among states and regions"—and that case should be sufficient to establish such a program.[8] After all such programs are added up (and state responses take place), we shall know what the federal share is.

7. Consider a society in which the only tax is a head tax—one man, one dollar. In such a society, the tax yield of a dollar spent on higher education would be nil (unless it increased the population) and a yield-maximizing government would never invest in education. Yet education in such a society could have a high rate of return even if measured by private money income.

8. Cartter also says that the federal tax structure is more equitable than that of the states and thus should militate in favor of expanded federal support. I do not quarrel with the assertion of relative attractiveness of the federal tax structure, yet it seems that the yield on that structure is already "spoken for" over the next few years. Thus one has to argue that incremental federal taxes are better than state-local taxes. Here the case is not at all clear.

PREPARING FOR THE 1980s

Allan Cartter's credentials as a seer are impeccable; his 1960s warning about an impending Ph.D. surplus cautions us to pay heed to his warnings about a stagnation of growth in higher education in the 1980s. My judgment is that Cartter will be right again—harder times are just around the corner—but I am disappointed with the commission's response to the challenge posed. As I read Cartter's work, two central themes emerge for planning for the decade ahead. First, Cartter outlines a massive revision of our education, social security, and manpower programs all for the sake of fostering "lifelong learning" and, not incidentally, filling the otherwise empty college seats of the eighties (I shall take this up in the next section). Second, Cartter and the commission stress the importance of narrowing the tuition gap between public and private education lest the "incipient financial crisis of the early seventies ... become permanent features of the landscape." Although I believe this view is correct, it directs too much attention to public versus private institutions. In a great many states, the private sector is small, non-competitive with the public colleges, and in many cases so heavily oriented to graduate education that undergraduate tuition differentials hardly matter.[9] Thus, it is important to focus on the public sector itself in justifying proposed new financial arrangements.

I believe that unless states and the federal government adopt the Carnegie Commission proposals for changes in public institution tuition and expanded federal and state direct student aid, the public sector itself will be in for enormous problems at the end of this decade. In most states public institution tuitions and fees are completely unrelated to the costs of education on the various campuses. Typically, tuitions are uniform across schools, resulting in large implicit subsidies to students at the costly state university, smaller subsidies at the state colleges, and smallest at the community colleges. Given the Carnegie Commission's proposal to keep per student general subsidies in public higher education constant through 1983, it is disappointing that it devotes relatively little attention to the redistribution of this fixed pie. If for no other reason, I believe tuitions in the public sector must be readjusted to allow rational planning in the 1980s.

As the 1980s approach, and undergraduate enrollments level off and decline, *some system will be needed to decide which public institutions*

---

9. For an interesting discussion of the outlook for private higher education, see Richard R. Spies, *The Future of Private Colleges* (Princeton, N.J.: Princeton University, Industrial Relations Section, 1973).

will contract and which will expand. Under the present public institution financing arrangements, inevitably attention will focus on the "high cost" public universities, whose undergraduate budgets will look as if they were an unnecessary drain on state treasuries. There will be strong moves toward shifting undergraduate enrollments toward "more economical" state colleges and community colleges, especially those that have large numbers of vacant seats. The effect of such moves will be to destroy public universities: with a cutback in undergraduate enrollments, teaching assistantships will be reduced and thereby reduce graduate enrollments in the public universities.[10] Barring a messenger from Queen Victoria carrying research grants, the outlook for the high-cost sector in public education is bleak.

If, on the other hand, the Carnegie Commission proposals were instituted, the outlook would be, at least, ambiguous. When the commission advocates setting public tuitions at a higher fraction of cost, I presume it means such a scheme to apply on a campus-to-campus basis.[11] Thus state universities would charge higher tuitions than state colleges, whose charges would exceed junior college fees.[12] State and federal scholarships would presumably be based solely on a student's ability to pay, not his actual costs. (The commission's proposals are not clear on this last point.)

In this kind of world, when the enrollment plateau and decline are reached, an entirely new planning device would be available to state authorities: the market. Campuses could be contracted or expanded according to whether or not they were enrolling students at the going (cost-related) price. The state university and other costly campuses as well will be able to justify expansion if they can find buyers for their

    10. For the relation between undergraduate and graduate university education see Stephen D. Dresch, "Perspectives on the Evolution and Financing of Graduate Education," mimeographed (Washington: National Board on Higher Education, 1973).
    11. A better rule for intercampus pricing would be to keep the dollar subsidy (cost minus net tuition) constant across public institutions. Such a scheme would make investment decisions of students more efficient. See Robert W. Hartman, "The Impact of Federal and State Policies on Prices and Efficiency in Higher Education" (New York: Committee for Economic Development, forthcoming).
    12. The implication of these tuition adjustments is that tuitions at public universities would rise much faster than charges in other parts of the public sector. In analysing the public-private competition in higher education, Cartter and the commission lay undue stress on the relation between *average* public tuitions and private tuitions. The well-being of the private sector depends much more, however, on the tuitions charged in the high-quality public institutions, especially the public universities. If the latter raise their tuitions at a higher rate than the rest of the public sector, the position of the private institutions will be even stronger than Cartter surmises.

services. The appeal of cutting back on the university because it offers high-cost education would become nullified: even though the cost is high, the students—not the taxpayers—would be willing to pay the price.

Whether the state universities or any other particular institutions would come out of a market test better off than if left at the mercy of state legislatures is hard to say. If the higher-cost schools can persuade students that their services are worth paying a higher price, then the market will help. If not, they will wither, as they will under present arrangements.

CONTINUING EDUCATION AND THE 1980s

Cartter's proposals for providing everyone with drawing rights to lifelong education raise some questions. I do not want to quarrel with the notion that it would be desirable for adults to have greater choice between spending their time working, studying, or in leisure pursuits. Surely as a society grows wealthier, it can afford some loss in output efficiency (if there would be any) to enhance the freedom of its people to live fuller, less scheduled lives. But the kind of program Cartter outlines contains hidden costs that raise questions about whether it is the best way to achieve the desired opening up of choices. The proposal is for an accumulation fund to be financed by a 4 percent surtax on earnings throughout a person's working life; the fund could be drawn on before age forty-five for educational purposes and thereafter for any purpose, including enlarging retirement benefits. The hidden costs of this proposal are threefold.

First, once the nation settles on a federalized plan of this sort, a new kind of lockstep is created. Everybody is forced to save at the same percentage rate; they all must obey the rule that "before age forty-five thou shalt accumulate capital; later you may sin." Such rigidities ignore the possibilities that educational and other needs may vary among occupations and that earnings patterns may so differ that optimal tax programs would not be uniform. In short, in this kind of area, industrywide bargaining might devise plans best suited to the needs of the various members of the labor force. Simply because such schemes have *not in fact* been established is no reason to federalize a program; it merely establishes the researchable topic "How come?"

Second, even if a federal program were desirable, a 4 percent surtax on earnings looks big enough to preempt other federal initiatives in the social area. It is often pointed out that societies less wealthy than the

United States are beginning to experiment with lifelong education programs—France, Sweden—but those societies already have national health insurance plans, reasonable welfare programs, and the children of their cities learn to read in school. If the U.S. taxpayer is unwilling to increase his payments substantially, we shall have to choose between continuing education and other social needs. Important as free choice for adults may be, it is hard to argue that it is our number one need.

Finally, linking continuing education with the problems of higher education in the 1980s in the public's mind is unwise. As yet there is no clear evidence that adults would choose to patronize institutions that are likely to find themselves in trouble in the 1980s, and wishing won't make it so. Moreover, the Carnegie Commission is faced with a need to do some fancy footwork on student aid if it undertakes to promote Cartter's plan. For the 1970s, it must argue (and has argued) for student aid that is targeted and based on need; it will be (and has been) criticized by those who believe only in "aid for everyone" through low tuitions. For the rest of the century, the Cartter plan suggests drawing rights for everyone, not based on need—precisely what the commission argues against in the 1970s.

One final word on the problems of implementation of the Carnegie Commission proposals in this decade. The report has already been attacked on the grounds that to call for higher tuitions in public institutions accompanied by larger student aid is to ignore the possibility that states will adopt the first, while the expanded student aid will be ignored. Cartter is certainly right when he describes these attacks as equivalent to doing "nothing because there may be dangers." But that is not a very convincing criticism.

Perhaps attention needs to be given to ways to improve our legislative processes so as to bring about linked changes in programs. Otherwise, the status quo will always look attractive to many people. Recently, several of my colleagues have proposed that the Congress adopt a multiyear appropriations process.[13] Under this proposal, Congress would vote on appropriations for higher education programs for, say, fiscal years 1974, 1975, and 1976. Unlike the present one-year-at-a-time process, a long-term perspective would allow for significant changes in national priorities to be expressed, allow the gradual phase-out of duplicative programs, and satisfy those who always fear the worst when any

---

13. See Alice M. Rivlin and Charles L. Schultze, "Shaping the Budget: A Way Out of Chaos," *Washington Post*, Sept. 9, 1973, p. C1.

change is proposed. Such modifications in how business is done in higher education, with appropriate adaptations at the state level, might go a long way toward answering the critics of the Carnegie Commission proposals. If, indeed, everyone can agree that higher public tuition *cum* higher student aid is a desirable end-result of the political process, it would be a sad day for that process if a way could not be figured out to achieve that desired end.

The Federal Stimulus in Postsecondary Education

CASPAR W. WEINBERGER

I AM PLEASED TO HAVE this opportunity to speak before an organization that for more than a half-century has contributed greatly to the high quality of higher education in America. During this span of time, our nation has made historic strides toward the cherished goal of assuring access to higher education to every American. The American Council on Education has played a vital role in furthering that national progress, an achievement in which the organization can take enormous pride.

THE ADMINISTRATION'S PROGRAM

This Administration remains committed to that great goal. Through the Education Amendments of 1972, and specifically through the Basic Educational Opportunity Grants program, it has sought to remove for all time the financial bars to quality education. The President, because of his overriding concern with the educational fate of young Americans, has asked Congress for nearly $1 billion to finance this program in fiscal year 1974. That amount would assure grants ranging upward to $1,400 for 1.6 million qualified but economically handicapped young men and women. Unfortunately, the Congress has voted only about half the amount requested despite obvious student needs. Also the Congress made even this small beginning contingent on the continuance of old and ineffective programs at high levels.

The legislative history of the Basic Educational Opportunity Grants illustrates several hard facts that affect higher education directly. First, it demonstrates the reluctance of Congress to terminate programs, whether or not those programs still are worthwhile or even necessary. The Basic Grants program was developed as an improved substitute for several other federal student assistance programs. But the Congress, while agreeing that the Basic Grants program is a step forward, refuses to cut loose the programs it was intended to replace.

This situation leads to point two. Both the Congress and much of the higher education community resolutely refuse to accept that—for the foreseeable future at the least—all of us must learn to live with the reality that our national wealth is not inexhaustible. Our resources are finite, and we must select priorities. We cannot fund everything in ever-increasing amounts. After decades of spectacular growth, sustained by a virtually unlimited supply of faith and funds, higher education institutions—and their counterpart institutions in other sectors of our national life—are finding it hard to adjust to the discovery that both the faith and the funds are finite.

And that stricture raises point number three. Having faced up to this new reality, we can either wring our hands and bemoan our fate, or we can address the more arduous but far more productive course of self-examination, self-reform, and self-renewal. Looking at ourselves against a backdrop of necessity will lead, I am convinced, to a fresh determination to make our limited resources count for more, through eliminating waste and inefficiency and by applying our savings to new approaches which hold greater promise.

I have used "we" and "our" because the problems that now face higher education institutions are in many respects similar to those facing the federal government.

Howard Bowen, chancellor of the Claremont University Center, was speaking of colleges and universities when he said, "The institution that can use fiscal necessity to prune the irrelevant, to find better institutional methods, and to achieve new cooperative relationships with other institutions, will emerge in the next decade as a leader." Chancellor Bowen's assessment applies to virtually all segments of our society.

The federal government, in several moves, has already begun to reassess its role in higher education and, as a result, to shift its priorities. The President's proposals to increase funding for Basic Opportunity Grants reflects the Administration's determination to place more emphasis on direct assistance to financially handicapped students. At the same time, we hope to improve the ability of postsecondary institutions to respond to the always evolving needs of students. The Fund for the Improvement of Postsecondary Education is designed to encourage greater diversity among institutions and a more effective use of resources within them.

The fund, another creation of the Education Amendments of 1972, is moving out briskly to fulfill its mandate. During July 1973, it awarded grants totaling $9.3 million to eighty-nine colleges, universities, state governments, and other providers of educational services to finance some interesting and innovative projects. Among them are efforts to demonstrate better ways of educating such nontraditional learners as homemakers, those isolated in rural areas, inner-city minority members, and prison inmates. Other projects financed by the fund are concerned with the award of degrees on the basis of specific competencies rather than number of hours spent in classrooms. Obviously, we are hoping through the fund to extend opportunities beyond traditional forms of postsecondary education. Many of the postsecondary institutions are still geared to assumptions that the nation in the 1970s will need only the same skills, motivations, and teaching styles that prevailed in the 1960s and that the 1960s structure of job opportunities will still maintain the 1970s.

I have described part of what the Administration defines as the appropriate federal role in higher education at this time: We want to provide the stimulus that will spur postsecondary institutions to reform and revitalize themselves. And we want to ensure educational opportunity for all. Again, it is the Basic Opportunity Grants program that best symbolizes the course we have chosen and the goals toward which we are working. Under the program, recipients of grants will, for the first time, be empowered to enter the postsecondary institution of *their* choice, whether it be a liberal arts college or a technical training institute. And if such freedom of choice induces some competition among institutions for students, that eventuality may not be altogether a bad thing.

When fully funded, the Basic Opportunity Grants in combination with the work-study and loan programs will constitute a package that will permit every aspiring student to afford the postsecondary education that he or she is qualified to undertake. That choice and that package mark a truly revolutionary change in the federal role in higher education. Together, these programs can guarantee genuine equality of higher education opportunity; at long last, disadvantaged young people will no longer face insurmountable financial barriers in the pursuit of either degrees or advanced technical skills.

But in establishing our new priorities, the Administration has been forced to curb or drop federal programs that we judge to be of less importance than others, because, as I have noted, we cannot and, indeed, should not try to do everything. Among the casualties are older forms of student aid, certain library programs, and funds for land-grant institutions.

I am, of course, well aware of the opposition within the higher education community to our decision to cut off some of the institutional support programs. Such decisions are, however, a necessity of governmental and of educational life in the 1970s. We are convinced that our most pressing responsibility is to put our money into programs of the highest priority and the greatest promise—programs to equalize opportunity and to generate institutional reform.

STUDENT LOAN PROGRAMS

I would like now to address a problem widely familiar: the drastic downturn in loans being made under the Guaranteed Student Loan program. Our latest statistics indicate that the number of loans is down 41 percent and the dollar amount down 35 percent from last year, a situation that is causing both students and institutions severe problems. The problem has stemmed in part from the implementation of a new means test to determine eligibility, as required by the Education Amendments of 1972, combined with the nationwide jump in the interest rates that lending institutions now charge.

We in the Administration are hard at work to resolve the problem. First, we are encouraging both lending institutions and college financial aid officers to interpret the means test more flexibly than they have in the past. Second, the Student Loan Marketing Association—Sallie Mae—has just issued its first public stock, in the amount of $100 million. This influx of new money, to be used to buy student loan notes from lending institutions, will ease the pinch and make more loan money available. Third, we are carrying forward an effort (long overdue) to streamline paper work and thus help cut the administrative time that banks must devote to processing the loans. Fourth, we are considering a number of approaches designed to encourage lending institutions to make more "nonsubsidized" loans available to students. Under the law, a student may obtain a federal guarantee and a 7 percent ceiling on interest charges without any means test of his family's finances. Such nonsubsidized loans are, in fact, advantageous to the student and his family.

In any event, although I am not attempting to minimize the difficulties being experienced by students and institutions, I am confident the situation is temporary and will soon be rectified. Any help the Council can lend to the Administration in generating wider understanding of the problem and working toward its solution will be welcomed. We look, in fact, to the Council and to other organizations in the field for advice and assistance in our continuing review of federal higher education programs and priorities. We solicit support when the education community feels it is warranted; we expect its opposition when that response is deemed appropriate. Although the government and the educational enterprise necessarily approach their common problems from separate perspectives, both should never forget that they share a common task—the unending search for ways to help the nation's educational institutions better serve both students and the society. This responsibility brings me to my last point.

QUALITY HIGHER EDUCATION

The key to giving the best service to students and society is the quality of education that institutions of higher learning provide. There is no point in encouraging students to go to college through generous grant programs if the level of education available at those colleges is not of the highest quality. There is no point in increasing grants to institutions to improve their buildings and other facilities if the lectures and seminars which take place in those buildings are not the best that the academic community can provide.

Obviously, quality education, which is the objective, means different things to different people. It may mean small classes and tutorials at one institution or large lecture courses at another. It may mean a strong liberal arts faculty at one institution or an excellent engineering school at another. We in the Department of Health, Education, and Welfare do not undertake to define quality education in such specific terms. Each institution has the responsibility for determining how it will provide the best education that it can.

Our concern at the federal level is to assure to each institution the freedom to provide what *it* feels is the highest quality of education. We firmly believe that the preservation of academic freedom is the best road to quality education. In its turn, academic freedom, like religious freedom, requires that the interference of the federal government in university affairs be kept to an absolute minimum. (The shift to the BOG program from institutional aid reflects this same desire to avoid "excessive entanglement" between the institution and the state.) I am confident that the essential decisions about curricula and academic appointments are best made by academicians themselves and not by the government. The preservation of academic freedom as a means to quality education is an essential part of our education program.

EQUAL OPPORTUNITY AND ACADEMIC EXCELLENCE

The Constitution obligates the federal government to guarantee civil rights and liberties to all citizens in all circumstances, specifically including faculty members and potential faculty members in academia. One of the most difficult problems with which the Department of Health, Education, and Welfare has had to deal during the past decade has been the need to guarantee to all citizens the right to equal opportunity for employment without compromising the equally important need to preserve academic freedom and, through it, quality education. I fear that at times our efforts in this connection have been misunderstood. I believe the two constitutional obligations should reinforce rather than oppose each other.

The greatest amount of misunderstanding pertaining to the Department's attempt to ensure equal employment opportunities in university faculties has involved the establishment of goals and timetables for minority hiring. There has been objection that the establishment of goals and timetables will result in coercive pressures to force the hiring of academically inferior candidates simply to achieve statistical ends and comply with formulas determined without reference to academic quality.

Erosion of quality is emphatically not the intention of the establishment of goals and timetables, nor has it been the practice of the Departent to apply the goals and timetables figures in such a way that lower-quality faculty appointments will result. As long as I am Secretary of HEW, that will not happen if I can prevent it.

It may seem a curious verbal paradox that, in practice, the establishment of goals and timetables called for under the law are but a means to the end of assuring equal employment opportunity. Providing equal opportunity for employment to all citizens is a process. It is a process that we all favor and that the Constitution guarantees. The establishment of goals and timetables helps assure the effectiveness of the process and provides a yardstick against which efforts to put the process into place may be measured.

We in HEW do not believe that failure to achieve the goals and timetables, per se, is evidence that the process has not been put in place. At the same time we do not believe that the establishment of goals and timetables, per se, requires a diminution of academic quality. Neither the educational institutions nor I would be fulfilling our responsibility if that happens. And it would imply an assumption, completely unwarranted, so far as I know, that the hiring of minorities and women would, in itself, result in lowering the quality of faculties. My firm belief is precisely the opposite. Guaranteeing equal opportunity for employment will enhance the quality of academic faculties across our nation and cannot diminish it. But it must be an equal opportunity for all. Inverse discrimination would be as invidious as any other kind of discrimination.

EQUALIZING EDUCATIONAL JUSTICE

Governmental Strategies For Educational Reform and Innovation

VERNE A. STADTMAN

REFORM AND INNOVATION are appealing activities. They promise improvement of conditions that are at best imperfect and sometimes unbearable. They may also seek to change practices that have become boring or obsolete in the mindless routine of their observance. But reform and innovation also have a darker side. They reveal dissatisfaction with the way things are and, therefore, may be the pursuits of malcontents who, unless carefully watched, could make a world that is merely imperfect into one that is totally intolerable. It was no doubt in this cautious spirit that the political antagonists of Justin Morrill called his Land-Grant College Act of 1862 an "Engine of Mischief."[1]

The strategy of innovation, wherever it originates, is actually the strategy of overcoming or outflanking the forces that fear the consequences of change more than they detest the conditions that reformers say need to be corrected. For many years, there was a framed inscription on the wall of the faculty club at the University of California that said, "When it is not necessary to change, it is necessary not to change,"[2] and Schein has observed that in professional schools:

> Without a feeling of psychological safety, the members of the system will increase in defensiveness in direct proportion to the amount of pressure brought to bear. We can see many examples of this mechanism operating in professional school faculties: new program ideas will not be tried because faculty members are afraid that students will learn less or be hurt by a new approach, or because they are unsure unless someone else has already tried it and can reassure them that it will work, or because they are reluctant to expose their fear of not being able to use the new idea effectively (e.g., computer-aided instruction). Fears will

---

1. "Senator Morrill's 'Engine of Mischief,'" *California Monthly*, March 1962, p. 6. See also Edward D. Eddy, Jr., *Colleges for Our Land and Time: The Land-Grant Idea in American Education* (New York: Harper & Bros., 1956, 1957), p. 31.

2. This quotation is attributed, in the *Oxford Dictionary of Quotations*, to Viscount Falkland, who uttered it in 1640.

often be rationalized in terms of economic arguments ("the innovation will be too expensive") or in terms of attributing problems to some other groups ("students won't know how to cope with that innovation"). In all these cases one must consider the possibility that what the person is really saying is that *he* personally is feeling threatened and/or does not see how to get there from here, hence he tends to resist on an emotional level and develop rationalizations for the resistance.[3]

Experiences with this kind of resistance to change throughout postsecondary education condition the observer to agree with Clark Kerr that many of the most significant innovations in the college and university originate as desires and demands of external groups.[4] And then one is sometimes tempted to go beyond that concurrence to assume that if a really significant change in higher education is desired, it must begin from some point outside the academic establishment. Moreover, because the most powerful external source of such action is the government, the place to start is at the highest possible level of government.

Two points will be argued from that assumption: First, the power of government as an innovator in higher education is more restrained than the assumption might suggest. Second, the government's influence on higher education usually is not directed at campus internal problems; it is, instead, exercised as public policy to which the affected institutions respond.

The Dynamics of Institutional Change

Schein suggests a model for the process of planned change that involves three stages: unfreezing, changing, and refreezing. The most important stage is the first, because it creates the motivation for changing. It involves (1) lack of confirmation or disconfirmation of present beliefs, attitudes, values, or behavior patterns, (2) induction of "guilt anxiety" by comparison of actual with ideal states, and (3) creation of psychological safety by the reduction of threats or removal of barriers to change.[5] It must take place not only at colleges and universities, but also in the centers of public decision making.

Only once in the history of American higher education (the last three decades of the nineteenth century) have the nation's colleges and universities been subjected to the kind of defrosting seen in the past

---

3. Edgar Schein, *Professional Education: Some New Directions*, Report for the Carnegie Commission on Higher Education (New York: McGraw-Hill, 1972), p. 78.
4. *The Uses of the University: With a Postscript 1972* (Cambridge, Mass.: Harvard University Press, 1972).
5. *Professional Education*, p. 76.

decade. The sharpest challenges to traditional attitudes, values, and practices on campuses were raised to national consciousness by the disorders of the late 1960s and early 1970s. The rigidities of academic policies, the inequality of educational access, and the ambiguities of campus governance—to name but a few of the issues—were all stridently proclaimed on campus quadrangles and library steps before they were taken seriously by the post-1960 institutional self-study groups that were the subject of Ladd's investigations.[6] Further awareness that something might be wrong with the nation's system of higher education accompanied the threatened withdrawal of the public's moral and financial support during the same period. To the extent that reduced financial resources reflected the disenchantment of the agents of governments—legislators, finance officers, and state and national education officials—governments contributed, as well as reacted, to the unfreezing.

Thus far, the unfreezing effort seems to have been successful in "confirmation and disconfirmation" activities than in inducing "guilt anxiety" over shortfall efforts toward either building an ideal institution or educational system or creating psychological safety for those who fear the consequences of change. The principal reason is that no agency or group has yet offered a comprehensive vision of the "ideal." And even if someone were to advance such an ideal, it is unlikely that there will be any consensus about its desirability—at least not soon.

The thaw of the past decade has eroded confidence in many long-standing practices in higher education. But our systems of higher education did not melt away. Innovation does not now involve complete reconstruction. It is still a matter of adaptation. And it has to begin with what remains confirmed after the recent challenges subsided.

For some time, however, the change process has been in the second stage, which Schein defines as "developing new beliefs, attitudes, values, and behavior patterns on the basis of new information obtained and cognitive redefinition."[7] Part of the changing activity began with the post-1960 institutional self-studies mentioned earlier. These soon became

---

6. Dwight Ladd, *Change in Educational Policy: Self-Studies in Selected Colleges and Universities,* Report for the Carnegie Commission on Higher Education (New York: McGraw-Hill, 1970). There are exceptions to this observation. In several institutions which survived the pressures of the period, self-examination had started in the golden era of the late 1950s. See David Riesman and Verne A. Stadtman, eds., *Academic Transformation: Seventeen Institutions under Pressure,* Report for the Carnegie Commission on Higher Education (New York: McGraw-Hill, 1973).

7. *Professional Education,* p. 76.

a part of a resonant swell of myth-abusing truths, speculations, and recommendations that were issued from campus-centered institutes of higher education studies, governmental agencies, institutional associations, national assemblies, presidential task forces, and commissions. And there is no doubt that our definitions of the universe and spectrum of higher education and its problems are changing in response to such efforts. The most comprehensive and conceivably the most significant redefinition expands the concept of higher education to include all postsecondary education—not only colleges and universities, but also scores of other educational institutions and activities. But while that redefinition may be the most dramatic, it is by no means the only one. Virtually every new report on education beyond the high school urges acceptance of new terms and/or fresh interpretations of old ones.

State governments have contributed to the change efforts by creating agencies to propose plans for reorganizing higher education systems. By 1971, twenty-one states had conducted such studies.[8] In 1972, at least twenty-three states adopted, or considered, legislation for some modification of their educational systems. This included bills to strengthen coordinating boards, the reconsideration of master plans, and so forth.[9] States have also contributed by supporting the research activities of such agencies as the Education Commission of the States. The federal government has been a major participant through financial support of research institutes at universities and other centers and through research and information programs of its own agencies. The recently begun work of the ERIC Clearinghouses—not as well known as it ought to be—is a particularly useful part of this effort. (All these efforts are discussed subsequently in another context.) In addition, the federal government has supported broad-gauge studies of its own, some of which have had important national impact. Among them have been those of the President's Commission on Campus Unrest and the U.S. Office of Education Task Force on Higher Education under the chairmanship of Frank Newman.[10]

8. Carnegie Commission on Higher Education, *The Capitol and the Campus: State Responsibility for Postsecondary Education* (New York: McGraw-Hill, 1971), p. 31.
9. Conversation with Richard Millard, Education Commission of the States, July 9, 1973.
10. *The Report of the President's Commission on Campus Unrest*, William W. Scranton, chairman (Washington: Government Printing Office, 1970). U.S. Office of Education Task Force on Higher Education, Frank Newman, chairman, *Report on Higher Education* (Washington: Government Printing Office, 1971).

The U.S. Office of Education Task Force was particularly adept at expressing the current status of the reform and innovation process:

> For a few years, while there is self-doubt in the academic community and uncertainty about the amount and form of public support, new directions can be established. Then the calm of business as usual will return, and the opportunity for change will pass.
>
> To reform itself before becoming hopelessly bogged down, to gain the solid support it requires to play a central role in American life, higher education urgently needs a sense of realism and a sensitivity to public concern as it recharts its future.[11]

The task force and the several other public and private investigative and deliberative bodies concerned with higher education reform since 1960 have been engaged precisely in discovering what is real and in creating public awareness of that reality.

The final stage of change identified by Schein is the "refreezing" stage. It involves the integration of the new ideas and definitions into the life of an individual or institution and is probably most readily recognized by another name, *implementation*. Evidence of this kind of activity throughout the country is abundant. But there is a fragility about many such efforts, as can be inferred from their designation as "experimental," "nontraditional," or "special" programs of the institutions where they are found. They do represent innovation; but they do not all represent permanent innovation. In many instances they appear to be fads or phases. Their special status allows them either to succeed or to fail without endangering the security or coherence of the institutions that initiate them. Schein insists that:

> The change agent who is genuinely concerned about effective refreezing, who wants long-run stable change as his product, must concern himself with the integration of new educational ventures into the total system of the school. Even if it is logical to start with an experimental cell because this poses the least threat initially, he cannot leave the matter there and hope for spontaneous diffusion. The matter of then integrating the cell must be actively managed, and often this will take more effort than launching the experiment in the first place.[12]

Government-initiated reform and innovation tends to create a condition for change rather than a program for change. Moreover, governments make rules that institutions must obey, and usually continue to

11. *Report on Higher Education*, pp. 62–63.
12. *Professional Education*, p. 83.

obey long after the initial excitement of an innovation is gone. An institution can survive a *demand* for change without genuinely changing as long as it is not *required* to change. Unlike student or faculty sentiment, governmental demands can *require* change. This power of compulsion renders to government the unique power of effecting change and simultaneously refreezing it. It is this characteristic that makes governmental action a favorite objective of the reformer. And it is also this characteristic that makes the government so potentially dangerous as a reformer. Fortunately, this type of reform is often awkward for governments to enforce and is, therefore, seldom attempted.

Two Domains of Change

The innovative power of government is mitigated in American higher education by a tradition that keeps government at a safe distance from the heart of the educational enterprise. The *Dartmouth College* case established the legality of the separation of private colleges from governmental control in 1819, and ever since that time—and surprisingly, when one thinks about it—similar autonomy has been claimed and rendered as indispensable to colleges regardless of the source of their basic financial support. Where public colleges have failed to win guarantees of such autonomy, in state constitutions or charters, they have usually managed to win it by practice and tradition. The public too has been educated to respect the principles of academic freedom, which infer a special sanctity for the campuses. By preaching the equation of "quality" with "autonomy" and securely implanting that concept in the public mind, they have succeeded in making government meddling unpopular. In his plea for Dartmouth's independence, Daniel Webster said it was "a small college, and yet there are those that love it." Public colleges may not all be small, but they have many alumni in every state—so there are all that many more who love them and might rise to defend their independence.

The Carnegie Commission has made the case for institutional independence in self-governance in two reports. It addressed the matter first in *The Capitol and the Campus*, issued in April 1971. In that report, the commission observed that institutional independence from government decreases the likelihood that internal controversies will become public issues. It stressed the role of autonomy in protecting academic freedom; in freeing members of colleges and universities of restrictions on their ability to comment upon, criticize, and advise about public policies and practices; in facilitating long-range planning; in making experimentation and innovation possible; and in making internal management easier. These and other justifications for autonomy were reviewed at greater length in the commission's seventeenth report, *Governance of Higher Education: Six Priority Problems*, released in April 1973.

One particularly relevant statement in the latter report is that "institutional freedom leads to freedom to innovate. But the record on innovation of unfettered higher education is not outstanding; in fact, historically, many and perhaps most of the major structural innovations have been largely initiated externally, like the land-grant movement and the introduction of large-scale scientific research."[13]

Some of the reasons innovation is likely to come from without, rather than from within, higher education are summarized in JB Lon Hefferlin's *Dynamics of Academic Reform*, in which he talks about one problem of reform that requires special attention here:

> Finally, academic institutions are deliberately structured to resist precipitant change. Besides their policies of academic freedom and tenure to protect against external vigilantes or internal dissention, most colleges and universities operate through a series of review and approval mechanisms: departmental faculty meetings, general faculty committees, administrative boards, senates, assemblies, and governing boards. This structure contributes to the deliberately slow adoption of change.[14]

Charitability aside and fears of the new and untried aside, at least one other reason is suggested for internal campus procedures to be change resistant. Such resistance slows the whole decision-making process to a pace that can be followed by faculty members, who have only part of their schedules free to participate in the governance of their institutions. Efforts to accelerate the process will succeed only at the expense of faculty participation.

We should also observe that resistance to change is not the same thing as inability to change. What Veysey calls the "academic revolution"[15] of the last three decades of the nineteenth century may have been inspired by practices of German institutions to some extent, but it was executed by institutional governing boards, presidents, and faculties.

The situation appears contradictory. Change in higher education is

13. New York: McGraw-Hill, 1973. P. 22.
14. San Francisco: Jossey-Bass, 1969. P. 16.
15. Laurence R. Veysey, "Stability and Experiment in the American Undergraduate Curriculum," in *Content and Context: Essays on College Education*, ed. Carl Kaysen, Report prepared for the Carnegie Commission on Higher Education (New York: McGraw-Hill, 1973), p. 1.

said to come most readily from the outside, but colleges and universities are internally structured to resist it. No change is easy from the inside, but some kinds of change can be effected *only* from within. But the "contradiction" is really an acknowledgment that there are two domains of change that can affect higher education. One domain can be altered by external forces, whereas the other domain can be altered only by internal authorities.

In the *externally alterable domain* lie such concerns as social justice, the welfare and security of the nation, and what might be called "national purpose." This is the domain of government at all levels. Changes induced here may not have college reform or innovation as their main objectives, but they may produce such reform because they force institutions to adjust or react to new policies. A good example is the provision of educational benefits for veterans. The policy was inspired by a public desire to compensate young men and women for foregoing learning opportunities in order to serve their country. The effect on campuses was to increase the size of student bodies, alter student-faculty ratios, require creation of new kinds of counseling facilities, and change expectations concerning student life styles and collegiate values. Many of the changes were made on an ad hoc basis without the deliberation to which most campuses were accustomed, and this very breach of long-standing tradition had the effect of reform: it changed things, often temporarily, but sometimes permanently. In the judgment of many who taught on college campuses in the postwar period, it also improved higher education.

The *internal domain* of change embraces such matters as admissions requirements, performance standards, methods of instruction, modes and style of campus operations, and the recognition of achievement. This domain is now the center of great attention by those reformists who are endeavoring to introduce greater flexibility into higher education and to alter its traditional notions of time, space, and modes for learning. Ironically, this domain is also the most resistant to change, even from within, and if the reformers are to achieve their objectives, they must look either to competing alternatives to conventional higher education or to governmental intervention.

Government can rarely intrude into campus decision making successfully. When it does, it must do so on grounds that are properly within the external domain. State-prescribed open admissions policies, for example, are in the external domain because they are designed to equalize human opportunities for achieving acceptable standards for living in the broader society. State-prescribed policies for public employees directly affect employees of public colleges and often set standards for private institutions.

STRATEGIES FOR REFORM AND INNOVATION

The task of government is to translate the external needs of society into policies and programs. When the policies and programs involve the work of colleges and universities, the task becomes one of inducing institutional decision-makers to accommodate externally perceived needs. There are five basic strategies available to government for this purpose: (1) information, (2) funding, (3) coordination and regulation, (4) imposition of sanctions, and (5) stimulation of competition.

Uses of information

The power of information is based on an assumption that institutions sometimes resist reform out of ignorance. They do not know how to do better what they do, or they do not know that other institutions are already doing what they assume is impossible. Government can seek to overcome such resistance in two ways: (1) by supporting research that will yield the new knowledge needed to improve policies and practices, and (2) by collecting data on current conditions and practices and making it widely available to decision-makers.

Since 1963, the U.S. Office of Education has funded numerous centers for research and development in education. The purposes of these centers, according to a recent study, were "not merely to expand the quantity of educational research. Instead, they were to break new ground, to bring together 'critical masses' of expertise to focus on major system-wide problems in education, and to develop new large-scale research and development technologies." When the study was reported upon in May 1972, there were eight university-based "research and development centers" and eleven "regional laboratories." [16]

The new National Institute for Education was created, according to the Education Amendments of 1972, to fulfill a "clear responsibility" of the federal government "to provide leadership in the conduct and support of scientific enquiry into the educational process." [17]

---

16. J. Victor Baldridge and Rudolph Johnson, "The Impact of Educational R&D Centers and Laboratories: An Analysis of Effective Organizational Strategies," mimeographed (Stanford, Calif.: May 1972), pp. 6, 7.

17. Enacted June 23, 1972; Public Law 92-318, title III, §405.

The federal government has systematically collected statistics on enrollments, instructional staff, and degrees conferred in higher education since 1870, has collected data on institutional expenditures since 1930, and on institutional income since 1890. The periodic reports issued by the National Center for Educational Statistics (created in 1965) are based on these surveys and other sources and provide the most comprehensive quantitative data available on higher education.

Another information link between government and educational policy-makers is the network of the Educational Resources Information Center (ERIC), which issues reports and other documents concerning new educational developments.

At the state level, the Education Commission of the States serves as a valuable clearinghouse for information and ideas.

This review of governmental information activity is far from complete, but it illustrates the character of the endeavor. The government's information strategy has not yet been spectacularly successful, however. It provides basic data that are helpful for comparative evaluations of institutional operations, at least on superficial levels. It provides a source of information about places where certain reforms and innovations have been tried and found successful. It helps identify a national cadre of persons who share interests in certain problems and certain kinds of reform and innovation. But it is not sufficiently coherent to induce specific reform or innovation, because it is usually neutral toward implementational objectives, often physically isolated from the mainstream of educational practice, or is conducted in a laboratory, nonoperational format. It is much better known to students of higher education than to teachers and administrators in the colleges and universities. Its treasures are available to the campus reformer, to be sure, but to use them, he must seek them out.

Funding

History's most dramatic example of innovation in higher education achieved through governmental funding is provided by the Land-Grant College Act of 1862. Most of the colleges established under its provisions were totally new. But some were preexisting private colleges and universities that had to adjust their programs before they could serve the new classes of students the law sought to accommodate, could offer the new kinds of practical instruction the law sought to encourage, and thus could benefit from the law's provisions.

When funding is considered as a strategy for reform and innovation, a distinction must be made between governmental initiative and governmental response. In general, all governmental policy is a response to public desires and needs, perceived by legislators and other governmental decision-makers. In the context of educational reform and innovation, however, institutions of postsecondary education can initiate funding transactions by requesting assistance for their respective programs. Such requests may, or may not, reflect needs for general innovation or reform in higher education. And the influence of specific innovation funded in this way is often felt only by the specific institutions assisted.

There have been examples of the government's providing incentives for specific innovation or expansion. Illustrations from the 1960s include encouragement of expanding programs of graduate education under the National Defense Education Act, strengthening of science education with the support of the National Science Foundation, and expansion of medical and dental schools by the National Institutes of Health. The effective strategy here was to offer financial rewards to institutions that undertook the desired programs.

The Education Amendments of 1972 are impressive at several points in proclaiming the federal government's interest in reform and innovation for its own sake. Such language appears in the sections creating the National Institute of Education. Even more dramatically, the amendments provide for explicit support for improving postsecondary higher education, with $10 million appropriated for the year ending June 30, 1973. Programs earmarked for support under this provision include:

1. Encouraging the reform, innovation, and improvement of postsecondary education, and providing equal educational opportunity for all;
2. The creation of institutions and programs involving new paths to career and professional training, as well as new combinations of academic and experimental learning;
3. The establishment of institutions and programs based on the technology of communications;
4. The carrying-out in postsecondary educational institutions of changes in internal structure and operations designed to clarify institutional priorities and purposes;
5. The design and introduction of cost-effective methods of instruction and operations;
6. The introduction of institutional reforms designed to expand individ-

ual opportunities for entering and reentering institutions and pursuing programs of study tailored to individual needs;
7. The introduction of reforms in graduate education, in the structure of academic professions, and in the recruitment and retention of faculties; and
8. The creation of new institutions and programs for examining and awarding credentials to individuals, and the introduction of reform in current institutional practices related thereto.[18]

The public interest in such reforms was manifested neither by a massive citizens' demand nor a concerted grass roots movement at institutions. Instead, the public's interests were asserted in the suggestions and persuasion of prestigious statesmen, congressional leaders, commissions, and associations concerned with higher education's future. The 1972 amendments probably mark the most direct action yet taken by government to affect reform and innovation.

If innovation is desirable, it should be undertaken not only on single, isolated campuses but also on any other campus where it is appropriate. Therefore, it may be hoped that governmental strategies for innovation in the future will increasingly favor proposals with built-in dissemination capabilities. Such capabilities may involve cooperative innovation by institutions jointly organized for the purpose. They may include demonstrations and workshops that require representatives of more than one institution to participate and to evaluate results. They may involve subject disciplines or functional activities (admissions, counseling, for example) that cut across institutional lines. Or, finally, they may involve organizations that are independent of institutions, but are permanently organized to help institutions achieve specific objectives. Cooperative enterprises are especially likely to attract government funding if the innovation to be supported is too costly for a single institution to sustain alone.

The Carnegie Commission has concluded that instructional technology will not develop fully in the United States unless it is facilitated extensively by government support. The costs of acquiring and utilizing some of the most sophisticated electronic technology for teaching and learning is out of reach for most colleges and universities. The commission has therefore recommended that the federal government not only support utilization of instructional technology at individual institutions,

18. Ibid., §404.

but also provide financial resources for developing and operating cooperative learning centers that would be voluntarily organized by participating higher educational institutions and systems, would combine the major forms of instructional and communication technology, and serve large numbers of institutions. In all, the commission recommended that the federal government appropriate at least $100 million for research, development, and application of instructional technology in 1973 and further recommended that the level of expenditures for such purposes rise to 1 percent of the total expenditures of the nation on higher education by 1980.[19] Given the sharp decline in all appropriations for educational purposes, such figures have little reality at the moment; nonetheless, the recommendation remains valid as an example of the funding strategy. Should such appropriations be made, institutions would obviously take a more serious attitude toward instructional technology than many of them now do.

The funding strategy is implicit in several other major recommendations of the Carnegie Commission. Among them are the calls for federal and state governments to preserve and strengthen private colleges and universities,[20] the recommendation that the federal government (and foundations) consider financial support of adult education programs in black colleges,[21] and the recommendation that the federal government provide construction grants and loans for university health science centers, area health education centers, and start-up grants for new university health science centers.[22] All such recommendations have the effect of focusing attention on one type of educational institution or one type of educational activity.

Coordination and regulation

Governments have special powers for regulating all institutions within their purview. State statutes define the systems of higher education under state jurisdiction and prescribe the functions for the institu-

19. Carnegie Commission on Higher Education, *The Fourth Revolution: Instructional Technology in Higher Education* (New York: McGraw-Hill, 1972), pp. 53–60, 62.
20. Carnegie Commission on Higher Education, *New Students and New Places: Policies for the Future Growth and Development of American Higher Education* (New York: McGraw-Hill, 1971).
21. Carnegie Commission on Higher Education, *From Isolation to Mainstream: Problems of the Colleges Founded for Negroes* (New York: McGraw-Hill, 1971).
22. Carnegie Commission on Higher Education, *Higher Education and the Nation's Health: Policies for Medical and Dental Education* (New York: McGraw-Hill, 1970).

tions within the systems. Enforcement of the statutory provisions inevitably requires that institutions adjust their admissions requirements, curricula, and enrollment limits whenever they are at variance with the statutory scheme for the jurisdiction. In many states, responsibility for overseeing the implementation of legal regulations imposed upon colleges and universities is given to coordinating agencies with broad powers. In *The Capitol and the Campus*, the Carnegie Commission suggested that they be authorized to approve or disapprove new institutions, branches or centers, and new degree programs, and allocate funds under state-administered federal programs. The commission further suggested that such agencies advise on effective use of resources, educational quality, access to postsecondary education, functions for various types of institutions, and articulation among elements within postsecondary education.[23]

Superficially, the coordinating agency's role seems to be that of preserving the status quo—of assuring that the law is not breached. But agencies like this are in a unique position to disseminate information about reform and innovation that might be advantageous to institutions within a higher education system. They also have responsibilities for remaining alert to innovations that might minimize waste and maximize use of public resources. Because these agencies are relatively new in American higher education and are still defining their roles, they may be slow to take up the cause of innovation.

On the other hand, there are a few current signs of the potential of direct governmental regulation for purposes of innovation. In California, one joint legislative committee has already concluded that existing institutions are not providing adequate adult and continuing education for the needs of the people. It therefore proposes investing part of that function in a new, independent, fourth postsecondary education component in California.[24] That would be innovation of an impressive and portentious order.

The federal government explicitly recognizes the role of coordination in the Education Amendments of 1972 by requiring that states which desire certain types of federal financial assistance form state commissions with powers "to make studies, conduct surveys, submit recommendations,

---

23. *Capitol and Campus*, p. 37.
24. "Report of the Joint Committee on the Master Plan for Higher Education," John Vasconcellos, chairman (Advance draft; Sacramento, Calif.: February 1973), chap. 8.

or otherwise contribute the best expertise from the institutions, interest groups, and segments of society most concerned with a particular aspect of the Commission's work."[25] The commissions may also be designated as the state agencies for receiving certain federal funds made available under the 1972 amendments. The legislation requiring the creation of these state—1202—commissions was itself innovative. It specified that the commissions be representative not only of traditional public and private colleges and universities, but also of proprietary schools, vocational schools, and technical institutions. Thus, for the first time, the federal government accorded equal recognition to the full range of postsecondary education institutions in the United States, and opened considerably wider than ever before the possibility that new interrelationships between segments of postsecondary education might develop. The result could be a much enlarged student capacity and vastly greater flexibility in an individual's learning opportunities after high school.

Imposition of sanctions

In contrast to funding and coordination, which can achieve reform by positive actions, *sanctions* withhold support for failure to adopt policies and practices considered essential to desired reforms. The most familiar current example of this strategy is provided by the Executive orders applied to all institutions with federal contracts (including grants) of over $10,000 and enforced by the HEW Office for Civil Rights. It prohibits discrimination in employment and requires that all private institutions employing fifty or more persons and receiving $50,000 or more in federal contracts have affirmative action hiring plans, including numerical goals and timetables. The institutions found in violation of the order are subject to having pending government contracts delayed and current contracts revoked.[26]

The imposition of governmental sanctions can be criticized on several general grounds. It interferes with the institutional decision-making process; it threatens (perhaps to a degree not warranted by the circumstances) the very existence of some institutions; and it usually shifts the burden of proof of guilt or innocence to the institution threatened with

25. P.L. 92-318, title x, §1202.
26. Carnegie Commission on Higher Education, *Opportunities for Women in Higher Education: Their Current Participation, Prospects for the Future, and Recommendations for Action* (New York: McGraw Hill, 1973), pp. 128–29.

penalties.[27] For these reasons sanctions may be a strategy that holds great risks for the self-determination of campuses and for the maintenance of institutional diversity, both of which have come to characterize American higher education.

It is worth noting that governmental recognition of established accreditation procedures involves what amounts to sanctions against some kinds of institutions. By restricting certain kinds of financial assistance to use only in accredited institutions, the government seeks to prevent public funds from being squandered at incompetent or fraudulent colleges or schools. But it may, in the process, withhold assistance[28] from certain kinds of institutions that may be competent and legitimate even though they fail to meet some accreditation standards. As a result, their resources are undoubtedly underutilized. Such institutions may require special evaluation in the future.

In the meantime, sanctions are a two-sided strategy for achieving change. If sanctions are imposed against institutions that fail to adopt reforms or innovation, the strategy might be viewed as positive. If the sanctions are imposed only to preserve existing practices and standards, it may deter innovation. Government must tread a fine line in deciding which course to follow.

Stimulation of competition

In the report of the Commission on Non-Traditional Study, two passages deserve attention here. The first observes that the Education Amendments of 1972 give students financial support so that they may choose more freely than in the past which institutions they will attend. This freedom has generated a new competition for students and prestige among institutions. The strong traditional institutions will continue to thrive, the report says, while some of the weak ones will "become so inadequate that there will be little reason for their continued existence." The report continues: "Meanwhile, an old member of the educational scene is emerging as a strong [new] competitor for students—the system of alternate opportunities for learning offered through business, industry, labor unions, proprietary institutions, the military, cultural agencies, and the like—a system that may cause a very serious drain of the pool of potential college students." The report concludes: "It would be better, especially in the short run, to help existing colleges and universities grant

27. Ibid.
28. And aid to certain students.

credits and degrees based on non-traditional approaches than to create new degree-granting institutions for this purpose."[29]

This discussion suggests a useful strategy for governments: watch for opportunities to assist competing types of institutions in order to advance government's innovations and reforms. This device might be particularly useful when the reforms can be readily adapted in all sectors of postsecondary education. In general, new competitors might be less tradition-bound and less resistant to change than most colleges and universities. The possibilities are therefore fair that the first major breakthroughs in instructional technology and more radical innovation of other kinds will take place in such institutions. By fostering such developments outside the colleges and universities, the government could intensify the competition for students and, at the same time, stimulate general self-evaluation by all institutions and more experimentation with new approaches to teaching and learning.

STRATEGIES AND OPPORTUNITIES

When society is placing numerous, often conflicting demands on institutions of higher education, governmental action may be required at times to determine which demands should take priority. The government's role in such determinations may be relatively simple when there is considerable consonance between the expressed desires of the public and the aspirations of the teachers and administrators on the college and university campuses. The task becomes more difficult, however, when the perceived needs of the public appear irrelevant to institutional goals, or when colleges and universities persistently thwart desired reforms.

Each of the five main strategies that are open to governments for effecting change in higher education has strengths and weaknesses. The strategy of information leaves the greatest discretion to internal decision-makers in higher education, but it is quite weak. The information generated must first be wanted before it will be sought and applied. Too often it exists, but in oblivion beyond institutional awareness. The strategy of funding is potent, but only in a time of national affluence and only when expenditures on higher education have strong public support. This is not such a time. The strategy of sanctions is somewhat awkward, but potentially strong; however, it poses great threats to institutional independence and the doctrine of institutional diversity. The strategy of coordination

---

29. Commission on Non-Traditional Study, *Diversity by Design* (San Francisco: Jossey-Bass, 1973), pp. xvi, xvii.

may be increasingly effective as governmental coordinating agencies become more certain of their roles and responsibilities. But coordination also poses possible threats to independence and may tend to strengthen the barricades that protect the status quo more than it facilitates innovation. The strategy of encouraging competition is certainly timely. It is not clear, however, that competition can be abetted with anything less than financial support for programs outside the traditional system. And whether or not the public will be even as enthusiastic in supporting educational expenditures in noncollege sectors as it is for expenditures on colleges and universities remains to be seen.

Although there are several strategies theoretically available for government encouragement of innovation and reform, the most effective strategies require either funding or actions that threaten institutional independence—and sometimes judicious amounts of both.

In the long run, the government must play a much greater financing role in innovation than it does now. Much of the innovation required in postsecondary education is too costly for the institutions to undertake themselves. Some of it, including the acceleration of postsecondary learning and the introduction of the more sophisticated information and instructional technology, can assist all institutions, not just a few. There should not be, therefore, any relaxation by postsecondary education's statesmen in their efforts to persuade government with respect to its financing responsibilities and opportunities. In the short run, however, it is doubtful that governmentally induced change will be great, or, at least in application of the funding strategy, as great as it eventually should be.

Some of the most interesting and promising innovations and reforms in the 1970s fall fully in the domain of internal decision-makers in postsecondary education. These reforms would promote some relaxation in the sequence and duration of instruction, the openness of the system to new kinds of students, the hospitality of higher education to older and part-time students, and increasing flexibility in the method and timing of instruction. In the 1960s and 1970s, the internal decision-makers have not achieved a good record in matters of reform and innovation, but they still have immediate and promising opportunities to initiate exciting changes now under consideration. If they take the initiatve in pursuing those opportunities—perhaps aided by greater governmental efforts to expose the new information and ideas already available to them—they will lessen the need for, and likelihood of, governmental intrusion. And they can perhaps realize some modest success at innovation on their own. Any progress they can thus achieve will do them honor until the time returns when more potent support is again available in the form of government dollars.

Procedural Reform: A Strategy

JOHN VASCONCELLOS

MY EXPERIENCE as a state legislator leads me to suggest that two strategies are available to government and governmental officials who wish to stimulate educational reform. I will call these strategies "substantive" and "procedural."

In substantive reform a specific policy objective is set, and government either mandates its implementation or provides some incentive to encourage voluntary compliance. This strategy is useful when educational and public policy issues overlap. Some examples are the establishment of statewide educational goals and objectives, the organizational structure of public education, the broadening of access, state policy with respect to private education, and patterns of state educational financing, including student financial aids.

The second strategy is procedural reform. Rather than dealing with the actual content or substance of policy, it is concerned with the processes by which decisions are made and institutions and systems of education are managed. Procedural reform often creates the conditions which make self-initiated substantive reform possible.

Government is responsible for protecting and maintaining the integrity of decision-making processes in all public institutions, including public educational institutions. This responsibility includes the right and obligation to ask whether institutions maintained and supported by the people conduct their affairs in such a way as to justify confidence and trust. Procedural reform is, therefore, a legitimate and necessary concern of government. Several examples will illustrate kinds of procedural reform, resulting developments, and some ramifications.

One specific example of procedural reform is the broadening of governance in higher education to bring persons of both sexes and of diverse interests and backgrounds—economic, social, racial, etc.—into the decision-making process, particularly at the governing board level. Such reform can improve the institutional ability to perceive and respond to the needs of its various internal and external constituencies. It can broaden the base of popular support. Finally, it can enhance the legitimacy of educational institutions in the public eye and strengthen the case for institutional autonomy over substantive matters.

Another procedural reform is governmental insistence on open disclosure of all information relating to colleges and universities, including the processes by which decisions are made. (I am, of course, not referring to confidential personnel matters, though the *processes* by which personnel decisions are made should be public knowledge.) Although this kind of disclosure will, of course, invite scrutiny and criticism by the public and its elected representatives, it can produce better public understanding and a more knowledgeable public, which, in turn, will lessen fear, hostility, and suspicion. It can also produce badly needed pressure to change practices which cannot be justified.

On the federal level, a significant procedural reform is the provision for state postsecondary planning commissions under section 1202 of the Educational Amendments of 1972. If the commissions become operative, each participating state will have a forum in which all the parties in postsecondary education can participate. The clashes between the representatives of the various interests may be many and heated. But the conflicts will be public, and they will take place within the state's decision-making apparatus. The states will then have access to a more comprehensive perspective on postsecondary education. This is a healthy development.

A procedural strategy available to fiscal committees of state legislatures is to raise *process* questions during budget hearings, to probe into how decisions are being made as well as into the decisions themselves. Such a strategy is touchy but nevertheless appropriate if utilized with care and sensitivity.

Procedural reform is not limited to postsecondary education. The California Legislature's Joint Committee on Educational Goals and Evaluation has designed processes and materials for use by school districts and individual schools that wish to involve their communities in a dialogue about goals. Use of the process is encouraged but not mandated by the legislature. Involving communities in goal setting may result in substantive reform as well as increased confidence in the schools.

Procedural reform should be given high priority in the 1970s. Governors and legislatures should stimulate and even mandate procedural reform particularly with respect to state, system, and institutional governing and coordinating boards. But the most important procedural reforms will not require legislative or governmental authorization. The need is for mechanisms to bring all those affected by institutional governance, including the public and the local communities, into the process at some point. Thus, much of the responsibility for procedural reform falls on the educational community itself. Self-governance is the ideal. Those who wish to minimize the involvement of state government in institutional governance should recognize that the more responsibility for reform taken by the academic community, the less the need for pressure from the outside.

During the past two years, I have chaired two joint committees of the California Legislature, one dealing with K-12 education, the other with the Master Plan for Higher Education. Both committees have attempted to involve the public along with students, faculty, administrators, and parents in discussions of goals. We often found that the greatest resistance was not to the discussions themselves but to the inclusion of the public. Such resistance tends to reinforce the notion that education is remote from the world of life, experience, and work where most people live. One reason for government to intervene in education is the perception by political leaders that the gap between education and life is widening.

The future of academic freedom, autonomy, and the credibility of public education depends, perhaps more than anything else, on the development of decision processes which are open, rational, and human and which are so perceived by the internal and external constituencies of public education.

A final word about the responsibility of government. If government leaders are to be involved in educational change, they have a responsibility to be well informed, well staffed, personally known, and credible to the education community. Sometimes the most effective change has come, not as the result of pressure or mandates, but from continuing dialogue between political leaders and educational leaders. If meaningful dialogues are to occur, political leaders must be sufficiently knowledgeable to ask searching and challenging questions. And the political leaders must be perceived—whatever their disagreements with professional educators—as deeply concerned with the process and quality of education.

Equity through Change

ELIAS BLAKE, JR.

THE ELEMENTS IN, and the strategies for, educational reform and innovation that Stadtman presents are, I believe, sound. My comments focus on what the framework he describes implies for social justice, equality of opportunity, and equality of access with respect to the goal of wiping out inequities for black Americans and others in similar circumstances.

A list of the issues that are critical to social justice and that require reform and innovation will include: admissions, financial support, academic support programs, curriculum responsiveness, major field distribution, decision making in administrative matters, decision making in policy aid, and governance matters. Under Stadtman's categories of external and internal forces, the issues other than admissions and financial support fall in the internal domain—the domain most resistant to change. These issues are also critical to equity for blacks in higher education. Equity sets a goal wherein inequity has disappeared. The issues related to academic support programs and curriculum responsiveness will determine whether blacks and other minorities, now enrolled in increased numbers, will in fact get out of the system with first-rate competencies.

If Stadtman is correct that one must look to alternatives to generate significant change, then blacks are in deep trouble in this decade. They need, not access to experimental alternatives outside the standard system, but rather access to experimental alternatives *inside* the standard system. What is taught, how it is taught, and the negative or positive attitudes transmitted to the student outside the many assumptions in the curriculum—all are critical to success or failure for many black students. Without a large pool of readily available administrative decision-makers who would bring about new ways of looking at teacher responsibilities, the quality of learning remains problematical.

So far as the internal reforms that blacks and other minorities need most, Stadtman correctly predicts resistance to change: the recent history in public schools suggests that institutions of education have more trouble adjusting to the problems of educating new groups than might be expected. Just as there are signs that the public schools in many major cities are deteriorating under the pressure of mastering the problem of educating blacks, so also some segments of higher education may possibly undergo a similar decay and deterioration.

Especially one segment of higher education, the community college, will have to fight doubly hard and be extremely creative and innovative. The economics of higher education and geographic accessibility now dictate that, of blacks entering higher education, the larger proportion go into community colleges. In this decade the struggle must be to create reform and innovation in those colleges lest they deteriorate into the sham, custodial institutions that many of the big city high schools have become. This view is not a prediction of what *will* happen. It is a prediction of what will happen if public policy and public funds are not set to flow in a pattern that demands consideration to institutional change as opposed to innovation.

An illustration of organizational and information dissemination strategies will make a point. Thirteen black colleges were involved in a program to develop an entire freshman-year program aimed to reduce attrition. The thinking was that if the existing enrollment could be sustained through to graduation, this accomplishment in itself would help deal with the problem of inequity. The first two years were regarded as critical inasmuch as most dropouts occur in this period. A comprehensive first-year program was put together. The reason for involving a number of institutions was that the program required an initial, major series of institutional decisions in order to install even a beachhead program on a campus. There were the enormous problems of whether or not students would get full credit and advancement toward graduation for a new program. Once these commitments were in place, however, the program had a significant impact.

The dissemination process required several elements: (1) The experimental model had to move into an implementation (institutional change) phase while other institutions were considering using adaptations of the program. (2) The model at this stage necessarily included (*a*) some new patterns of teaching and learning, and (*b*) conceptions of how to confront the problems of institutionalizing the new patterns of teaching and learning. (3) The model that produced reductions in attrition and changes in teacher behavior was still in existence and thus able to interact with new institutions.

Twenty-two other institutions are now in various stages of adapting this first-year program to their own uses. This step is expensive but offers more possibilities in the long run. First, however, there must be an institutional commitment, as opposed to an individual professor's commitment, for otherwise the program cannot even be started on a campus.

Institutional commitment is a key factor both in the use of demonstration and pilot program approaches and in the dissemination approaches.

The strategy of the black colleges' freshman-year venture exhibits a significant difference from the strategy of the National Science Foundation teacher institutes, which cultivated new skills and new knowledge in individual teachers. In the former case, the teachers were involved as a result of a prior series of institutional commitments. The undertaking is inherently difficult: it requires consensus that the problem is sufficiently severe to warrant the commitment, and it requires some changes in the patterns of education.

My illustration of strategy brings me to my final problem with change and innovation in relation to social justice. Stadtman indicates that when there is considerable consonance between the expressed desires of the public and the aspirations of teachers and administrators on college and university campuses, the likelihood for change and reform are increased. But when public needs appear irrelevant to institutional goals or when colleges and universities persistently resist desired reforms, change becomes much more difficult. Currently there is no agreement on the part of the public with respect to fundamental issues involved in equitable higher education opportunity for blacks and other minorities. Dealing with this problem is not in the normal aspiration pattern of mainline teachers or administrators, and it is of questionable public need in this particular political period. Counterattacks that undercut relating reform and innovation to the needs of minorities are everywhere to be seen: Counterattacks on open enrollment are made under the guise of protecting the quality of higher education. An essentially merit system argument is invoked when discussing access to higher education for blacks and other crippled and neglected groups. There is a canard in equating quota systems with the setting of numerical goals to keep the pressure on and to force positive responses within the systems of higher education (it is as if one is arguing that his personal integrity will be sacrificed in trying to promote a positive social good).

We also see legal counterattacks on some of the compensatory methods in admissions and in special support programs for blacks and other minorities. The argument goes that if whites are not getting any of the earmarked scholarship money, for example, they are being discriminated against on the basis of race. The same argument applies if a black is admitted to a college and a white is not. Thus we see cases being brought under the Fourteenth Amendment by whites saying that their rights are being denied by efforts to compensate for past injustices against blacks. The legal question is difficult and will require that legal scholars in the black community work very hard to define the uses of the Fourteenth Amendment for uplifting and protecting the interests of blacks.

My comments have not been particularly optimistic, but then this is not an optimistic time. I think Stadtman's analysis is essentially correct and implies that the interaction between the motive of getting blacks into higher education and the promotion of reform and innovation is breaking down. As Vernon Jordan, executive director of the National Urban League, has said about keeping up the momentum for blacks in all areas: the battle plan for blacks has shifted from the marching songs along the streets and from exhilarating demonstrations to the trenches where they will have to dig in to avoid a retreat and stay there, and they may have to make their progress with pick and shovel.

The City and the Campus

VIRGINIA B. SMITH

OVER THE PAST SIX YEARS, I have worked with the Carnegie Commission on Higher Education and assisted in preparing certain of its reports. Three of the reports concerned relationships of higher education to different levels of American government or to various subsets of the American public. *Quality and Equality* dealt chiefly with the national interest in higher education, particularly as the commission felt it should be defined through federal policy and legislation. *The Capitol and the Campus* explored similar questions at the state level. And in *The Campus and the City*,[1] the commission considered the relationship between higher education and the city.

This third relationship proved to be by far the most difficult to deal with, and indeed seemed to elude any reasonable analysis. The terms *state* and *nation* have relatively well-accepted meanings, at least within the American federal structure. But "city" is a chameleonlike concept whose meaning shifts with the subject under review. *City* may be used loosely to refer to the entire metropolitan area; or it may be restricted to mean the inner city or the central city exclusive of the suburban areas or secondary cities within a major metropolitan area; or it may simply be a broad allusion to an urban, as opposed to a rural, setting. It may refer to a geographical area, to a set of circumstances, or to a group or groups of people. In matters of higher education, city rarely refers to the governmental unit.

Discussions about federal and state relationships with higher education usually move quickly to governmental roles and to the influence that state and federal legislation and fiscal policy have on colleges and universities. Thus the analysis becomes quite concrete, acquires specificity,

---

1. *Quality and Equality: New Levels of Federal Responsibility for Higher Education* (New York: McGraw-Hill, 1968), 54 pp.; *The Capitol and the Campus: State Responsibility for Postsecondary Education* (New York: McGraw-Hill, 1971), 154 pp.; *The Campus and the City: Maximizing Assets and Reducing Liabilities* (New York: McGraw-Hill, 1972), 205 pp.

and develops a focus that permits the exercise to be productive. Central issues may be delineated and positions taken. Temporary resolutions of issues are usually expressed through governmental action.

Discussions about city and campus relationships, on the other hand, more frequently both begin and end with rhetoric. Governmental expressions of policy do not provide a focus, and thus discussions range over the complex and often amorphous interaction between higher education and the larger society in which it exists. Analysis of the interface between colleges and universities and their local environment, of necessity, leads to an exploration of ever-widening circles of concern: What is the responsibility of the institution to its students (both those it has and those some think it should have)? What public services can the institution provide for urban needs? What are appropriate research responses to urban problems? How should the institution act as a corporate entity in the community? Under the rubric "city and campus," the topic frequently broadens to the appropriate purposes, functions, strategies, and content of higher education in a society that is rapidly becoming concentrated in metropolitan areas.

As a result, city-campus dialogues not only often seem unfocused, but may also appear to be without clearly designated participants. Almost everyone is an eligible participant and almost any aspect of the institution and its program would be considered as lying within the scope of discussion. An examination of the range of activities listed in the *Urban Affairs Newsletter*[2] supports this view, as does also the range of topics for the case studies in *The University and the City*. Nash, the principal author, points out, "Most universities, academicians, and scholars who try to deal with the vast urban landscape wind up specializing and concentrating on a few promising areas. My own history is a case in point. The Twentieth Century Fund asked me to write a book on the whole subject of the university and the city, but the resulting description of activity in the field was not focused enough to result in a book."[3] Nash instead wrote case studies of one or two facets of urban involvement at eight institutions.

While parameters may be difficult to ascertain and conceptual frameworks are sorely missing, there does exist a generally sensed need

---

2. Washington: American Association of State Colleges and Universities.
3. George Nash et al., *The University and the City: Eight Cases of Involvement*, Report prepared for the Carnegie Commission on Higher Education (New York: McGraw-Hill, 1973), p. 2.

for urban involvement by the nation's colleges and universities.[4] Today's economic and social problems exist in both rural and urban areas, but take on their most intense expression in the high-density population urban areas, where more than two-thirds of the nation's population lives. Thus, if higher education is to have an impact on the quality of American life, that impact must ultimately be demonstrable in urban areas.

The need for many colleges and universities to make an urban commitment is strong; the general willingness to respond also seems clear. Yet few institutions emerge as being largely characterized by their urban commitment. Major land-grant institutions, with their strong commitment to agriculture, provided symbols of commitment for their era. Higher education now faces the more formidable task of identifying and implementing those activities and programs that, collectively, would symbolize a parallel commitment to urban America.

As inventories often reveal, colleges and universities believe they are serving urban needs when they provide programs in adult education, teacher training, criminal justice and law enforcement, business training, and consumer education as well as a range of other programs related to the needs of city dwellers. In actuality, however, their diffuse programs rarely form an aggregate that signals a cohesive urban commitment. Partly in light of this lack, the Carnegie Commission on Higher Education recommended, in *The Campus and the City,* that the federal government establish an "Urban-Grant program ... which would provide 10 grants to carefully selected institutions for the purpose of undertaking a comprehensive urban commitment for their institution. These grants should not exceed $10 million each for a ten-year period with reviews every two years."[5]

Certainly, in this period of financial stringency, risk capital would be needed to support a comprehensive move toward an urban commitment. Even if the money were available, there would still be the problem of how the particular institution could be most responsive to urban needs. Should it simply continue to respond to diverse urban needs and define its urban mission as the aggregate of those responses? Should it seek definition of the most urgent needs through external structures? And, more particularly, in keeping with the conference theme, "Education and the State," what should be the relationship of higher education to the

---

4. In a survey by the American Association of State Colleges and Universities, 81 percent of the responding institutions (some of them located in rural areas) saw urban involvement as a major or important function. See *Urban Affairs Newsletter,* June 1973, p. 1.

5. *Campus and City,* p. 101.

city government in seeking to identify urban needs and demands in setting priorities among those demands, and in developing appropriate responses? Is the city government a useful agency for aiding the university or college in implementing a comprehensive urban mission? It is this aspect of the city-campus relationship that I explore here.

As already noted, the focus on city governments in city-campus discussions is rare. One could review numerous case studies of college or university special projects designed to "serve the city," yet find no reference to interaction with city government in either the development or execution of the projects. In most instances the omission is far more than authors' oversight: few of the activities required involvement of the city government, and none was sought.

OBSTACLES IN CITY-CAMPUS RELATIONS

For several reasons the relationships between city governments and colleges and universities, despite proximity, are characterized by remoteness.

First, few city governments contribute directly to the operating expenses or capital expenditures of the institutions. Many public two-year colleges are supported from local tax funds, although in most cities these funds are not part of the city budget but, rather, are collected and disbursed through an independent legal entity established to govern the community college district. The district area often does not coincide with the geographical area of the dominant city. Thus, for example, the community college theoretically should have its closest ties to the city in order to respond to community needs; instead, it responds through a special-purpose legal entity whose jurisdiction is limited to community colleges and whose interaction with other higher education institutions in the metropolitan area is minimal or absent.

There are notable exceptions to the above generalization about support. New York City still contributes to the City University of New York, and Cincinnati contributes to the University of Cincinnati under a formula of two mills of every assessed property tax dollar collected by the city. A few other cities earmark special-purpose grants in their city budgets.

College and university relationships with federal and state governmental units have largely been shaped by budgetary matters. At the state level, an added influence has been the state licensing and regulatory powers. For the most part, however, both the degree and the nature of interaction have stemmed from funding transactions. Thus the federal government's intense involvement with the campus at the graduate level and in scientific fields stemmed from the federal funds provided for these purposes. Similarly, state relationships with private institutions have begun to take on a new character as private institutions have sought state subsidies.

City-campus fiscal relations are further complicated when a major institution in a medium-sized city actually has a larger budget than the city government itself. That city finds it difficult to think about allocating funds to its "rich" inhabitant. Many cities do contribute indirectly to collegiate institutions through property tax exemptions, but even this form of city subsidy to higher education is increasingly coming under attack. Reverse payments from the institutions to the cities for public services received can be a lively local political issue.

Second, in an era when many major universities and consortia of small colleges have their "man in Washington" and their liaison in the state capital, few institutions have assigned anyone to cover city hall down the street. And most cities assign no higher education expert as liaison with the cities' colleges and universities.[6]

Third, problems and concerns to which colleges and universities might address themselves usually concern the entire metropolitan area, or the interactions between the inner city and the suburban areas, or particular neighborhoods within the city, but rarely involve exactly the area of the city government's jurisdiction. Furthermore, college and university interactions are typically with special-purpose groups, either narrower or broader than the city.

While many of today's social problems must be solved on a metropolitan basis, the governmental structure of most metropolitan areas can best be described as something of a "maze."

> The boundaries and jurisdictions of cities, counties, school districts, and special districts typically overlap and conflict in a complex maze. For example, the Chicago Standard Metropolitan Statistical Area (SMSA) has over one thousand local governments; Philadelphia has over eight hundred. The interdependent activities of people in the metropolis cannot be dealt with comprehensively by any one government. The result is said to be inferior services, economic inefficiencies and disparities, and lack of responsiveness to popular control.[7]

6. Ibid., p. 190.
7. Dale Rogers Marshall, "Metropolitan Government: Views of Minorities," in *Minority Perspectives,* The Governance of Metropolitan Regions, no. 2 (Washington: Resources for the Future, 1972), pp. 10–11.

Fourth, most city governments (with notable exceptions, for example, New York City's move for open admissions) do not appear to see themselves as representatives of the city's people in seeking specific types of education or public service or research from higher education. During the preparation of *The Campus and the City,* I asked the mayor or city manager in each city in a major metropolitan area to identify those public services supplied by area colleges and universities which they considered valuable and those which were not being provided but probably should be. Many of the responses suggest that "service" was defined as service to the city government as an agency (special training for city personnel and the like) rather than service to the city's people. Interest groups seeking services appear to act directly on the institutions rather than pressuring through the local government. And higher education, in a sense, is forced to deal with a number of local-level, fragmented pressure groups and then, itself, sort out the priorities and competing demands. All too often its service to one group may be viewed as a disservice to another group.

ADVERSARIAL ELEMENTS

These four reasons go far to explain why formal, constructive relationships between city governments and higher education are so limited. And the tendency is reinforced by the nature of the few interactions that do exist: from the city's standpoint, many of the interactions contain adversary and negative elements that are hardly good training for a collaborative, developmental approach. Illustrative are three types of interaction, all connected with the institution's physical presence in the city.

1. In recent decades, colleges and universities have grown dramatically. In a city, one consequence has been the institution's physical expansion into the city's scarce space. Unless the expansion was jointly planned, the institution might well find itself asking a city agency to authorize an activity that at least some city officials would perceive as permission to intensify certain of the city's biggest headaches—parking, traffic congestion, loss of tax property, student-community interactions, and housing problems. Questions about better use of existing space, modified schedules, and the like become almost inevitable. In this vein, the publication chronicling the development of the University of Wisconsin—Milwaukee as an "urban university" has only two index references to the city of Milwaukee, both of which relate to UWM's plans for

physical expansion and the resistance thereto of certain groups in the city. As chronicled, the major plans for UWM were developed at the state level—the level with funding potential—and the only city interaction mentioned in the detailed story concerned physical expansion. In the course of that interaction, both the mayor and the director of Milwaukee's Economic Development Division suggested that if the expansion did take place, the university should compensate the city for resulting tax losses.[8]

2. Concern about tax loss from institutional expansion is a second kind of city-university interaction that includes adversary elements. The tax-exempt status of college and university property has often been, and continues to be, a source of friction between the city and the campus. As noted in *The Campus and the City*,[9] increasingly colleges and universities, even though tax exempt, are making some payments for services received from the city. And in order to reduce some of the friction, efforts have been made to consider the tax loss in terms of the total economic impact of the institution on the city. In this connection, Caffrey explained that

> In one large city . . . 58 percent of the land is excluded from the tax roster. Of the tax-exempt land, local, state, and federal governments own more than half and use it for such purposes as schools, roads, parks, waterways, offices, and storage areas. Churches are the second largest nontaxpayers. In addition to houses of worship, church-owned properties such as schools, parks, cloisters, residences, libraries, and competitive businesses are not subject to taxes, simply because they are church-owned. Private schools, including colleges, come third. One may question

---

8. J. Martin Klotsche, *The University of Wisconsin, Milwaukee: An Urban University* (Milwaukee: The University, 1972), pp. 98, 102.

9. Pp. 85–86: "The American Council on Education recently reported that one out of three institutions of higher education now pays taxes or makes cash payments 'in lieu of' taxes and/or provides direct services in addition to or instead of those provided by local government agencies ["City Taxes and Services," an Urban Observatory Report, *Nation's Cities*, August 1971]. Of those institutions making such payments, amounts of payments were determined on the following bases (percent indicates percent of institutions for which the basis of determination was used):
'38% Estimated cost of services provided by local government
'32% Fixed proportion of assessed value of tax-exempt property
'20% Fixed contribution based on some arbitrary assumption
'15% Locally determined real-estate tax
'14% Fixed proportion of revenues from nonacademic, auxiliary enterprises
'5% Fixed per capita (per student) rate per annum
'1% Fixed proportion of total-annual revenues.'" [John Caffrey, *Tax and Tax-Related Arrangements between Colleges and Universities and Local Governments*, A.C.E. Special Report (Washington: American Council on Education, Aug. 12, 1969), p. 3.]

both the volume of the loss occasioned by removing colleges from the tax rolls and the justice of criticizing them and not the government and the churches.

Furthermore, many colleges are actually substantial taxpayers. In Cambridge, Massachusetts, Harvard and M.I.T. come second and third only to the Cambridge Gas and Electric Company as the largest taxpayers; fourth largest is the Boston and Maine Railroad. Princeton University is the largest single taxpayer in its community.[10]

Studies have also been undertaken to show that the institutional presence produces economic gains that potentially offset loss in tax revenues. The following conclusions were reached in certain of these studies:

Indiana University—treating foreign students as an export industry, it was estimated that they constituted the fourteenth largest exporter in the state.

University of Oklahoma—attraction of out-of-state students results in creation of new jobs at substantially little cost.

University of Washington—the university's operations result in a ratio of business actively generated to tax support of nearly 6 to 1.

University of Wisconsin—the university community pays more than its share of property taxes relative to the rest of the community.[11]

University of Pittsburgh—economic benefits generated by the university more than offset the hypothetical amount which the city would receive in tax income if some other type of enterprise were located on the campus.

But the friction continues. The several studies are perhaps more theoretically persuasive than practically valid. A university may bring net positive economic gains to a city without improving the revenue situation. It appears that the friction can be reduced by only two possible actions: (a) significant revenue sharing; that is, the institution would be willing to design the expansion so as to permit the property to remain on the tax roles (example, the Paul Mellon Center for British Art, at Yale), or (b) would conclude agreements that services would be paid for in lieu of taxes, at least for expansion (example, the University of Pittsburgh Law School).

3. A third form of interaction with some negative overtones, particularly during the 1960s, is the responsibility that many cities have of

10. John Caffrey and Herbert H. Isaacs, *Estimating the Impact of a College or University on the Local Economy* (Washington: American Council on Education, 1961), p. 41.
11. William A. Strang, *The University and the Local Economy* (Madison, Wis.: Bureau of Business Research and Service, 1971), pp. 5–9.

maintaining law enforcement in the campus environs. In some instances interactions between the campus and the city police force have been positive, but many others have been characterized by lack of common understanding and a degree of mutual distrust.

ALTERNATE PATHS

The picture I have drawn of city-campus government relationships may be overly pessimistic. Despite disagreements about the degree of importance and intensity of the characteristics described, it must be concluded that, at present, opportunities for positive, constructive interactions between city governments and campuses are severely limited because: (1) The city either lacks funding potential or does not perceive itself as having funding responsibility for higher education. Either situation shifts the initiative to other governmental units that do exercise funding responsibility. (2) Few cities or campuses are organized internally to interact with each other. (3) Problems or concerns either go beyond the confines of the city to the entire metropolitan area or are limited to groups or segments within it. Few metropolitan regions have a governmental unit that embraces the entire metropolitan area. (4) The limited interactions that do exist between city and campus have certain adversary or negative overtones.

If these conclusions are accepted, then colleges and universities, in their pursuit of urban activities, may pursue one or more of the following alternative courses of action:

1. Accept the notion that the city government is rarely the appropriate agency for many urban activities and continue to interact directly with a number of special-interest groups. This alternative is characterized by lack of coordinated structure within and outside the institution.
2. Recognize the need for some stronger focal point for the institution's urban involvement, and develop a direct relationship with the city government for a much broader range of interactions.
3. Support forces that call for some type of metropolitan regional government.
4. Recognize the need for coordination of higher education within the metropolitan region, and create a special-function agency for this purpose.
5. Confine the activities of the institution to student-centered education, and, through the students, utilize the range of educational resources within the city to serve the student.

The first alternative describes fairly accurately what happens in most city-campus relationships today. It has numerous drawbacks. The college or university is subject to direct pressures from a variety of special-interest groups. And, more often than not, the institution finds itself serving as arbiter or mediator (either deliberately or through the responses it chooses to make) among vocal competing groups. Its urban involvement is characterized by a lack of focus and by diverse individual activities which may be catalogued to show urban involvement but which may in fact dissipate resources without making any substantial urban impact. This fragmented pattern is often reinforced by governmental funding patterns that do not make available single grants for comprehensive missions but usually provide funds for specific programs or specific numbers of students.

The University of Cincinnati recently recognized some of these characteristics in its own urban involvement. Hoping to develop a more effective overall approach, the university and the city took steps to move it along the road to the second alternative—development of a broader working relationship with the city government. In December 1972, the city manager of Cincinnati and the president of the University of Cincinnati jointly called a two-day "University/City Retreat." Twenty representatives from the city and the campus reached the conclusion that a new "mechanism" was needed to facilitate a closer, more mutually beneficial interaction. The two agencies are now attempting to bring the mechanism into being. Membership on the coordinating mechanism's governing board will include both city and university representatives. The mechanism's tasks will include developing constructive involvement among the people of the city, its government, and the university, identifying high-priority projects, and generally steering their interrelationships. Within the university, an Office of Metropolitan Affairs, headed by a vice-president for metropolitan affairs, will provide institutional focus for the mechanism. The federal Fund for the Improvement of Postsecondary Education recently provided a grant to aid the University of Cincinnati in undertaking certain aspects of this renewed effort to establish an urban mission. Only experience will tell whether the new mechanism will produce the desired effect. But the move is a deliberate act to bring positive leadership to an activity in which the university is usually reactive rather than active.

Assuming that an external governmental framework is needed to help focus efforts in those institutions that seek more intensive urban missions, the third alternative—support of a rational metropolitan regional government—might be the logical choice. Revenue-sharing programs are highlighting the need for such agencies. But institutions alone can do little to bring such agencies into existence, and, realistically, the choice of this alternative can be little more than a waiting action. Yet this alternative, particularly if combined with a strong revenue-sharing program, would have the greatest impact on city-campus relationships.

The fourth alternative—the development of a higher education council for the metropolitan area—is more clearly within the power of institutions to bring about. In effect, it would create another regional special-purpose agency. The reasons for bringing such an agency into existence are many:

- While an overall shortage of college spaces continues in many metropolitan areas, excess capacity at higher tuition private institutions is increasing, while public-college enrollment grows.
- Metropolitan institutions, many severely hit by the new depression in higher education, can alleviate in some measure their financial problems by sharing facilities with other colleges and universities.
- In some instances coordinating agencies may seek to obtain agreement on differentiation of functions among institutions within the region to avoid unnecessary duplication and/or to protect particular markets for certain institutions.
- A consortium or metropolitanwide agency may be organized to provide certain educational or service programs beyond the scope of the individual cooperating colleges.
- Growth of population in the central cities has either declined or slowed considerably in the last decade while population continues to grow rapidly in the suburban areas within the metropolitan regions, thus suggesting that the location of today's institutions might not be desirable for population patterns which will exist a decade or so in the future.
- The nature of the central-city population is also changing and the capabilities of some central-city institutions may not fit the particular educational needs of the residents of the area. Cooperation with other institutions in the central city could provide the desirable range of educational services.[12]

The Carnegie Commission saw the development of a metropolitan higher education council as a key need in improving higher education's ability to serve urban needs. The commission defined the functions of this new council as follows:

- Act as primary market-research agency for educational needs in the metropolitan area and as central focus for planning for higher educa-

12. *Campus and City*, p. 106.

tion in that area. The council would work closely with any existing state coordinating agency on assessment of needs and in educational planning. With its primary focus on the metropolitan area, however, it would play a key role in the continuing evaluation and implementation of recommendations for higher education in the area.
- Create a vital, working system of interaction between industry and education in the city. This could be accomplished in a number of ways: (1) working with industry and appropriate colleges and universities to institute in technical and professional fields a series of work-study programs in which employees alternate periods of work with intensive seminars on academic material related to that work; (2) arranging with colleges and universities a series of later afternoon classes in factories or office buildings; (3) helping industry assess its educational needs for its various positions and by working with placement officers to develop new screening techniques with reduced reliance upon degrees as sole screening devices.
- Develop a cooperative working relationship between appropriate metropolitan colleges and universities and the public school system to develop projects designed to (1) improve inner-city teaching, (2) facilitate early admission and advanced-placement programs for high school students, (3) act as a placement agency for student teachers in the city schools from all the city's colleges and universities.
- Serve as the coordinating agency for student service projects in the community. This agency would perform a function similar to that proposed by the Atlanta Service-Learning Conference. It would act as receiving agent for work-study funds to be dispersed through community agencies and would be responsible for placing students with various agencies and providing supervision in the appropriate use of these students. While the agency would provide some general orientation for students on service projects, it would not provide educational programs or grant credit in connection with any service activities. The educational content of any program or supervision of the student in his service assignment for educational purposes would be the function of the college or university at which the student is matriculated.[13]

Perhaps more important than the above functions is the role the council would play in serving as a lay board representing the educational interests of the metropolitan area. It, not the individual institution, would be the focal point for pressure by special-interest groups. Its secretariat could provide many of the same benefits for the area's institutions that the University of Cincinnati hopes its new mechanism will provide for the University of Cincinnati.

To many, the dimension of urban involvement that distinguishes a university or college which has an urban mission from one which does

13. Ibid., pp. 109–10.

not is the institution's willingness and demonstrated ability to serve inner-city students. A closely linked function is the relevance that the institution's educational program has for today's urban society. Taken together, these two educational expressions are intricately related to the educational needs of urban America. Adequate response to either need will have a pervasive impact on the total institution.[14]

There are many who argue that today's society requires both a new set of educational goals and a new structure to facilitate achieving the goals. Increasingly, specific goals are determined by the individual student within a broad institutional framework. Thus, an appropriate response can be made to the diverse student body. But such a response is not wholly adapted to the traditional college structure, where a defined clientele has been served through relatively well-defined programs. If the urban student is to have full use of urban educational resources, there must exist an agency that brings the student and his particular educational goals together with the appropriate educational resources.

It is hard to see how either the education of inner-city students or the provision of relevant urban education—two highly important urban missions—could be aided by closer interaction between existing city governments and institutions of higher education. However, at least the second educational goal and perhaps the first also might well be served by the creation of institutions like the Minnesota Metropolitan State College, Empire State College, and Vermont Community College, structures that permit the student's educational goals to define his program and that include as part of that program the use of the area's educational resources.

A similar educational need prompted the Carnegie Commission to recommend a metropolitan educational opportunity counseling center, which would be learner-centered and encourage more effective use of educational resources in the area by the educational consumer. As envisioned by the commission, the new centers would "Act as educational and vocational adviser to the citizens in the metropolitan area, regardless of their age or past educational preparation.... Act as adviser to the higher education council on the need for new facilities and on any discernible shifts in student educational demands."[15]

The present form of interaction between city government and

14. See, for example, the case study of Our Lady of the Lake, in Nash, *University and City*, pp. 59–72.
15. *Campus and City*, p. 111.

campus does not substantially aid higher education in defining its urban mission. The presence of a functional government unit or quasi-governmental unit at the local level could help institutions focus their urban involvement. Thus, colleges and universities that are serious about their urban mission should seriously consider giving strong support to alternatives 2, 4, and 5 enumerated above. Structures alone will not ensure translation of a desire for urban commitment into a reality. They may, however, provide the necessary vehicles for marshaling both governmental and institutional interest at the local level.

In turn, government policies, particularly funding policies, must be developed in the light of public needs and institutional capabilities to serve the growing needs of two-thirds of our population now centered in the standard metropolitan statistical areas. These policies must address the diverse needs of the college-age and adult populations for a variety of postsecondary educational aspirations. The merging of public policies and institutional alternatives poses a challenge to the cooperative development of solutions which will deliver educational services to an expanding and diversified segment of our population.

The City as Campus

DAVID E. SWEET

WHEN CITY-CAMPUS RELATIONSHIPS are being considered, two questions need answers. First, what kind of education does a *citizen* (literally, a member of the city) require? Second, what forms and systems can best provide that education? It is insufficient to seek out mechanisms to improve coordination among existing educational institutions, not only if the institutions are not meeting the educational needs of citizens but also if their structure contributes to that failure. Improved coordination of essentially irrelevant institutions may perpetuate what ought to be eliminated and may prevent the development of suitable alternatives.

Our higher education system has been shaped by several forces. The public colleges and universities, most of them established during the nineteenth century, were designed for a rural society and thus located in small towns rather than the few large cities. When educational resources were sparse, it was sensible to concentrate libraries, laboratories, and teachers on a campus to which students and researchers must retreat in order to have access to facilities and events that were under institutional control. In such a setting, education was viewed as a hiatus—a withdrawal from life in order to prepare for life. These historic, economic, and philosophic forces created educational communities that intentionally were set apart for the larger community.

But times have changed. Recent American history has been characterized by the urbanization of life and by the explosion and dissemination of knowledge. No longer is this a nation of small towns or a people with few educational opportunities. Our society has become a teaching-learning society, rich in learning resources. Education has come to be provided through churches, community groups, YMCAs and YWCAs, proprietary schools, governments, business, industry, and labor organizations. An alert and aggressive person can easily pursue lifelong, self-directed learning. It is now not practical to isolate learning resources on secluded campuses.

Today, a danger lies in perpetuating an educational system that attempts to remain separate and self-contained. Too often the campus is still not envisioned as an integral part of the city, an essential element in whatever it is that makes a conglomeration of human beings into a city. Too often, even today, educational institutions are politically and philosophically "in" the city but not "of" it, arrogating to themselves a "separate but equal" status in the society and particularly in relation to the cities. They demand that they be separated from the society's political system, that they be allocated resources for which they are held only minimally accountable, and that they be allowed to serve with impunity as society's severest (and, often, not even friendly) critics. Increased "citywide" coordination of such higher education institutions might, in my judgment, even increase higher education's isolation from the city and exacerbate hostilities between higher education and the city.

Are there alternatives? Both Virginia Smith and the Carnegie Commission on Higher Education have cited the Minnesota Metropolitan State College, Empire State College, the Vermont Community College, and the College for Human Services as models suited to urban areas. It seems to me that they view each of the cited institutions as offering a viable alternative to the traditional form and content of higher education. These new educational systems share a prime characteristic: each is more a *system* than an *institution*—a process more than a tangible entity. They *disperse* educational resources out into the city, both in space and time; they become educational catalysts for the teaching-learning activities that permeate every contemporary urban environment.

Because I know MMSC best, I shall offer some highlights about its program. We are attempting to teach students to design their educational programs to acquire demonstrable competencies through utilizing all the resources of the city rather than depending on "experiences" or "events" determined by the college. We contend that it is dysfunctional to teach students to rely on the college as the authority for selecting appropriate competencies and as the primary agency for cultivating competencies. We want to discourage our students from that kind of dependent relationship, and prefer that they design their own education and implement it by using all aspects of their lives as essential elements in their education—work, home, leisure and recreational activities, civic and social commitments.

To achieve this end, we have no "campus" in the sense that educational resources are not concentrated in a single place within the seven-county Twin Cities metropolitan area which we serve. If we need space for college-sponsored learning opportunities, we draw on the array of unused and underutilized facilities scattered throughout the metropolitan region. We introduce students to the area's libraries, museums, theaters, laboratories, and research centers, rather than creating new facilities. Increasingly, we rely on noncollege-sponsored learning activities. The college makes inventories of learning opportunities conducted by a host of agencies, institutions, and corporations and disseminates information about these teaching-learning events to our students.

The heart of the MMSC effort to base education in the community is the community faculty. These faculty members constitute the central teaching personnel and are also persons who have major commitments, not to the college, but to their noncollegiate lives. As a group, they do not hold the conventional credentials; they have, however, demonstrated competencies which our students want to acquire and they have shown an ability and willingness to share those competencies. The community faculty is a major educational resource, one which must be at the heart of any reconciliation between urban educational needs and a system of higher education to meet those needs—between city and "campus."

In addition to using the city as a campus and the community as a learning resource, MMSC advises students to acquire civic competence. Man is, for the most part, a social creature, he lives in communities with other people, and, if he is to be truly self-governing, he needs to know how that community makes decisions—all kinds of decisions: political, economic, social, religious, aesthetic—which impinge upon the individual. The self-governing individual understands how the community makes decisions, has the skills to influence that process, and, furthermore, believes that participation in community life is worthwhile. I think it imperative that educational institutions urge students to demonstrate competencies related to the effective functioning of the urban community as a self-governing society of self-directed individuals. In this way educational institutions and their graduates can serve the city.

Lest my earlier comments about coordination be misconstrued, I affirm that I am committed to improving coordination in education. My concern about establishing higher education coordinating agencies in metropolitan areas, as advocated by Smith and the Carnegie Commission, is that the boundaries of coordination have been defined too narrowly. I would plead for metropolitanwide agencies which embrace all levels and types of educational systems, from preschool through the graduate and professional schools, and include proprietary schools and in-house staff development programs conducted by industry and government. The coordination effort should have as its purpose, not the greater rationalization of what already exists, but rather the dismantling of much that exists in order to construct in its place systems of dispersed, competency-focused, community-based education. To that end, I endorse the principle that such coordinating agencies be kept out of the hands of those who direct and operate the existing institutions and be given to those who seek and need an *urban* education.

One final point. It appears that the "urban grant university" is an idea whose time has come. I have reservations about simplistic application of the land-grant model to the urban situation. The land-grant institutions contributed greatly to the increase in agricultural production—a specific, technologically manageable goal. A question now being asked about land-grant institutions is whether or not they have made a balanced contribution to the development of rural society as a whole. Even rural areas exhibit a complex configuration of life styles, economic and social forces, and human needs. In comparison, the contemporary urban environment is many times more complex. The land-grant movement could focus on serving the needs of individual entrepreneurs in order to increase agricultural production. No such defined target group is available when it comes to the development of rural society as a whole—and this situation is even more true of the city.

Smith stresses that the complexities of urban society make it difficult to identify urban needs and then to articulate urban missions for higher education based on these needs. Perhaps for this reason, new institutions such as MMSC lay stress on permitting students to design their *own* educational goals in competency terms, using the college as a resource for advice and counsel but not permitting the college or its faculty to substitute its judgment for that of the individual citizen.

The Dynamics of a Metropolitan Community College

PETER MASIKO, JR.

VIRGINIA SMITH HAS SUMMARIZED WELL the problems of coordination among postsecondary institutions to meet the needs of metropolitan constituencies, especially governmental units and agencies. Suggestions are offered to help colleges define and achieve their urban mission, with primary attention given to established institutions—public and private—in downtown and near-downtown areas of our larger and older cities and metropolitan areas. The emphasis is proper: inasmuch as large numbers of the potential college clientele live or work in the city, city-campus relationships need to be cultivated so that appropriate educational services can become available to expanding, more diversified segments of the population.

The proposal to develop formal metropolitan higher education councils may be sound for many metropolitan areas. I suggest, however, that the objectives may be achieved without a new bureaucratic organization on top of the present superabundance. My experience—in a city of 3.5 million with at least thirty postsecondary educational institutions and a metropolitan county unit of 1.4 million that includes at least ten postsecondary institutions—leads me to conclude that *mandatory* coordination, even by essentially local boards or commissions, is the least desirable method of achieving the objectives sought.

There is a movement in this country toward statewide coordination of postsecondary education. Although the thrust is concerned with the public sector, the private sector is not ignored; and legislation, both state and federal, virtually assures that the entire higher education enterprise will be included in considering future expansion of existing institutions and the development of new ones. Certainly, enrollment projections for the next ten to twenty years have caused greatly increased demands for better utilization of existing plants and for limitation of expansion, particularly in areas where private nonprofit institutions have excess capacity.

Many metropolitan multicampus community colleges are already performing inner-city functions emphasized in the Smith paper. They have filled long-standing vacuums by serving large numbers of students for whom traditional four-year college programs have been either inappropriate or out of financial reach. They work closely with all levels of government, in physical plant development, site acquisition, program development, and so on. Many kinds and levels of coordination take place: at both state and local levels, with all segments of public and private postsecondary education, and with business, industrial, civic, and political leaders. Let me illustrate with examples from Miami-Dade Community College.

Miami-Dade is one of twenty-eight community colleges in the Florida community college system, a system which provides the first two years of college within commuting distance of more than 95 percent of the state's population. The state furnishes all basic capital construction funds and 72–75 percent of the operating funds. The state director of community colleges, who is under the Florida commissioner of education, coordinates the operation of the community colleges, each of which has its own board of trustees. The board has legal responsibility for its college, and has wide discretion in meeting local needs.

The state plan for community colleges was developed in 1955, and the twenty-eighth unit began operation in 1972. The growth has been systematic, and in each case a new community college has required the active support, financial and otherwise, of local political leaders, public school officials, and important business, industrial, and civic leaders. Until July 1, 1968, the community colleges operated under the respective local (county) boards of public instruction. Since then the colleges have operated independently under their own boards. The change did not alter the close cooperative relationships between the community colleges and their originators and supporters.

Miami-Dade Community College and the Dade County public schools cooperate on many fronts for the advantage of the people. The college uses twenty or more public school facilities throughout the county for late afternoon and evening extension classes, at no cost to the college.

In turn, Miami-Dade houses their computer operation. The college waives fees for employees of the county's public schools, and in 1972-73 the fees waived for 3,270 registrations were valued at $165,000. A joint Committee in Career Education has the task of avoiding duplication of programs and of determining the appropriate level and location of new career programs.

In the allied health (paramedical) programs, Miami-Dade has cooperated with all related hospitals, clinics, and other health facilities, with appropriate professional personnel and organizations, and with all levels of government, in developing the programs, in arranging for physical facilities, and in meeting the personnel needs of the community in this growing field. Every hospital in the county provides time, space, and trained personnel in our clinical experience requirements. The college provides special career ladder programs under contract with the local Veterans Administration hospital. We do the same with the huge county-owned hospital, where we also provide instructional personnel for the hospital's three-year R.N. program. A private Miami Beach hospital has built a $2 million paramedical educational facility on its grounds which the college leases for $1.00 per year; more than 1,500 students are enrolled. We are ready to let the contract for our own paramedical facility, valued in excess of $5 million, across the street from the county hospital and within easy walking distance of the University of Miami Medical School and a large number of other health facilities, including the huge VA hospital. Many different groups have been involved in the development of this project, including the state and county governmental units, the public school board, the University of Miami Medical School, Florida International University, the county hospital, and representatives from all professional fields that will have programs at this location.

Perhaps the best illustration of what can be done on a voluntary basis is seen in the Institute for Criminal Justice, a specialized facility nearing completion on our North Campus. This facility and the program required the active support, financial and other, from every level of government, ranging from the twenty-six incorporated municipalities in Dade County to the federal government. Each municipality, the City of Miami, and Dade County have independent police forces. The county, the City of Miami, and several other cities have had their own police training programs. Under the new arrangement, the community college will provide the basic training, both pre-service and in-service. In addition, other aspects of the criminal justice system will provide educational and training opportunities at the community college campuses. Federal funding for construction was achieved, but the undertaking required much work with the county, the state, and the regional office. The money in this case must go to a local governmental unit, but Dade County transfers these funds directly to the college to meet construction costs.

It was no small task to get all of the independent police agencies to work together to develop with the college the educational specifications for the institute, nor was it easy to secure agreement on the curricula. But all this has been done, and an Advisory Committee will watch closely the results of this coordinated community enterprise.

Miami-Dade Community College has also responded to the special needs of the many different groups in the county, including the blacks concentrated in the Model Cities areas as well as those in scattered clusters throughout the county. For the Spanish-speaking residents, mainly Cuban, instruction is provided in bilingual modes in off-campus centers in the heart of the respective populations. Nor are the Miccosukee Indians in the remote Everglades neglected. Our board of trustees has adopted a liberal waiver-of-fees policy so that no interested student is denied access because of economic factors. In 1972–73 the board waived fees for 10,551 different students, in the amount of $1,835,000.

The newest addition to the Miami-Dade Community College complex is the $10 million downtown campus, which was opened in the fall of 1973. On land cleared by the U.S. Department of Housing and Urban Development as depressed business property, we have built an outstanding architectural structure designed to help rebuild the downtown area and to provide much-needed services to people who work in the downtown area or who must rely on public transportation. I wonder whether a metropolitan higher education council could have done the same.

City and Campus: Scrutinizing the Alternatives

CHARLES Z. WILSON

THE EMERGENCE OF THE MODERN CITY as the hub of our civilization is a complex social and cultural phenomenon that cannot be ignored by institutions designed to further the development of humans. The position of the city in the affairs of man during this and future centuries may well exceed its eminence during the Middle Ages. It follows, therefore, that the problems of such a massive social and technological structure are and will continue to be enormous and ill-organized. Faced with the task of contributing to human development in the setting of urban communities, universities and colleges have too often become engulfed with fear and uncertainty.

Academic communities appear to live in awe of cities and the problems they bring. Yet projections are that within twenty years as much as 75 percent of the population in highly developed countries may be centered in urban communities. All universities and colleges, whether located in urban centers or in rural areas, must in one way or another become involved with the questions of city and campus.

In most city-campus discussions, the subject stimulates considerable apprehension, and those speaking for postsecondary education appear to be cautious, critical, and extremely tough on themselves. Virginia Smith writes with regard to the performance of colleges and universities on the urban scene: "Yet few institutions emerge as being largely characterized by their urban commitment." "In actuality, however, their diffuse programs rarely form an aggregate that signals a cohesive urban commitment." Both statements reflect the institutionalized impatience of scholars, administrators, and students alike. We expect too much too soon.

I propose an alternative framework for viewing the relation of colleges and universities with the city. I would like to posit that: (1) The problems of the city, the nature of universities and of cities, and the desired interaction patterns between the university and its large urban task environment are too complex and ill-structured to be approached except through a learning-by-doing heuristic. (2) The limited experiences of universities and colleges to date are sufficient only to raise question about the range of problems and issues confronting universities and colleges in dealing with urban settings and possible heuristics for seeking solutions.

Indeed, given these propositions, the fact that universities are not "characterized by their urban commitment" or that "their diffuse programs rarely form an aggregate and cohesive urban commitment" may be a healthy development. The most important qualities for college and university efforts are an openness to change and a willingness to search, to act, and to learn—in short, to look for insights into what (or what doesn't) works and what has been learned. The nature of a feasible urban commitment for colleges and universities must evolve through experience.

When one applies a learning-by-doing heuristic to the alternatives for colleges and universities pursuing activities with cities, as developed by Smith, what are seen as alternatives become elements of a broad strategy for developing effective relations between cities and universities. Consider each of the alternatives listed in the Smith paper.

1. *Accept the notion that the city government is rarely the appropriate agency for many urban activities and continue to interact directly with a number of special-interest groups.*

Being an agency of loosely coordinated, diverse groups, a university or college should not find it difficult to interact with other entities of diverse groups. The challenge to universities and city governments is to search for organizational frameworks that will facilitate interaction between such groups. We should be experimenting with community-based corporations, new systems of delivering public services to diverse community groups, and new formal organizational relationships of city government and university that will provide umbrellas for relations between the many interest groups of communities and universities. At the University of California, Los Angeles, we have experimented with "storefront" facilities, "student-community-faculty" problem-solving coalitions, and community-based research and public service cooperatives. And we are still experimenting and learning.

2. *Recognize the need for some stronger focal point for the institution's urban involvement, and develop a direct relationship with the city government for a much broader range of interactions.*

This particular element is not different from the first. If colleges and universities raise the right questions about structures, their relative efficiency in promoting interaction between universities and urban communities, and their abilty to endure the stress and strains generated by interactions between universities and urban communities, and city governments, *per se*, have to be considered seriously. Experience, however, suggests that relationships with some city governments can paralyze the university's capacity to relate with a whole range of important decision units within urban communities. In a university-city applied research project between UCLA and Compton four years ago, it was the shortsightedness and traditionalism of the city government and not "conflicts between special-interest groups and the university" that undermined the project. Today, we believe the newly elected administration of the City of Los Angeles will be a source of strength and will give new directions to relationships between the city government and universities in urban problem solving and public service. Instead of assisting the need of more focus between city government and universities, we should be experimenting and assessing current and past experiences to determine conditions when such a move is useful in our efforts to interact more effectively with urban communities. We should be evolving empirically based decision rules that will help campuses shape policy.

3. *Support forces that call for some type of metropolitan regional government.*

Promoting metropolitan regional government is certainly consistent with a learning-by-doing approach. Helping city governments reorganize and move toward more centrality is one way to reduce the problems of coordination. It represents one way to develop a more efficient mechanism through which interest groups may be forged into working coalitions. Committing the energy of the university to this direction does not preclude other efforts on the part of universities and colleges to establish relationships with the city and its environment.

4. *Recognize the need for coordination of higher education within the metropolitan region, and create a special-function agency for this purpose.*

This proposition points to an assertion that we all believe to some extent: coordination through consortia, superboards, and higher education associations can improve *some* working relations and *some* interactions of universities and urban communities. This is not an alternative to the first, second, or third propositions. At best it represents an additional element in a strategy to promote more interaction and coordination. Again, the question is not whether there should be regional organization in higher education, but, rather, under what conditions can such organizations contribute toward better interaction between universities and cities. On the urban scene there has been little experimentation with interorganizational structures. At UCLA, we have initiated a five-college consortium around special education programs. More than six hundred students have gained access to UCLA through the consortium. In still another consortium, we are developing an applied research project involving at least two other universities and nonprofit corporations. We do not have the answer as a single institution; collectively, however, we can raise the question: What have we learned about superboards, consortia, and cooperative interorganizational efforts? This question deserves a place in discussions of "The City and the Campus."

5. *Confine the activities of the institution to student-centered education, and, through students, utilize the range of educational resources within the city to serve the student.*

As presented by Smith, this particular activity is placed in competition with other activities, but it need not be so. There is nothing inconsistent with pursuing a student-centered effort while seeking more focus with city government, experimenting with applied research efforts across many groups within the city, seeking regional coordination across several higher educational institutions, and promoting coordination among city governments in a given region. Indeed, some mixture of these elements, rather than any one element, may represent a more accurate picture of the strategies followed by large urban universities today.

The tenor of Virginia Smith's paper is to minimize the accomplishments of many urban universities. The author prematurely poses some very difficult questions. The problems of our cities are too complex to design strategies for effective working relationships between universities and urban communities from our present limited experiences—inefficient *role* definitions, mistrust, protection of interests. It would be unfortunate if the trial-and-error responses of the past seven years (many emanating more out of fear than wisdom) were allowed to shape the long-term urban commitments of colleges and universities. I suggest that urban institutions of higher education more consciously engage in further experimentation, assess the outcomes, and slowly develop empirically based policies and directions.

MANAGEMENT AND GOVERNANCE IN HIGHER EDUCATION

The Management Systems Challenge: How to Be Academic Though Systematic

EARL F. CHEIT

FOR ALMOST A DECADE NOW, a small but growing number of specialists have been working to bring to administration an advantage which on campus had previously been associated with the hard curriculum: systematic thought. It was early in the 1960s that the possibilities for improving administration in higher education through the use of systems approaches and rigorous analytic techniques began to attract a few researchers. Although they did not know the style of the strong, one-man administrator of the pregrowth era, most had some acquaintance with the practices of his "chief administrator" successors. These systems researchers knew that administrators had established ways of counting income and expenditures; that they were orderly—if not highly analytical —about keeping track of staff, buildings, and some program activities. Every campus had its folk methods of administration. Though unobtrusive, these controlled well enough to make scandal rare, yet they were visible enough to cause faculty irritation about bureaucracy. By and large, they worked fairly satisfactorily for stable, one-campus institutions.

But in the early 1960s, the condition of higher education was not one of stability. It was one of rapid, almost explosive growth. Within a decade, college and university enrollment had doubled. As academic administrators labored with their old methods to provide space and teachers for new students and to develop policies to govern their growing, multicampus institutions, some of their colleagues who were system advocates began to think about the possibilities this growth created for new methods of management and planning. The old ways were already being successfully challenged under somewhat similar circumstances in

I owe thanks to several persons who read and criticized an earlier draft of this article: Carl R. Adams, David W. Breneman, Mariam K. Chamberlain, Robert H. Cole, Harold Howe II, Walter L. Johnson, Joseph W. McGuire, Roger G. Schroeder, and Burton I. Wolfman.

the Department of Defense and in many business corporations. Why not on campus? If information on income, expenditures, and activities could be defined, gathered, analyzed, and presented in new ways that developing techniques were making possible, then more sophisticated management and planning tools would be available to academic administrators. Colleges and universities could be made efficient and more effective.

That was the goal of the systems work which began about 1964. It may, in the retelling, seem to lack drama, but, early on, academic administration qualified as a problem worthy of elegant solutions and, as such, inspired prodigious effort on its behalf. By the end of the 1960s, the efforts to design systems for planning and management had created a new field of specialization, complete with research organizations, conferences, and technical publications. And it had produced a product line of analytical techniques and systems whose acronyms have become an integral part of the compleat administrator's technical vocabulary (replacing, it seemed, the initials of radical organizations that for a time were essential to the administrator's lexicon). It is probably a mere coincidence of timing, but no less a small irony for that reason, that during the late 1960s when many campuses were at their most disorderly, raising serious question whether they were governable, studies aimed at improving their management and planning were most prolific. If this work has not solved the planning and management problem, it is not for a lack of output.

One measure of that output was provided in 1972 when the Education Commission of the States sponsored a national conference on the state of the art of the new planning and management systems.[1] The magnitude of the field led conference planners at first to limit the discussion to "systems and approaches actually in use today rather than theoretical discussions by systems developers of what may be available tomorrow." In this fast-moving field, that is a major limitation. Yet, even with the limitation, not all the systems currently available could be included. So a second limitation was set: an illustrative sample would be used. A committee of specialists found that the range of systems could be illustrated by a sample of twenty-seven systems falling into four major areas: (1) data base management systems, (2) basic operational systems,

---

1. The proceedings volume, *Planning and Management Practices in Higher Education: Promise or Dilemma?*, Education Commission of the States Report no. 26 (Denver, Colo.: The Commission, May 1972), is a good reference and bibliographic source on this subject.

(3) planning and resource allocation tools, and (4) communication base tools.[2]

Additional conferences could well be held on the large number of systems omitted. In the field of operational systems alone—areas such as admissions, registration, student aid, alumni records—so many systems are available that an exchange has been organized to facilitate their circulation to administrators interested in using them. Created just a few years ago, the College and University Systems Exchange has already distributed in excess of one thousand systems abstracts and five hundred sets of systems documentation to member institutions, and its scope is limited to operational systems.

This systems work goes on in all parts of the country and, as befits a development increasingly dependent upon computer technology, in a variety of institutions—public, private, and profit making. No physical or intellectual center exists, although the National Center for Higher Education Management Systems (NCHEMS) at Boulder has become a focal point because of its size and the increasingly public direction of its projects. But equally important contributions to the concepts have been made by the Systems Research Group in Toronto, the Analytical Studies group at the University of California, the Program for Research in University Administration at Berkeley, several Big Ten institutions, the Florida state system, and by men and women in public accounting firms, in consulting organizations, and in research institutes.

HISTORY AND DEFINITIONS

Overall, this prodigious systems effort is directed to many technical questions, and its products function at various levels of sophistication. In higher education, the movement had at its point of origin a single impelling motive—to hasten the conversion of academic administration from folk to systems methods. Academic administration was far from the first subject singled out for this attention. Efforts to effect the same transition have been under way for several decades in business organizations and more recently in the government.

2. Examples of the categories and uses cited at the conference are: (1) a budget system that tells administrators whether the budget is being implemented as planned; (2) a student information system that helps students select their academic programs; (3) a planning system whose reports show effects of policy changes on budgets, enrollment, and program; (4) a system that records basic data in sophisticated ways such that planning and budgetary staff at state levels can use it to allocate resources to various state institutions.

Similarly, it is not unique to higher education that management methods became part of a struggle for power. In an important book on this subject, Ida Hoos observes that the earliest applications of the systems approach and its arsenal of sophisticated tools were made in World War II, where they "became a potent weapon against the prevailing defense management styles."[3]

Interest in the use of the newer analytic approaches was also developing rapidly in the private sector. Robert McNamara's early work at the Ford Motor Company is well known, and there are many other examples. Since the early 1950s, there have been lively discussions in business journals about "scientific" decision making. From the mid-1950s to the early 1960s, the *Harvard Business Review* published more than fifty articles on the new decision-making tools.[4] In the federal government, the momentum of the approach carried beyond the Department of Defense into other departments, in what Alice Rivlin calls "a quiet revolution in the government."[5] Thus, the systems approach is relatively new to higher education, but late in the general development of the movement. The purpose, however, has been the same as elsewhere—to apply "systems analysis" to an enterprise.

No precise agreement prevails about what "systems analysis" is or, indeed, whether in higher education that is the appropriate term. One convention has it that "management systems" is the broad term encompassing all processes used in decision making and operations. This delineation would leave "systems approaches" as the more technical term, referring only to the modern tools and techniques. If the field were to be described in the manner of the traditional biological science departments—by reference to the tree of knowledge—it could be called a leafy branch of management science. In fact, no single name has as yet been accepted as definitive.

In consequence, then, *systems approach* seems to mean, on the one hand, the use of techniques such as program budgeting, management information systems, and resource allocation models. On the other hand, it also seems to mean a framework of thought designed to help decision-

3. Hoos, *Systems Analysis in Public Policy: A Critique* (Berkeley: University of California Press, 1972), p. 44.
4. Edward Bursk and John F. Chapman, eds., *New Decision-Making Tools for Managers* (New York: New American Library, Mentor Books, 1965), p. viii.
5. *Systematic Thinking for Social Action* (Washington: Brookings Institution, 1970), p. 3.

makers select the best choice in a complex situation containing a number of interdependent variables. Sometimes it means both. I shall use "systems" with and without "approaches," as the context seems to require.

One sensible way of avoiding ambiguity was used by Lawrence Bogard in his Carnegie Commission essay; he did not try to define the systems analysis approach but, rather, stated precisely what he considers to be the preconditions for its goal of effective management: (1) institutional research, (2) a planning-programming-budgeting system (PPBS), and (3) a computerized management information system.[6] At the Education Commission of the States conference (referred to earlier), George Weathersby, a pioneer in this field, called the output of "the last seven years a number of analytic techniques, computer programs and new presentation formats.... These techniques," he observed, "have been referred to variously as models, program budgeting, management information systems, budget generators or predictors, and cost-benefit (effectiveness) analysis.... I include all of these techniques under the rubric of analytic planning tools or techniques as distinguished from formal organizational planning structures."[7] This is a useful distinction although, as discussed below, the organizational structures and analytic planning tools and techniques are becoming increasingly related.

In using the assigned title "management systems," as does NCHEMS in its name, I include in it three elements: (1) the full kit of analytical tools available for use in institutions,[8] (2) the related but more comprehensive techniques designed for statewide and even national use,[9] and (3) the conception of organization, not as structure, but as process: a process of goal designation, formulation of alternative plans, identification and selection of the best choice, evaluation of results, and continuation of the cycle.[10]

---

6. Bogard, "Management in Institutions of Higher Education," in *Papers on Efficiency in the Management of Higher Education* (Berkeley, Calif.: Carnegie Commission on Higher Education, 1972), p. 12. Not everyone would agree with this list. I suspect most critics would find it a bit short.

7. *Planning and Management Practices,* p. 80.

8. The best recent survey of these tools is found in Roger G. Schroeder, "A Survey of Management Science in University Operations," *Management Science,* April 1973, pp. 895–906.

9. Such as Statewide Student Flow Models. See Western Interstate Commission on Higher Education, *Annual Report, 1972* (Boulder, Colo.: The Commission), pp. 16–17.

10. See, for example, Vicki Kessel and Oscar G. Mink, *The Application of Open Systems Theory and Organization to Higher Education: A Position* (Durham, N.C.: National Laboratory for Higher Education, 1971), 70 pp.

Techniques versus Their Consequences

Management systems came to higher education the way new technology tends to arrive these days, fast, without arousing general questions about its future effects. Futurist Alvin Toffler describes the general phenomenon: "All of a sudden a new technology arrives on the scene. Then there is a big push to get it out fast. That means there is very little time for the society to make the subtle kind of adaptation necessary before it has committed itself to the use of the technology. Maybe the consequences are trivial. But who knows and who asks? Nobody."[11]

Until recently, not many questions about the general consequences of higher education management systems were asked on campus. Management systems commanded little attention from nonspecialists. PPBS may today be as commonly understood on campus as FTE, but certainly it was not five or even two years ago. In those earlier days, except for technical reports or small conferences of specialists, the principal forums for discussion of management systems were the meetings of task forces and committees to advise the Western Interstate Commission for Higher Education (WICHE) and, later, its NCHEMS, with members appointed precisely because of their specialized skills. When the specialists returned to their campuses, they would write memoranda to their presidents explaining the developments in a growing list of technical projects. If such subtleties as an "induced course load matrix" and a "resource requirement prediction model" escaped presidents during those days of student protest and campus upheaval, they might be forgiven. Like their faculty members, they knew something about management systems but did not give the subject much sustained thought.

As a consequence, the work on management systems was subject to considerable scrutiny, but almost entirely scrutiny of a technical nature. A flourishing literature developed.[12] Competent work was done in designing varieties of systems and in identifying their technical defects,

---

11. *New York Times Magazine*, June 10, 1973, p. 38.
12. Schroeder's "Survey of Management Science" is an excellent source. He covers eighty-six highly selected works (70 percent of them specialized, unpublished reports) and has several references to bibliographies (the two on PPBS each have more than a thousand titles; the one on management information systems, more than five hundred). Another comprehensive source is *State of the Art: Review and Evaluation of Educational Simulation Models* (Toronto: Systems Research Group, 1972). See also Paul W. Hammelman, ed., *Managing the University: A Systems Approach* (New York: Praeger, 1972), 139 pp.

but little writing (that I know of) raised questions about the possible larger consequences of management systems for higher education.[13]

Partly in recognition of the need to broaden perspectives, the Western Interstate Commission on Higher Education, in September 1972, for the first time called a national assembly to provide a forum for a full discussion of management systems. More than seven hundred persons attended. Yet in the three days of meetings, with but a single exception, the discussions were of a technical nature. The exception was a thoughtful session on policies about the release and exchange of information. All the right questions were raised,[14] but the greatest excitement was caused by the distribution of the "Fullerton Report"[15]—an account of the first effort to apply on a single campus the various analytical products developed by NCHEMS. The discussion was lively. The topic was "how to do it."

When the Education Commission of the States convened the national conference referred to earlier, it too had sought to put management systems into a larger context. The program subtitle asked whether these systems offered "Promise or Dilemma." Several good policy papers introduced the systems discussions. But the questions that followed suggest that the technical aspects commanded the interest. The first question signaled the discussion: "Where and how do I get my executive trained?"

AN ALIEN SUBJECT; GROWING CONCERN

Most nonspecialists, whether or not they have had to deal with the special problems of academic institutions in recent years, have found the whole subject of management systems less than gripping. Their relative indifference stems neither from indolence nor from fear of computers, however. There are other reasons.

To begin, for all the talk about management systems, they did not appear directly to affect the academic life of institutions. There was little contact between systems researchers and operating administrators. The

---

13. The valuable article by Peggy Heim, "Management Systems and Budgeting Methodology: Do They Meet the Needs and Will They Work?" *NACUBO Studies in Management*, September 1972, 4 pp., is the first I know of that has dealt with the larger organizational issues of management systems.

14. See especially the speech by Donald R. McNeil, "Who's Afraid of the Information Wolf? Caveats of a University Administrator" (Reprint; Boulder, Colo.: NCHEMS, September 1972).

15. *Implementation of NCHEMS Planning and Management Tools at California State University, Fullerton* (Boulder, Colo.: WICHE, August 1972), 99 pp.

early attempts (for example, by the California legislature) to impose measures like program budgeting had few practical consequences for faculty members. The burden fell instead on harassed budget workers who had to change the entire format of their budgets. The University of Michigan reports that it took three man years of work to make its data conform to the new state budget system requirements. The new formats are often not used, and, indeed, the California state agencies originally required that budgets be submitted in both the new and the old forms so that the materials could be understood. It appeared that the new format was mostly an exercise in communication between technical people.

Other techniques—student flow models, the resource allocation models—were conceived essentially as planning devices. Their perspective was the problem of future growth. Enrollment-driven, these models assumed a continuation of those conditions that provide a set of happy worries for academics, but do not attract their attention.

Academics have long called their enterprise a "system." "Our system of education" refers primarily to a hierarchy and its relationships, not to its internal workings; the "system of influence" means the informal organization, not a research technique. But the fact is that we *call* it "system," and announcements that it was now going to be *treated* as a system had no effect as long as no one felt a difference. Another reason academics took little notice of management systems, despite extensive technical work on the subject, is that applications have not progressed very far. The Bogard survey for the Carnegie Commission in 1971 revealed that, of 1,873 responding institutions, only 2.8 percent had institutionalized all three elements noted as his precondition for effective management.[16]

Even where institutions have moved to adopt management systems, academics have been slow to take notice because of the unusual nature of college and university organization. They have, as E. D. Duryea points out, become organized, not in a single large bureaucracy, but in two of them. One is a loose collection of professionals, the faculty hierarchy. It claims "rights of control over the totality of the academic function," leaving, in effect, a separate administrative hierarchy "to grapple with the immense tasks of management, . . . not the least of which are budget and finance." In this situation, Duryea notes, the lines of relationship have become tenuous, with different values, attitudes, and not

16. "Management in Institutions," p. 35.

much communication or understanding of the overall mission of the academic enterprise.[17]

The last year has produced impressive evidence that this general indifference to systems is changing, that academic men and women are becoming aware of management systems and increasingly concerned about their possible implications.[18] Why this growing concern now? Partly, of course, it takes time for technical matters to be understood, analyzed, and commented on in print. Yet it is more than simply passage of time. A visit to campuses today reveals a kind of foreboding about what this new development might bring. The main reason for the aroused concern is that conditions have changed.

The most basic change is that the problem of dealing with growth has become the problem of adjusting to the steady state. This transition is the subject of extensive discussion, for it has many dimensions, of which none is more significant than management systems. Under steady-state conditions, the methods of management are having impact on organization. Planning models, or even simple exercises to develop goals, bring to the fore certain objectives that had been assumed but never made explicit. Now they must be not only revealed but also defended. Without growth, the interdependence of decisions cannot be ignored or left to be absorbed by future changes. The method of change becomes substitution or even contraction. This squeeze places great stress on

17. "Evolution of University Organization," in *The University as an Organization*, ed. James A. Perkins, Report for the Carnegie Commission on Higher Education (New York: McGraw-Hill, 1973), p. 35.

18. Evidence of interest is the session on the subject that the American Council on Education included in its 1973 annual meeting, which, by tradition, is devoted to issues of broad interest to academics. As a continuing activity, the Council is spending some of its relatively scarce resources on its recently reactivated Office of Administrative Affairs, whose first priority is work on management systems, a further indication of a conclusion that the implications must be examined. The Academy for Educational Development has recently issued various helpful publications on the use of models for planning in higher education and on the uses and limits of business management practices in higher education: of special interest are William A. Shoemaker, *Systems Models and Programs for Higher Education* (Washington: Academy for Educational Development, 1973), 20 pp., and *The Contributions of Business Management to Higher Education* (Washington: The Academy, 1972), 16 pp. Other evidences of the growing consciousness appear in the popular periodicals of higher education. *Change Magazine*, in its first treatment of the subject, devoted its lead editorial to the dangers of the cult of efficiency in education: see Stephen Bailey, "The Efficiency Cultists," *Change*, June 1973, pp. 8–9. *The Chronicle of Higher Education* printed (June 18, 1973, p. 16) parts of Harold L. Enarson's strong statement on the threats posed by the "managerial revolution" on campus. Mrs. Hoos's *Systems Analysis in Public Policy* contains the strongest critique to date, and its comprehensiveness makes it an influential volume.

choice. Decision points become more formal. Criteria for judgment are more often those that are measurable. In short, the basic questions of goals, governance, allocation of funds, and measurement of results now are coming within the influence of management methods, whether folk or systems.[19]

A second stimulus for this new awareness is the changing role of the state governments in higher education. As the states have become an increasingly important source of funds, they have begun to demand more information, more coordination, and a larger role in planning and even in governing. Management systems originally developed for institutional use have become the most readily available tools to assist the states in carrying out their own purposes. Thus, the formal organizational structures and the planning and management systems of higher education are coming into closer relationships. Suddenly, campuses discover that they are now part of a large systems network. Information is flowing out, and consequences are hard to predict.

Recently the federal government has indicated it intends to condition much of its financial role on information gathered by management systems. Legislation which would make support for higher education conditional on the availability of cost data was defeated, mainly because such data are not available. But the Congress then created the National Commission on the Financing of Postsecondary Education, whose charge requires that it report on methods for determining cost data per student by level and by type of institution. Its report to the Congress is due in December 1973, and within sixty days thereafter the Commissioner of Education is, by statute, obligated to make recommendations for congressional action.

A final reason that the technical field of management systems is attracting greater interest on campus is that "everyone is doing it." When campus administrators compare experiences, they all report expanded management effort. Thus pressure is stimulated on each campus to evaluate the adequacy and effects of its own efforts.

Everyone in the higher education enterprise can be grateful that this concerned awareness is coming early enough in the history of higher education management systems so that Mr. Toffler's concern—that no one asks about or has time to care about eventual effects until it is too late—

---

19. For an informative and competent demonstration of what can be done in applying systematic techniques of analysis, see *Budgeting and Resource Allocation at Princeton University* (Princeton, N.J.: The University, 1972), 390 pp.

need not apply here. There is still time to care and to do something about the impact of management systems, for most are future consequences.

INTENDED CONSEQUENCES OF MANAGEMENT SYSTEMS

I shall try to specify what these consequences might be and discuss them briefly. I shall begin by looking at two intended consequences of management systems: first, improved management and planning of higher education; and second, improved attitudes toward higher education through rebutting the presumption that its institutions are inefficiently run. Next I shall consider three unintended (or mostly unintended) consequences: increased centralization, reduction in diversity, and the influence of systems requirements on decisions.

I find that although the intended effects on management and planning are potentially beneficial, their value to date, though little studied, appears to be quite limited. Even when the application of management systems proves successful, I doubt that the results will produce favorable public attitudes toward education. The unintended consequences raise a growing challenge for higher education: Can colleges and universities be academic though systematic? After analyzing briefly the origins and nature of this challenge, I conclude that management systems are generating still another unintended consequence: they are creating new requirements for academic leadership. If academic leaders are to meet the growing challenge of management systems, they must begin to influence the design and application of the tools, techniques, and processes.

1. *Has the work on management systems produced better management and planning on campus?*

I believe that the answer is tentatively yes, but that is more an impression than a conclusion drawn from evidence, because relatively little has been done to evaluate the impact of management systems. A major implementation program started by NCHEMS will provide some information. I know of other plans for evaluative studies, but if any studies have been completed on the use of management systems to determine their effects, I am not aware of them. It may be too early to make convincing comparisons of costs and benefits. Moreover, in this context it is hard to know just what measures of improvement are best. If the degree of interest in management systems is indicative of the possibilities for improvement, then perhaps evidence for a yes answer will be available soon.

At the Education Commission of the States conference, a question was raised about the impact of systems. Ben Lawrence, director of NCHEMS, replied:

> We recently had a consultant group at the University of Colorado ask a number of you across the nation some hard questions about new management tools. I would say that we have no way at the present time of indicating their impact on the higher education process, but we know that we can measure the impact [on] institutions and agencies that are attempting to use these things or are getting ready to use them. A large number of institutions and agencies are attempting to gear up to use these new tools in their decision making process. This conference evidences that in itself. However, it will be several years yet before we know that these new management concepts can make a significant improvement in our decision making capabilities.[20]

In the meantime, what indications of improvement are there? Testimonials of those using management systems, for one thing. Every developer of systems has its list of satisfied users or experimenters. *Management Forum* (the new publication of the Management Division of the Academy for Educational Development) presents one such account, "Success Is Projected by a Systems Approach to Planning."[21]

Beyond interest and testimonials to actual use of management systems, evidence that would indicate improved planning and management is sketchy. Although there are, as I noted at the outset, many systems products available, except for operations systems the number in use seems to be small, and it is not uncommon to find campuses where early users or pilot testers of various planning models have stopped using them.[22] The latter can be a matter of some sensitivity. A visitor may be told that the use was a research effort, not an attempt to incorporate the system into the continuing, decision-making part of the organization. Experts in the field have different views about why management systems are not in wider use. As Mr. Lawrence's statement notes, newness is one explanation. Dissatisfaction is another. Carl R. Adams and Roger G. Schroeder, two education systems specialists with Defense Department experience, contend that "the record of successful implementation is poor" because the systems have tended to be solutions seeking problems,

---

20. "Questions and Answers, Transcript from Work Session," *Planning and Management Practices*, p. 150.
21. April 1973, p. 1.
22. Some of the main weapons in that "quiet revolution in government" have been discarded. See Leonard Merewitz and Stephen H. Sosnick, *The Budget's New Clothes* (Chicago: Markham, 1971), 318 pp.

and are not designed to help with day-to-day problems of operating control and efficiency.[23]

Has the actual use of systems, whether for research or operations or planning, increased campus efficiency? The great range of current practice makes it difficult to say. On occasional campuses, the dean of a school, by using an information system available in an office console, can determine in minutes the implications of a number of moves that might be made with courses, faculty, new programs, enrollment, tuition. Yet some institutions apparently still do not even know exactly how many students they have enrolled. A university recently defended itself against HEW charges of discrimination by responding that it did not know its employment patterns because it did not have an overall count of its employees. In this situation, it is hard to generalize about efficiency for all institutions. It seems clear, however, that simple management information systems and a variety of operational systems are increasing efficiency in a growing number of colleges and universities, much as they have helped business organizations. Beyond the realm of operations and simple information systems, the challenge is for potential savings. But the form is still unclear.

Are management systems improving planning? When this question is posed to systems advocates, the discussion often shifts to the increased awareness gained by planners or potential planners. A favored criterion seems to be the extent to which models require an institution's members to look at the interrelatedness of a large number of variables and thereby increase their awareness of the value of planning. Users are forced to look at problems they otherwise would be unaware of until a crisis arose, so the benefit, the explanation goes, lies in requiring them to look at the future in a more orderly way.

Does awareness lead to greater effectiveness, that is, to the doing of the "right" things? Unfortunately, there are no means at hand to measure effectiveness. Perhaps the only measure here is satisfaction. Using this criterion, the answer would seem to be a guarded yes.

The Carnegie Commission reports bearing on these aspects of management systems seem to warrant three conclusions. First, substantial changes in attitudes, practices, and policies concerning institutional man-

---

23. "Design and Implementation of Improved Management Systems in Postsecondary Schools," Working paper (Minneapolis: University of Minnesota, Graduate School of Business, June 1973).

agement are occurring on campuses. Although the Bogard study found that only a small percentage of institutions had all three preconditions he had set for effective management, it also found that significant changes were being made in the use of operational systems and in the development of long-range plans. Bogard concludes that change and innovation are taking place but that their success may not be known for some time. That finding is confirmed by the Carnegie Commission study, *The New Depression in Higher Education—Two Years Later*.[24]

A second conclusion is that the most immediately visible impact of these changes is a substantial reduction in the rate of expenditure growth, as reported in *The New Depression in Higher Education—Two Years Later*. According to campus administrators, the rate of expenditure growth was reduced primarily through applying established methods, not management systems approaches. In response to the question "Have you found that modern management techniques for planning and decision making are helpful in solving your cost-income problems?", administrators were cautious. Their responses suggested possible short-run benefits, but real evidence of an important impact on expenditure is yet to come.

The third conclusion follows logically. Perhaps the most important impact of management systems approaches is on thought processes about the future. Almost all institutions in *The New Depression* study have adopted or soon will adopt an overall strategy in their cost-income problems. Management systems have helped some of them emphasize output-oriented planning, but no one can say how much or to what effect. Thus, the response to the question posed at the outset is that management systems appear to have some short-term, though limited, benefit; they promise greater future benefit, but it will take several years to test that promise.

2. *Will the use of management systems help develop more favorable attitudes toward higher education (by rebutting the presumption that colleges and universities are inefficiently run)?*

The following excerpts from congressional hearings, which eventually led to the Education Amendments of 1972, illustrate how the issue of "inefficiency" apparently influences attitudes toward higher education.

> CONGRESSWOMAN GREEN: I am very disturbed over what seems to be an absence of any concern on the part of the Office of Education and

---

24. Earl F. Cheit, a technical report sponsored by the commission (Berkeley, Calif.: Carnegie Commission on Higher Education, 1973), pp. 59–70.

HEW over the plight of our private colleges and other institutions that are experiencing such great financial difficulty. . . .

CONGRESSMAN BRADEMAS: Madam Chairman, May I simply say, "Right on!"

SECRETARY RICHARDSON: . . . we are concerned about the plight of institutions of higher education, and, as I indicated earlier, we are giving very intensive thought to the question of what the response of the Federal Government should be. We are convinced that among most inefficiently administered institutions in the United States, by and large, are our institutions of higher education, and that before we turn to means of providing help to them we ought to be clear about what help is needed.

CONGRESSWOMAN GREEN: May I interrupt there, Mr. Secretary. Would you want to refer to institutions of higher education as the most inefficiently administered? Would you compare them with Lockheed and Penn Central?

SECRETARY RICHARDSON: I have no means of comparison. I suspect their facilities are used a large percentage of the day and more months per year.[25]

Whether those are Mr. Richardson's views today, given what has happened since then, or to what extent they are shared by others, they clearly represent in some measure attitudes held by the public and by legislative bodies. The reluctance of Congress to fund the Education Amendments of 1972 suggests that view is persuasive in the Congress.

Will the use of management systems rebut the presumption of inefficiency and lead to greater support? Probably not. My conclusion is based on three grounds. First, there is little evidence that once the accusation of inefficiency is made, accused institutions can get credit for taking steps to increase efficiency. Such measures, rather than producing a vote of confidence, tend to evoke the response that they should have been taken earlier. Public agencies that attempt to demonstrate their efficiency by cutting costs more often than not are penalized for it. Because few incentives exist for public agencies to save, the wonder is that they make as many serious efforts at efficiency as they do.

Second, public agencies that have won fiscal confidence have done so by other means than claiming to be efficient. Stephen Bailey, in "A Comparison of the University with a Government Bureau," points out that the government agencies most successful in gaining solid support

---

25. U.S. Congress, House, *Hearings before the Special Subcommittee on Education of the Committee on Education and Labor*, 92d Cong., 1st sess., March 2, 1971, pt. 1:128–29.

(the merits aside) have been remarkable in retaining autonomy in using their funds. He suggests that university administrators "might well turn to selected government bureaus. . . . The Corps of Engineers, the FBI, the Atomic Energy Commission, selected regulatory commissions [are agencies that] have learned the art of attracting appropriations while preserving an astounding independence from political surveillance."[26]

Third, my judgment is that use of management systems will not do much to foster favorable attitudes toward higher education because unfavorable attitudes are based primarily, not on questions of efficiency, but on questions of purpose. Bailey puts it better: "Only the woefully naïve contend that the real problem is efficiency—that government bureaus and universities will receive votes of confidence in new dollars when they can master PPB (program planning budgeting) and related cost-benefit techniques and thereby can be held accountable. The basic issue is political and psychological—a growing belief that what government bureaus and universities do is not worth the cost."[27]

Higher education is expensive. Given its high costs, increased efficiency is an important objective in its own right, one that administrators and faculty members must take very seriously. An efficient operation can also rebut an excuse for nonsupport. But even the most successful application of management systems alone is unlikely to inspire better funding.

Unintended Consequences of Management Systems

3. *Will management systems accelerate the trend toward centralization of higher education?*

On grounds of theory, behavior in the business sector, and some early signs in higher education organizations, the answer is almost certainly yes. The theory is well understood by anyone familiar with organizations: Power goes with information. As information goes to higher levels in the organization, the power to decide and the practice of deciding goes there too.

If systems were being built from the bottom up, with information about the organization and its requirements rising from departmental to school or college and then campus levels, and only then beyond the campus level, a trend toward centralization would not result unless by

26. In Perkins, *The University as an Organization,* p. 134.
27. Ibid., p. 133.

deliberate choice. That is not the main pattern, however. Systems are being built on top of governing structures or at the headquarters level; therefore, centralization of decision power is occurring, and the power of informal collegial systems and even of the formal organization at lower levels is declining. At the same time, the agenda at the top is growing. Under these circumstances, governing easily becomes managing. Examples in industry are numerous. In a typical situation, the corporate office, as a consequence of its new information system, receives production data before they reach the department or divisions responsible for the production. A careful survey of forty top corporate executives by Carl R. Adams of the University of Minnesota Graduate School of Business asked the executives whether management systems had led to increased centralization in their organizations. The answer was overwhelmingly yes.

As already noted, although many system products are available, actual installation and use of management systems is more limited in higher education than in business, and therefore experience is quite limited. I am predicting from early signs rather than confirmed facts. Yet these small signs suggest that a survey of academics would produce results no different from the business survey. Let me elaborate on one example—the evolution of the work and purposes of NCHEMS.[28]

The evolution of the purposes and projects at the Western Interstate Commission for Higher Education, first under its management information systems project, and then through its National Center for Higher Education Management Systems, seems to bear out the concern that, in a fast-moving field like management systems, the "top down" phenomenon becomes inevitable. In 1970, Western Interstate Commission for Higher Education—Management Information Systems began work on thirteen projects, of which twelve were designed to help institutions. One—on statewide student flows—was for state or federal use. The overall list of projects revealed the main question WICHE was asking: How can management and planning of institutions be improved? In 1971, NCHEMS was formally organized, and started ten projects in its first year, of which three bore directly on earlier work, five were primarily for state or federal use, and one was a reporting application. This ratio set the pattern for 1972, when twelve projects were started, of which six are primarily for state or federal use and one primarily for reporting.

28. For help on this section, I am indebted to a management systems specialist who prefers no identification other than being "a dedicated WICHE-Watcher."

The project lists, when compared by years, reveal a sign I noted earlier in discussing the shift toward centralization caused by systems. In this case, the emphasis changed from almost exclusive interest in institutional management needs to state and federal needs. Does this changed project mix reflect a changed perspective? Or is it accidental? Consider the statement of objectives in 1969: "(a) to significantly improve the capability of local institutions and agencies to more effectively allocate resources; (b) to provide the cooperating organizations, on a continuing basis, comparable data throughout the region and elsewhere on the cost of instructional programs by level of student, level of course, and field of study." By 1971, WICHE's annual report stated the goals for its new division working on management systems as follows: "(1) the improvement of institutional management; (2) the improvement of statewide coordination of higher education; and (3) the improvement of decision-making processes on the highest national levels." Two of the three goals have now been stated to serve constituencies other than the colleges and universities. The statement is repeated in its 1972 report.

This brief analysis is not a comment on the relative merits of the shift in emphasis, for it can be argued that state systems are designed to help institutions. Nor is it an argument about the merits of the work at WICHE, for its staff is competent and has made important contributions to the effort to improve the resource allocation process in higher education. I simply suggest that the shift toward giving state and federal needs a priority equal to, or a priority greater than, institutional needs is an example of the centralizing tendencies of the management systems effort.

There are other reasons for this centralizing tendency. In comparison with the campuses, the higher levels of authority—the state government, the federal agency, the superboard—all have more money for systems work and are more inclined to use it for that purpose. Finally, I noted earlier that centralization is *mostly* an unintended consequence of systems. I refer to the much observed fact that some of the shift of authority away from the campus to higher levels is not accidental, but the result of conscious policy. It is the unintended acceleration of centralization that should be the concern of system planners, and it is my concern here. Without realizing the situation, colleges and universities may be cooperating with systems to be used by centralized agencies to monitor the costs of higher education without apparent reference to quality. Until similar efforts measure benefits, there is reason to be cautious.

4. *Will the use of management systems reduce diversity in higher education?*

The task force that worked on the NCHEMS Resource Requirement Prediction Model 1 (RRPM)—one of the thirteen projects initiated that year—was from the start concerned about the problems of making meaningful comparisons of data from various types of institutions and the hazards to diversity that forced comparisons create. The task force adopted a resolution that states in part:

> Institutions of higher education differ widely among themselves. They have different approaches to teaching, different degrees, different requirements for the same degree, different course mixes within a single institution to satisfy the requirements for the same degree, different course contents, different methods of awarding and computing credit hours, different support activities, different student-faculty ratios, different goals, and other differences too numerous to enumerate.

The value of diversity in meeting the diverse needs of the student population of more than nine million is generally recognized, and in the last few years has been stressed by study groups who fear diversity may be declining. The fear is that, by copying a certain model, institutions may tend to reduce diversity. In recent years the higher education establishment has become sensitized to that fear. But little thought has gone to the growing danger that diversity may be reduced, not by faculty aspirations for a prestigious academic model, but through the natural tendencies of management systems.

The inherent threats to diversity appeared acute to the task force. In another paragraph, its resolution warned of dangers in the resource allocation process:

> In a variety of ways, including references in publications, training seminars, and casual conversations, the erroneous impression has been given in many areas of the higher education community that data (such as unit costs) developed under RRPM and Cost Finding Principles will be comparable among institutions of higher education and result in directly meaningful information which would likely be used as a basis for the allocation of resources among institutions. The RRPM Task Force believes this conclusion to be erroneous and submits that this impression must be eliminated now before serious damage is inflicted upon higher education.

That resolution was adopted by the task force in 1970, and my impression is that the concern expressed then has become more widespread and greater today.

Persons who work on information exchange projects know the difficulties of obtaining meaningful definitions of *course load* and *work load*. Unit cost measurement is even harder. In addition to the technical problems, questions of cost can be answered only when all the alternatives are considered. To its credit, NCHEMS has recognized the problem of normal variations among institutions. It asked institutions to provide examples of the difficulty, and I quote from one response, that of a group of experts in institutional analysis who gathered data from five comparable institutions in different states. It took them two days to define exceptions, limitations, qualifications. Their report states in part:

> One measure compared was an unweighted FTE student per faculty ratio. For one department in the five institutions the values were 11, 15, 16, 17, and 33. Upon investigation the 33 was attributed to bad data, an occurrence for which one must always allow. The small number was associated with a new program; a new program might easily have half the student-faculty ratio of an established program. In Art the student-faculty ratio was quite consistent for all institutions except one, which had half the ratio of the others. This was attributable to the fact that their academic policy called for all their art classes to be taught in small studio sections. This also had the effect of reducing the budgeted support per faculty to less than half the level of the other university art departments. A general undergraduate art requirement contributed to a very high student-faculty ratio in one institution.[29]

Examples such as these are familiar to persons who understand academic institutions. The fear is that variation and diversity will be lost when data are generated for statewide and even national comparisons. Budget officials will want a standard. There will be a demand for a standard Art figure, and the consequences, as applied to FTE or to work loads, cause concern to the task force experts. Once an average is set, its powers are great. An early example of a phenomenon a labor economist once called the "orbit of coercive comparison" was cited by Bogard in his survey for the Carnegie Commission: "One school system found that a dollar purchased 238 pupil recitations of French but only 5.9 pupil recitations of Greek. The conclusion drawn was that unless the *price* of Greek was reduced, the school system should invest in something else."[30] Although this is not a recent example, most experts in this field have modern horror stories of their own. The challenge to diversity appears to be growing.

29. Given to me with the request that its authors and their institutions not be identified.
30. "Management in Institutions," p. 7.

When examples of systems rudely overriding academic goals are discussed, systems planners shudder. They see the dangers, but say that they can be avoided. The problem remains: systems planners like to design systems, but they do not run them.

5. *Do systems requirements themselves tend to influence decisions about education?*

The process by which a question is developed is usually the major influence in determining how it will be answered. That axiom may now be understood in the social sciences, but it may still be learned the hard way in higher education planning. That hazard arises from two aspects of management systems: first, from the premise that models can be developed to predict behavior, and, second, from the need to derive quantifiable, standard answers from data, which, as Peggy Heim observes, "usually do not come in appropriately adjusted form."[31]

The danger posed by the first hazard is that planning will never catch up with its moving target, or may simply be wrong. The cost will be money wasted as a result of relying on systems-influenced decisions.[32]

A potentially more serious problem is posed by the second way systems requirements can influence decisions, that is, by defining the problem and producing a quantified answer. When they compete, things that can be quantified are accorded more importance than things that cannot. An instructive example of the need to be alert to the influence of systems requirements on decision making was provided in a new University of Minnesota publication sent to its alumni and friends. A legislative inquiry about work loads was phrased, "How much time do university faculty members spend in the classroom?" In response, the computer produced an average ICH (instructor clock hour) for each department. Analysis by the university director of budget planning re-

---

31. "Management Systems," p. 1.
32. In his article "On the Use of Large-Scale Simulation Models for University Planning," *Review of Educational Research*, December 1971, pp. 467–78, David S. P. Hopkins observes that cost simulation models have drawbacks that are not well understood by prospective users. He concludes that "perhaps the single most troublesome aspect of these large-scale simulation models is their inability to distinguish institutional variables, administrative controls, and environmental parameters from one another.... [A]n overwhelming quantity of computer output serves only to obscure one's understanding of the structural relationships between important variables in the system.... Indeed, based on cost considerations alone, the author would argue that the use of mathematical models for making resource projections at the departmental level is simply not appropriate. The cost of new educational programs can be predicted far more directly, inexpensively, and accurately if we use the judgment of experienced educators to estimate the student demand for courses."

vealed two facts about the average ICH: (1) "the simpler the department, the more accurately it read out"; and (2) "for most departments, narratives with documentation tell far more about each department's teaching effort than a computer printout." An ICH basis for decision making would tend to discriminate against large, complex departments offering both undergraduate and graduate education. John G. Darley, chairman of the Psychology Department, commented on the problem of using such systems data for decisions about complex, high-quality academic departments: "The computer isn't designed to generate data in the right form . . . and the trouble with using misleading data is that the truth seldom catches up with error."[33]

According to newspaper accounts, the concern about this aspect of decision making led to the downgrading of the Pentagon's former Office of Systems Analysis. Ironically, it fell to Secretary of Defense Elliot Richardson to reveal (on April 11, 1973) that this lodestar of management systems would no longer be the guiding force on DOD decision making. According to the *Wall Street Journal,* the decision was "dictated by White House officials much against his (Mr. Richardson's) wishes."[34] The key factor apparently was congressional dislike of the office, which was seen as substituting method for the judgment of generals and admirals in making national security decisions.

As of now, the extent to which systems requirements have influenced decisions about higher education is a matter of conjecture and of great concern. The tendencies noted earlier become particularly evident when systems used for management and planning in institutions are elevated to statewide use and thereby become meshed with the aspirations and procedures of statewide governing structures. Will the systems' questions—which require simple, standard answers—tend to influence decisions about education? As President Harold L. Enarson reports:

> Around the country, right now there is pressure in one or more states for the following: standardized course offerings for "general education" in the first two years; a standard calendar for all state universities; round-the-clock (7 a.m. to midnight) operation on a 12-month-a-year basis; legislatively mandated teaching loads of nine hours at the graduate level, 12 hours at the undergraduate level; a single computer system, a single library system for a state; a job classification system locking every professor and employee in an appropriate niche; space-utilization and build-

33. *Update* (a University of Minnesota news publication), Spring 1973, pp. 3–5.
34. April 12, 1973, p. 8.

ing construction standards that treat all universities as if they were alike in all respects.[35]

THE MAIN CHALLENGE

6. *Can colleges and universities be academic though systematic?*

If the preceding discussion fairly represents the unintended consequences of management systems, being academic will be an increasingly difficult task. Perhaps I overstate the dangers of these unintended results. A recent study suggests that early predictions of somewhat similar dangers to civil liberties posed by computers and record-keeping systems have as yet not been borne out by experience.[36] I certainly hope that worries about the effects of management systems on higher education will also prove unduly pessimistic. Yet given the trends discussed, one is led to conclude that an understanding of the dangers now may reduce the need for worry later. That is a necessary step. But an emphasis on promised benefits or possible dangers is an inadequate context for developing intelligent policies about management systems. The larger context should include some facts of recent history, an examination of systems against that recent history, and, finally, a consideration of the implications for academic leadership.

Recent history

1. In the recent past, being academic was facilitated by the folk methods of academic administration. As alumni and friends of institutions discovered during the period of campus disturbances, colleges and universities were not poorly managed; they were undermanaged. Far from being a reason for concern, this undermanagement was one of their great strengths. They have been decentralized, largely autonomous institutions, relying on shared values and assumptions for their coherence and their ability to operate, and relying on individual academic entrepreneurship for innovation and development. Despite the duality of organization noted earlier, these values and assumptions worked well. These loosely organized collections of professionals we call colleges and universities served the society well. They responded to demands for greater access, for variety and diversity, for science and graduate study for

---

35. "University or Knowledge Factory?" *Chronicle of Higher Education*, p. 16.

36. Alan F. Westin and Michael A. Baker, *Databanks in a Free Society* (New York: Quadrangle Books, 1973), 501 pp. This issue is far from settled, however, for there is evidence to support the opposite view.

national purpose, for language and research for national defense, and they have, since the end of World War II, converted American higher education from an elite to a mass enterprise.

2. It was not growth that challenged folk methods; it was the coming to terms with growth. The pressure to abandon what Peggy Heim calls "ivy-halled personal-factor administration" in favor of "rationalistic resource-allocation administration" was not produced by a short-run crisis of failure, but rather by a long-run change in condition. That changed condition is partly economic. The colleges and universities continued to do things the larger society once wanted but whose current cost it is no longer willing to pay. This problem is exacerbated by the decline in the enrollment rate, and both are affected by changes in attitude about the value of education.

As a result, leaders of colleges and universities face a new task. They must help their institutions to live within new financial limits. A new style is emerging on campus. Unlike the old one, which sought improved quality mainly by adding income, the new one relies mainly on control, planning, evaluation, and reallocation to promote institutional strength within fiscal constraints. This new style means converting loose collections of professionals into managed institutions, using more formal approaches to decision making, relying more on systems. A difficult task in any organization, but in academic institutions it is doubly so. I have never met a faculty member who felt the need to be managed.

The injection of systems

3. Systems are an essential component of the managed institution. Awareness of them must extend beyond the dangers to a realistic understanding of their necessity and possibilities. The changed conditions that make systems so important also make unlikely, and even irresponsible, the counsel of combating them, unless there is a demonstration that alternative methods are equally sensitive to the high costs of education and to a better definition of educational purpose.

The states and the federal government recognize the state of affairs and are doing what governments tend quite naturally to do: assert their own interests. They have a legitimate desire for information, an understandable concern about the credibility of figures provided in the past, and a legitimate demand for justification of apparent cost differentials. Faced with the demands of competing claimants and with the growing costs of education, governments are going to ask more questions, seek more information. It is a coincidence that these pressures are being exerted at the time of the burst of activity in management systems. But they do coincide, and in consequence institutions are being forced into state and perhaps federal systems. The second task for academic leaders is to develop a strategy for dealing with these growing systems requirements.

4. Management systems, whether used at the state level or on campus, are "tools" but they are not "neutral," that is, independent of their setting. Systems are meaningful only in the context of their environment. On campus or off, the old methods of governing are being challenged. As a result of systems, the power of the formal structure is increasing. It need not follow that values of the old (informal) environment—the concern for diversity and quality—are threatened. But as the above discussion shows, style is the key to good systems use. There is reason to fear that without much broader participation in the systems movement, the environment will produce a style that is not particularly academic.

It is sometimes contended that a measure of progress is the speed with which society can convert its ideological or policy problems into technical ones. Here the rush of management systems presents the higher education enterprise with a somewhat different situation. Can we resolve our educational policy issues before a technical system decides them for us? Can we be academic though systematic? The answer depends largely on the quality of academic leadership.

A FINAL CHALLENGE: NEW REQUIREMENTS IN LEADERSHIP

The management systems movement is creating new requirements for academic leadership. Some of these requirements—for example, the need to understand the technical operations of management systems, the ability to provide the academic dimension to what could become a mechanical process—are by now fairly obvious. These requirements emerge from the circumstance that the diverse, unorganized world of higher education is for the the first time being defined. It is being defined, not by an educational master plan or design, but as a result of the growing struggle for scarce resources. Higher education, once an obvious investment, is increasingly regarded as a consumer good. The rate of growth of its public financial support is declining. As this occurs, efforts to establish position become intensified. For employees, the instrument is collective bargaining with its centralizing tendencies; for the state and increasingly for those institutions that have not been in positions of influence, the instrument is systems, accompanied by the intended and unintended consequences observed earlier. Academic institutions have reason to be concerned about this process, and it appears that the complex, high-quality institutions are particularly vulnerable. Apparently reluctant to be arbiters of quality, they have done little visible, normative academic planning and increasingly face the prospect of finding themselves the dependent variable in a systems calculation.

To be academic though systematic requires that systems thinking be liberated from technical or partisan concerns and made a true systems approach—one that embraces all aspects of education, not just those interests for which there are paying customers. Such an approach could increase the range of options and, at the same time, reduce the arbitrariness of decisions that make systems advocates appear to be efficiency cultists with little regard for education.

The leadership tasks needed to achieve this goal are formidable. Academic leaders must:

1. Work to develop public awareness of the emerging situation. To help develop their awareness is a classic leadership task, and Mr. Enarson's strong speech (noted earlier) is a classic example of a leader doing his work. There are encouraging signs that such awareness may be developing. In some states—Nebraska is sometimes credited as an example—state systems are said to be used intelligently and with restrained concern for the role, initiative, and integrity of the educational institutions.

2. Devise effective ways to monitor higher education management systems. The federal government recently created an Office of Technology Assessment. It is designed to help the nation escape the unintended adverse consequences of technology. Higher education needs its own methods to assess its own systems. Ways must be found to bring informed judgment to bear on systems data and on their uses. Ways should be found to publicize good uses of information exchange and to help higher education avoid becoming a prisoner of centralized systems.

3. Demonstrate, perhaps even in the style of the strong administrator of the pregrowth era, what it is that institutions of higher education should be doing. There are signs today that in higher education a feeling is growing that its members are trapped in what one of my colleagues calls "the systems syndrome"—systems are inevitable, so submit to the one about to define you or someone else will cause something worse to

happen. What is needed is a renewed sense that academic men and women are willing and able to assert a larger measure of control over the course of educational events. If institutions of higher education are determined to earn the freedom to serve in academic ways, in ways that are—by systems terms—unusual and do not lend themselves readily to simple systems requirements, now is the time to act.

A Proper Role for Management Systems

ROBERT B. MAUTZ

EARL CHEIT HAS WOVEN A FABRIC that not only fully clothes but even envelops the subject. The woof is logic and the warp is broad conceptualization based upon factual knowledge. Although I might have stated some of the background differently, and I might quarrel with some of the sentences, I find no disagreement with the paragraphs. My remarks therefore are by way of perspective and addenda emanating from my experiences of watching developments from both the institutional level and the state-governing level.

In a practical sense, universities are responsible for the trend toward centralization of governance. The competing demands and inconsistent claims that universities have made on legislators and on the federal government raise questions about the validity of their claims. The facts presented by university claimants were frequently competing and contradictory. How many times has the justification "but we are different" undergirded an attempt to obtain more funds so that universities could become more nearly alike? How many grant requests have been submitted for identical "innovative" programs that were tired rewrites of each other and of requests from earlier years or even decades.

The creation of a coordinating or governing board for a state may be viewed as a delegation to academicians of the right to settle competing claims. The legislature has departed the field of interinstitutional battle and turned instead to the battle between higher education as a totality and other state functions.

The delegation of responsibility for the academies to academicians may be a plus, particularly if the legislature can have confidence in the integrity of figures submitted to it by higher education. I agree with Cheit that the use of management systems has not noticeably increased the public's confidence in higher education, but I have also noticed an increased confidence on the part of knowledgeable legislators. The level of argument before legislative committees has been upgraded, and the political logrolling that sometimes featured appropriations to individual universities has been substantially reduced. Legislators have been freed to focus on general policy questions, and many of them are doing so. This depolitization can only benefit higher education.

A systems approach as defined by Cheit included as an important element the definition of standards. We work with standards in every phase of our daily lives. We measure distances, quantities, values, and other items and functions. Indeed, one of the principal functions of the National Bureau of Standards is to assure a standardization of units used for measurement. Yet the use of standard measurements has not brought about uniformity of activity, of taste, of life. A necessary concomitant of the use of standards to measure activities in higher education is not that such diversity as exists now will disappear. It does not automatically follow that a decision by a higher administration about allocation of resources on the basis of a uniformly defined measure will deprive academicians of decisions with respect to academic function.

In Florida, for example, we have derived techniques for measuring activities as a basis for allocating resources to universities, but we have not attempted to control the reallocation of those resources within institutions. Each institution must have a method of determining the amount of money allocated to each college, and each college must determine the division of the sum allocated to it among the departments for which it is responsible. The department must subdivide available resources to programs and individuals. An allocation to organic versus inorganic chemistry must have some basis however inchoate, unwritten, or political. Indeed, unless the legislature uses a line-item method of appropriating funds or unless appropriations are directed to departments, universities and colleges are always forced to make judgments with respect to distribution of resources.

Administrators have always made decisions based on available information. The use of systems will not displace that function. The question becomes whether a systems approach produces better or poorer information, whether it leads to better or poorer judgments, to a more purposeful or less beneficial use of resources.

Inasmuch as judgments with respect to academic and fiscal matters must be made, a second question is the appropriate level for each judgment. The appropriate level for decision making has been and forever will be a debatable subject. The new factor introduced into this eternal debate is the computer. The computer renders possible the rapid assimilation of vast quantities of facts and the communication of aggregated information. The computer has not abolished the debate over the level of decision making. The computer has made it possible to centralize more decisions. I emphasize the word "possible." Computers do not force centralization. They remove a constraint on upward mobility of decision making.

The "top down" syndrome is not inevitable. A systematic approach to the definition, "gathering and use of information and the tool which makes possible a more detailed analysis," should not shift or obscure discussion about the desirable level of decision making.

Faculty and administrators adjust to the use of standard units of measurement within the institution. No reason exists why the same adjustment should not be made when the allocating agency is outside the university or is a central office of a university. Again, it is important to note the difference between a basis of determining need and a resulting allocation of resources as against the utilization of funds in an operating mode. I agree with Cheit that in a period of constrained resources and declining enrollment, systems analysis will increase. In addition, I believe more intelligent decisions will result.

It is clear that no system of resource allocation should be permitted to dictate some academic decisions. Systems must be used to analyze what is done in the academic area, not to control how it should de done. Faculty need not, should not, and perhaps cannot be managed in the crucial academic areas of teaching methods, content of course, and similar matters.

I shall make one other point. In recent years I have seen the strength of central state educational authorities grow in almost geometric progression in terms of legislative authority. The legislature will insist that this authority be exercised. This factor will be of growing importance in the academic world.

As Cheit points out, now is the time for leadership in academe. Leadership must be constructive. It must recognize new forces in our environment and mold these forces to serve the academic world, not control it. Central offices must be staffed with men and women who are part of, and who understand, the academic world with respect to which they must make decisions. Central agencies, like the central authority of universities, should be staffed with persons of wisdom and strength. The institutions of higher education should help in that staffing.

If I permit myself certain flights of fantasy, the specter raised by systems analysis is terrifying. But the specter does not petrify me, and, in a calmer mood, I see no alternative. Decisions must be made. They cannot be made without information. There cannot be an absence of management structure. A nonstructured, nonsystematic method of allocating resources among or within universities is not a feasible plan. We must accept new instruments and new methods as the tools they are, and focus our debate on the fundamental issues which remain unchanged.

The Challenge to Academic Managers

PAUL C. REINERT, S.J.

ONE CANNOT QUARREL with most of the conclusions in the Cheit paper, and I agree with much that he says. In one area, however, I have a different opinion. In discussing the *intended* consequences of management systems, Cheit expresses his judgment that "the use of management systems will not do much to foster favorable attitudes toward higher education because unfavorable attitudes are based primarily, not on questions of efficiency, but on questions of purpose." This statement may hold for government opinion of higher education, but in my experience it is not equally true with respect to the opinion held by business and industrial leaders. On the contrary, I am convinced that the recent improvement in the business community's attitude toward my own institution (Saint Louis University) is directly traceable to the reputation we have gained, locally at least, for improved efficiency. No matter how serious the need, businesses were outspokenly reluctant to contribute as long as they believed, correctly or not, that there was waste and inefficiency. As the business community has become satisfied that the university is willing and able to make the difficult and unpopular management decisions necessary to streamline operations and improve efficiency, they again have come forward with their help.

I shall explore several aspects of the issues discussed by Cheit. From the standpoint of institutional management, the financial crisis that hit higher education in 1969 had at least one far-reaching side effect. When university administrations were forced to make difficult decisions on an emergency basis, they were brought to realize that they were poorly equipped to do so. Traditional methods and tools for decision making were found wanting just when the margin for error had all but disappeared. Not only did decisions have to be made quickly but also they had to be the correct ones. Governing boards and university administrators became nervous as they realized that they lacked ready access to the kinds of information needed to make sound decisions. They welcomed with relief, therefore, those specialists who offered a solution to this problem. The promise was that one day soon everything would be better and they would have at their finger tips instant access to reams of pertinent data, in exactly correct form, including data assessing the results of alternative decisions. Decision making in academe would be easy.

However, with the press of day-to-day worries, university administrators did not have time to talk with their computer and systems specialists. To paraphrase an old joke, when one is busy fighting off alligators, he is not inclined to worry about the philosophical aspects of an induced course load matrix. For want of a better ear, the specialists talked to each other, with the result that data management systems became both increasingly more complex and further removed from the real-world management needs that gave them impetus.

Meanwhile higher education, and particularly private higher education, came to the realization that federal and state financial assistance is an indispensable part of the total mosaic of funding needed for the fiscal health of the institutions. Higher education pressed for more and more direct assistance, and the state and federal governments, in turn, in an attempt to assess the validity of these requests, sought a sound basis on which to measure institutional efficiency and on which to make interinstitutional comparisons. They listened with interest to the plans being developed by the systems specialists and began to influence the direction in which systems development was moving. This influence accelerated the trend toward standardization of measurement and toward centralization of management, about which Cheit so correctly warns.

These are the elements of the dilemma that higher education faces: On the one hand is the indispensable need for direct federal and state funding, and on the other hand is the belief that this help will not come without standardized methods of measuring what some perceive to be efficiency. Moreover, we in higher education dare not oppose the trend toward standardization of measurement systems lest our opposition be interpreted as an attempt to hide inefficiency. As we struggle with this dilemma, we need to bear in mind that our own needs for improved information and information systems are as real and as urgent as they ever were.

There is, moreover, one dimension to this dilemma that strikes private higher education in a special way. Traditionally, private higher education has argued that it is an integral part of the total academic scene. As such the private institutions pressed to be included in and have a voice in statewide planning for higher education. Until recently, such pleas seemed to be ignored and the planning was concerned only with the public sector. Now the situation has changed and private institutions are indeed being included in the evolving systems approach to higher education. However, the machinery of the system is such that potentially it could threaten the distinctiveness that is the private sector's very reason for being. Historically, in American higher education, private higher education has been the force for variety—the counterforce against uniformity. This value places a special responsibility on those of us in the private sector to become fully involved in the implementation of the systems approach to statewide planning and decision making. We must do this, among other reasons, in order to safeguard against measuring and reporting systems that might be badly designed or misapplied to eliminate beneficial differences merely for the sake of uniformity.

Finally, those involved in the higher education enterprise should keep in mind an essential difference between the academic manager himself and the methods and tools he uses. The widely used term "management systems" perhaps is unwise because it tends to obscure this difference. It must be understood that the developments in information systems are, after all, no more than the fashioning of the tools that the managers will use. It is up to us, the academic managers, to tell the machinists what kind of tools we need—not vice versa. So far, we have not spent enough time or effort in doing so. It is high time that we correct this lack—time that we, the users, now give the needed guidance. If academic management abdicates its responsibilities and transfers its authority to computer technicians, it is indeed likely, as Cheit says, to find itself "the dependent variable in a systems calculation."

Today our information systems do not measure *output*—do not measure quality or benefit. Rather, they concentrate on *input*, on the cost of producing a unit of education without regard for the quality of the education produced or, for that matter, for whether or not the education should have been produced at all. In times past, the traditional academic manager made decisions based on experience and judgment. His intuition was good, and his experience and judgment served subtly to factor into the decision equation those parameters that measure output. Until our information systems also are able to do likewise, we shall have no true measure of efficiency because efficiency, in management science just as in the physical sciences, is defined in terms that include both input *and* output.

There is a great deal at stake for the institutions in seeing to the proper implementation of the systems approach to higher education in America. If properly applied, the benefits can be enormous in restoring public confidence and in gaining for higher education the investment of the nation's resources essential to meet the challenges of the 1970s. We must be diligent, however, to ensure that, in the process, the best values of higher education are not subjugated to expediency and uniformity. I am optimistic that we can do so.

Management Systems: An Aid, Not an Answer

JAMES F. KELLY

EARL CHEIT HAS PRESENTED a scholarly summary of the development of management systems in colleges and universities and a provocative analysis of the usefulness of the technique; he posed many apposite questions. Although I cannot agree with all of his conclusions, I shall use his base to take a somewhat different approach.

The basic question, Can academe be systematic?, is not in my opinion the proper question, for higher education has a long history of being quite systematic. To it can be credited the extent to which man's knowledge has been subdivided into disciplines, and disciplines into recognized and discrete areas; the extent to which a system has been designed in terms of schools, majors, programs, and, in turn, subdivided into interrelated courses; the extent to which there have been established the concepts of semesters, credit hours, and periods of study. It is, indeed, a formidable achievement that such complex and imponderable problems have found such a high degree of consistency and methodology for the provision of education. What could be more systematic than the achievement of a system that is followed in more than twenty-four hundred institutions in the United States, with great capability and mobility within the system. Academe has thus, in fact, long directed its energies and attention to systems of fulfilling their objectives of expanding man's knowledge, of imparting that knowledge to students, and of providing public service.

No, the real question is: Can the academic community accommodate a new discipline—the management systems analyst—in its midst? It has already demonstrated the capability of developing the skills and capabilities of this new discipline. What we are now asking is, Can the academic community effectively adapt the discipline which it has developed to relate to its own environment? The application of the systems management approach through this new discipline, as I see it, is not a question of whether we discard all the management techniques that have heretofore been developed, but, rather, whether we can expand those techniques and approaches by still more sophisticated approaches to our complex and difficult task.

Much has been done and much needs to be done, but clearly the new discipline has been perceived by the academic community as a threat, and it has met much resistance. In part there are illustrations and anecdotal stories indicating that the new discipline is sometimes too aggressive, arrogant, and not fully comprehending of the problems being addressed. On the other hand, there are illustrations and anecdotal stories which indicate that some academic administrators and some academicians have been unwilling to look objectively and with greater insight into the operations for which they were responsible. Neither of these criticisms constitutes a generalized condemnation of the network of academic administrators and academicians. They do, however, reflect a basic problem for effective utilization of new techniques and new approaches.

If an academic administrator perceives his mission as the expansion of man's knowledge, the provision of quality education—within the resources available—to those seeking access to the educational resources of his institution, and the provision of limited public and community service, I suggest that a close alliance between that administrator and the new management systems discipline will further those objectives. On the other hand, if the administrator perceives his objective as survival and the maintenance of the status quo, I cannot conceive how use of the new management systems discipline will prove helpful.

It is frequently contended that the new technique of management systems can produce substantial savings in ongoing operations. I seriously question that hypothesis. If financial circumstances require that substantial savings be effected, I believe that the new systems analysis technique may help to identify where reductions can be made with minimum erosion of basic objectives. In any event, if savings must be effected, some decision-making process must be employed. The question then becomes, How good were the decisions? The systems approach offers some assistance to improving the decision. It did not effect the savings; rather, the *decisions* to effect reduction were responsible for the reduction and probably were occasioned by lack of resources.

Too frequently new techniques are adopted in an institutional environment simply to satisfy the academic administrator and external groups that the institution is modern and progressive. Certainly this phenomenon is abundantly illustrated by the computer and, currently but to a lesser extent, by management systems analysis. At best the new techniques assist the academic administrator, but are not a substitute for him. Thus, if he does not use them as an *aid* to understanding and solving the problems that confront him, he should not be surprised when they do not achieve the objective he expected. A new discipline placed in a staff role within a university, undirected and left to its own initiative and inclination, is likely to be a disaster. The new techniques are not likely to create an appropriate dialogue with the faculty, department chairmen, and deans. They are not likely to analyze and evaluate the issues on which decisions are going to be made. They are likely to become a competing and separate channel of influence within the university rather than rendering effective staff assistance to line management.

Frequently it is contended that systems management can deal only with quantifiable areas and therefore quantification capability will take precedence in the decision-making process. This will be true only when the results of systems analysis become *the decisions* rather than one of the inputs to the decision-making process. The academic administrator who effectively uses systems analysis as *one* of his sources of insight will add to those results his own background, knowledge, and wisdom, and the attitudes and views of the people he normally consults before he arrives at his decision.

Earl Cheit warns that systems analysis results are tending to move decision making to a highly centralized level, and he appears to question the wisdom in the activity for higher education. Two features of this conclusion bear comment.

First, the only reason the higher levels of government are concerned with college and university decision making is that colleges and universities are seeking public funds. Were this not the case, the federal government, the Congress, the governors, and state legislators would probably be little interested in systems analysis data and little interested in making any decisions with respect to it. The phenomenon of increased decision making by centralized public bodies is a function, not of systems management, but of the increased demand by higher education for public support. These public bodies feel entitled to information and accountability that will assist them in rendering their judgments.

Second, all too often I have heard the academic community indicate a desire not to develop and disclose information about higher education and their institutions lest it be used against them. I am affronted by this view. I do not understand a system of educated men, dedicated to the search for truth and its wide dissemination, that could develop a frame of mind that says the truth should be hidden. This attitude should be quickly dispelled. I can understand the concern about disclosure of half-truths that result in ill-informed and ill-advised decisions. Does not that very hazard place on the academic community the responsibility for expanding half-truths into full-truths? And should we not devote our energies to improving and projecting systems analysis accounting and management to achieve full truths?

It is argued that systems analysis—the development of comparable data for all institutions—will destroy the diversity within higher education that we hold in such great pride. Did we not begin to destroy diversity before we ever heard of systems analysis? Institutions have worked so hard to emulate each other that, in my view, almost every year has seen diversity diminished. Should diversity occur by unplanned decision making which is hidden in the woodwork? Or should diversity result from a decision to approach a particular program in a special way, with the decision being reached on the basis of full knowledge of the facts relating to it? Planned diversity can be fully explained and fully justified: not diversity for diversity's sake, but diversity for thoughtful reasons related to institutional objectives.

It is sometimes argued that the public is not really interested in efficient management of higher education. I doubt that. Development officers have given me the impression that, in approaching a prospective donor for funds, they find it important to illustrate that their institution is operating in the black, that management is in control, and that the operation is efficient and effective. Potential donors who are convinced that the institution has this managerial capability and the ability to live within its means may then be willing to discuss support for the institution. They will not finance an activity which they did not stimulate or concur in. They are refusing to pay deficits; an activity already under way without its own funds is almost impossible to use as a fund-raising objective. I believe that the development people in the colleges and universities all over the United States might well be the strongest exponents of good management in institutions of higher education.

Coordinating Federal, State, and Institutional Decisions

JAMES A. PERKINS

THE TITLE FOR THIS PAPER is an elliptical expression for complex processes. Because federal and state governments and universities and colleges rarely make conscious decisions, the coordination of the rarely made decisions is a somewhat limited exercise. The title can, nevertheless, prove illuminating. Illuminating, for its analysis brings into high relief both institutions involved: their internal processes, the nature of their relationships, and the real manner in which accommodation of policies is achieved. Such a canvas is obviously too large to cover in detail, but a few points will be instructive, stir up some discreet controversy, and point the way to further clarification.

DECISION MAKING IN UNIVERSITIES AND COLLEGES

Four general propositions about decision making in institutions of higher education are in order. First, real decisions are made by a minority, sometimes a minority of one, in the form of a proposal, project, or program that the individual or a small group wishes an institution to support. The decision to initiate an internal action rarely flows from a conscious weighing of alternative choices—the classic view of the process of decision making. However stated, the tactic and strategy of securing institutional approval rarely force a conscious choice. Far more likely, approval will be reached through tacit acquiescence, without requiring explicit commitment on the part of every individual in the community. Most "decisions," therefore, are the silent approval of the majority to a minority initiative.

The second proposition: The more important or sensitive the issue, the more likely the process of silent acquiescence and the less likely the process of open discussion, debate, and decision. In universities, at least, the delicate etiquette of the intellectual community requires careful attention to protecting the right of the faculty member to avoid public commitment to intellectual positions. In an unpublished paper on the teaching of undergraduate political science, a Stanford professor observed that an effort to produce an agreement or make a departmental decision on the purpose of political science instruction would shortly destroy the fragile and anarchic community that makes up a department.

A third proposition: In academe, large decision-making bodies generally try to avoid making decisions of an institutionwide character. They much prefer to deal with specific measures and allow the general policy to be implicit in, or to grow out of, individual decisions. To make the general policy explicit is to bring into the arena of debate other parties with different interests. An academic senate, for example, usually wishes to debate and possibly may even oppose a specific decision if its members think the general policy implied will be held against them. An implicit general policy can always be interpreted or modified at some later date when, as stated in the first proposition, an individual's or a minority's interests require institutional approval.

A fourth proposition: Decisions are not static but dynamic. Once made, they are not established facts of life but are immediately subject to the very forces that brought about the "decision" in the first place. The decision will require interpretation, then amendment, then inevitably will be superseded by a new decision. In periods of rapid change, the process of decision modification is vigorous and continuous. Higher education is in one of those periods.

Finally: There are many levels of decision making. Nearest the surface are decisions on individual student affairs. Should a paper be graded A− or B+? Should John Doe receive a $500 or a $750 scholarship? Should a federal loan be limited to $1,000 or $1,500? It is at this level that decisions are the most marked and visible.

At the next level, decisions involving the general student body are less visible and the policy more general. Loans or grants, agriculture or the liberal arts, a two-year or four-year college? At this level of decision, policy seems to evolve from historical precedent, or social requirement, or institutional standards, or student demand. The result seems more an expression of the operative forces than a decision by any individual or group of individuals. At the deepest level, "decision making" and "coordination" are almost grotesque ways to describe the process of academic development. Who "decided" or who "coordinated" the decision to expand postdoctoral study, or to make legal education a postbaccalaureate discipline, or to admit more black students into higher education, or to abandon the general education sequence? Obviously, no one made a decision. Higher education has slowly changed its collective mind on some important matters, and is still changing its mind on these same matters.

The process described above may seem overly subtle and even precious to the uninitiated, yet starkly familiar to those who have lived in the center of a college or university. Such governance may strike the interested observer as irresponsible, but the initiated will recognize a process that stems inevitably from the fundamental structure of the academic institution and the style of an Anglo-Saxon heritage, more recent external pressures notwithstanding.

University Governance Structure

Universities are structured in two modes. The intellectual-academic mode is associational, egalitarian, pluralistic, and individual. Learning and research are inward disciplines; teaching and administration are a sometimes awkward means for dealing with the young. Since the intellectual enterprise is, in gist, singular, lonely, and selfish, it follows that dealings with large institutional concerns are unlikely to summon much individual attention. It also follows that inasmuch as the individual professor feels essentially disinterested in activities that do not affect him, he finds it difficult to believe that others should legislate with respect to his own activities. The university in its intellectual-academic mode is, therefore, essentially and profoundly anarchic. Decision making in the academic area is almost a contradiction in terms.

Agreements in institutions of higher education are, nevertheless, achieved even if not by the process of formal decisions. There can be agreements not to try to agree. In the multicollege university there is a tacit agreement not to agree on uniform standards for graduation. The disruption and animosity that would result from formal agreement precludes the most daring academic innovator from even starting the process. To do so would compel faculty members to pass judgment on other faculty members, a situation an academic community finds almost immoral.

In its academic mode, the university is structured to prevent institutional decisions, to localize them if they cannot be prevented, and to keep any generally derived policies tacit and implied rather than specific and visible. But the university, like the double helix, is constituted in a second mode—the administrative-institutional. The mode of the academic community is horizontal and individualistic; the mode of the institution is hierarchical and social. Thus decisions do get made on dominantly institutional issues such as buildings and investments. Budgets are more likely to remain in the institutional mode when they are rising than when they are falling.

But when the two modes are both substantially engaged on a specific issue, when academic and institutional interests are simultaneously involved, when intellectual and social considerations must be adjusted, then decision making becomes extremely complex and often protracted. The institutional mode presses for general policies that can serve as a firm guide for future decisions. The academic mode presses for limited commitments that can be reinterpreted or changed. Decision making in this setting could be better described as a process of accommodation between parties with different backgrounds, different values, and different objectives. Thus the university, when regarded as an institution to have its decisions coordinated, represents, at best, a moving target.

GOVERNMENTS AND PUBLIC HIGHER EDUCATION

There is an enormous difference in both style and function between the public and the academic process. Between the federal and the state governments there is less difference in style but considerable difference in function, although the functional differences are becoming blurred.

Traditionally, the states have had the responsibility for public higher education. They are responsible for establishing healthy institutions and thereafter for encouraging programs that can be identified with the state and its people. Private higher education, though requiring state charters, has until recently not been regarded as a state responsibility. For a variety of reasons, not the least of which is the rapid expansion of high-quality public education, the states have changed their attitude toward private higher education from a detached indifference to a reluctant concern and hesitant financial support.

Simple views are dangerous in their oversimplification. It can be said, however, that the states have had the primary role in supporting the institutional growth of public higher education, to which has now been added a growing support for private higher education.

Coordination of higher education at the state government level has two separable but often interrelated elements—the public institutions and private institutions. With respect to the public institutions, the coordination of state and institutional decisions is, of course, a complicated matter. The state university or college is a creation of the state but is granted a measure of independence from its creator. In areas where the state does not pretend to function—curriculum, standards of work for degrees, and the like—the state is not likely to make decisions that must be "coordinated" with those of the institution. In other areas, such as admissions, internal budget allocations, and salaries and benefits, the relationship is more that of accommodation, with eventual positions being arrived at by compromise and sometimes by confrontation. At the other extreme, decisions on monies for state institutions are a state responsibility except for funds from private endowments and gifts, which fall more directly under the control of the regents or trustees.

In short, it is somewhat difficult to picture the state institution and the state each making decisions that must then be coordinated. Agreement being the necessary condition for survival, the public college or university is not likely to persist in or even make independent decisions that are known to endanger relations with, and therefore support from, the state. Rather, on institutional issues, the public institution is likely to assure itself of support before making recommendations, let alone preliminary decisions.

In contrast, on issues with respect to the academic community—academic functions and faculty standards—the institution expects to take the lead and receive the confidence and support of the state. If the state adopts measures that intervene in the internal delicacies of the academy, resistance can be expected and opposing or contradictory views must be composed. Yet the line between the two modes is not precise and is subject to change, and accommodation between the state institution and the state government is usually the name of the game.

THE STATE AND PRIVATE HIGHER EDUCATION

Coordination between the state and the private universities is something else. Until recently the problem hardly existed, and in many states it is still largely nonexistent. But the rise of the public universities in the East and the financial difficulties of private institutions everywhere have required state governments to interest themselves in admissions policies, building costs, professional programs, and so on. It has come as a great surprise to private colleges and universities that public financial support brings with it public accountability. Public universities have viewed this tortuous period of education with compassion, mixed with amusement.

And state coordination of public and private institutions involves something more than coordination of the decisions among the institutions in the two systems. It involves long-range plans (five years or more) to articulate future entrance demands with prospects for increased spaces in both public and private institutions. Of necessity, the total-systems approach has led to the creation of some kind of planning and coordinating instrument in almost every state. Public bodies fit within these instruments far more easily than do their private sister institutions. But fit they must if they would expect financial contributions from the state.

There is no easy way to justify public support for private high-cost quality education while, next door, a public standard-quality institution is bursting at the seams. One of the great unresolved problems is how the highly disparate and individualistic private colleges and universities shall be fitted into a statewide system of planning and coordination. The resolution will probably evolve like Topsy or, if you will, by a series of small adjustments that will be accepted because no one of them is large enough to frighten any of the parties concerned.

THE FEDERAL GOVERNMENT

At the federal level, government has expanded its role and responsibilities to produce one of the fundamental changes in the educational landscape. The increase in support of education in higher educational institutions has been phenomenal, with appropriations jumping from $526 million in 1947–48 to $5.9 billion twenty-five years later.[1] And from an earlier practical role as keeper of statistics, it has spread its influence and support through an increasing number of programs administered by an increasing number of federal agencies. There are three important things to be noted about federal decision making.

First, with respect to higher education, the federal government has made no decision. It has made bits and pieces of decisions about specific and limited issues.

Second, the higher education establishment cannot decide whether a federal position and policy with respect to higher education are developments devoutly to be wished or stoutly to be resisted. Thus far federal support and decision making have been scattered throughout the executive branch and various committees of the Congress. There have been times when this has been described as a happy state of affairs. Indeed, the autonomy of higher education and its institutions has, in the eyes of many, actually required a spreading authority and an uncoordinated

---

1. U.S. Office of Education, *Statistics of Higher Education, 1955–56: Receipts, Expenditures, and Property* (Washington: Government Printing Office, 1959), p. 6; USOE, *Projections of Educational Statistics to 1981–82* (Washington: Government Printing Office, 1973), p. 174.

power. On the other hand, the absence of a top-flight Cabinet officer for education, or even higher education, has sometimes been lamented as the source of much uncontrolled evil. As in so many areas, educators have not decided whether they are Jeffersonians or Hamiltonians. The higher education establishment appears to regard freedom and autonomy with a Hamiltonian cast when federal action is desired and in the Jeffersonian style when federal action is feared. This ambivalence of attitude about the proper federal role in higher education has not been resolved. Small wonder that national associations like the American Council on Education have found that demands for leadership come from a constituency that has not made up its mind what it has elected its leaders to do.

In truth, the federal government has not made decisions *about* higher education, but various parts of the federal government have made decisions to *use* parts of higher education. Thus, the Atomic Energy Commission has been concerned with research and study in physics; NASA has supported expansion in astronomy; the Defense Department, a whole variety of applied and basic research activities; the National Science Foundation, the scientific and engineering aspects of higher education with a modest bow to the social sciences; the National Endowment for the Humanities has supported its designated field, and so forth. Surely the federal government regards itself as supporting higher education in that it supports important parts of it. But compared to the attention state governments give to supporting the system of higher education, no such attitude, no such plan, no such capability yet exists at the federal level.

Only once in recent years has the federal government come close to making a decision with respect to higher education: in the recent legislation for federal funding through student scholarships that would bring financial aid to the institutions, the recipients. There was a classic debate about the wisdom of institutional support through students or directly to institutions. The legislative decision was, in general, to take the former course which, as discussed below, has been the traditional stance of the federal government. However, in this case, the federal government has not funded the program and, thus, institutional support remains moot. In retrospect, it seems strange that a national debate on the funding of higher education should have produced such great heat and been followed by such great silence.

In some quarters, the Land-Grant College Act is regarded as a federal government decision. In this important case, however, the federal government made a decision that permitted the *states* to establish state universities. The federal government intended that under no circumstances would it monitor this basic decision.

The third point about federal support, or decisions with respect to higher education, is suggested by the preceding sentence. The federal government has only recently even considered that one of its roles was to support the institutions of higher education or the system of higher education as a whole. Rather, it has responded to a variety of emerging social needs stemming from a concern with matters of social justice, national defense, economic growth, and foreign affairs. Since federal responsibilities are, generally speaking, programmatic and specific, it follows that federal support has traditionally been categorical and limited. As a result, the federal role has resembled that of a foundation, concerning itself with matters of geographical balance, with innovation, with specific and pressing need, but not concerning itself with the institutions or the system as such.

There have been real advantages in this arrangement. The states and the private sector have given the institutions financial help and stability, while the federal government added funds that have made possible the injection of concern for groups disadvantaged by racial or geographical origin. But this division of responsibility has become increasingly imprecise. Now that institutional financial problems have increased (at least in part because of the impact of federal programs), the matter of institutional health has been presented to the federal government as requiring attention beyond that given by the states and by private supporters of private higher education. The concept of federal support to institutions has been the latest large issue. The need is present, visible, and vital, but the federal decision to give institutional support, particularly federally directed institutional support, has not yet been really made, nor have the negative consequences been thoroughly examined.

It is fair to say, then, that federal decisions, or the idea that the federal government makes decisions about higher education, must be approached with great care. The federal government is divided not only between the executive and legislative branches but also between the parts thereof. Each part has developed its own special clientele in the universities. Each believes it is supporting higher education through support of its particular interests and concerns. Consequently, the federal government, as such, can hardly be said to make decisions; and if it cannot make decisions, then the problem of coordinating them evaporates.

The dilemma of decision making in the federal system is not singular with the United States. Other federal governments face somewhat similar problems. Indeed, West German colleagues, both in and out of government, find it convenient to talk with their opposite numbers in the United States because their experiences concerning federal structures have much in common. Western Germany has been trying to find a way to coordinate public and private interests through advisory bodies like the Wissenschaftsrat and coordinating bodies like the Bund-Länder Kommission. In the former council, federal, state, industry, and academic representatives are trying to develop a consensus on the allocation of funds. The Bund-Länder Kommission, on the other hand, made up essentially of federal and state ministers of education, tries to coordinate these two levels of government. Cutting across this coordinating effort, the political parties have enormously complicated the business of federal-state deliberations.

In Australia, the federal system is also facing acute problems because the states are currently resisting strongly the federal efforts to expand its authority commensurate with the demands for federal financial support. In Canada, the situation is complicated by the French-English relationship. There, the federal support to institutions is allocated on a per capita basis. Aside from the most difficult problem of French Quebec, educational policy and programming at the federal level have moved toward institutional support activated through the states.

SEARCH FOR AGREEMENT

There are three ways in which accommodation and agreement are, in fact, accomplished. (At least there are three ways I wish to mention.) They are: (1) coordinating organizations, (2) independent functional organizations, and (3) professional connections. I will probably not be able to resist a reference to nondecisions and noncoordination through automated systems.

Coordinating organizations

In today's institutionalized world, it is natural to look for organizational solutions to organizational problems. When two or more organizations find their activities to be more than casually connected, they instinctively try to resolve their problems by assigning responsibility to another organization or by creating a new organization if it is needed.

In the field of higher education, organizational solutions have taken diverse forms, ranging from loose associations to legal entities backed by a force of law. The Ivy League and the Southern Regional Education Board illustrate the range of regional solutions; the arrangements between the State University of New York and the state's private colleges and universities highlight a range of intrastate solutions.

A loose association of institutions rarely has power to ensure compliance with its decisions. In the United States, where the organized aspect of higher education defies a precise taxonomy, some associations do exercise power and many do not. None of them remains in a fixed state, but change as the nature of the educational environment changes. It takes no special insight to observe that, as time goes on, associations are inclined to become less permissive, more consensus-minded, and more concerned with "impact" and "effectiveness." This seemingly ineluctable drift of affairs stems, not from power-hungry administrators, but rather from the growth and increasing complexity of higher education, the increase in federal and state responsibilities, and the consequent public demand for large-scale planning and the consequent need for institutions to concert their interests.

But the drive toward coordinating systems as a means of long-range planning and of resolving problems has a built-in paradox. As noted earlier, "decision making" in the university is a grossly inaccurate phrase to describe the enormously complicated process by which the administrative and intellectual modes of the university are accommodated. Presidents and deans of colleges and universities find themselves, on the one hand, with greater involvement in increasingly vigorous associations, but, on the other hand, without any equal increase in internal power over intrainstitutional affairs. Any considerable change in recent years has probably reduced presidential power and influence and increased the power and influence of other elements of the academic community.

The stark and central fact is that administrative representatives (or any other representative on coordinating bodies) are acquiring more responsibilities as coordinators with less power or even right to commit their own constituency. This disjunction of power and responsibility places a severe limitation on coordination by the organizational route.

Independent functional organizations

The limitations of formal coordinating organizations has long been recognized—if not explicitly, at least implicitly. The consequence has been a rise in the importance accorded special-purpose organizations which are independent of the institutions, but work closely with them and provide the uniformity of procedure that interinstitutional negotiation could never achieve. Two examples of this institutional but external form of handling similar problems are the Educational Testing Service (ETS) and the Teachers Insurance and Annuity Association (TIAA). ETS has provided a standardized performance of high quality which cuts through the whole process and procedure of interinstitutional agreement. It may be that the ETS appeared on the agenda of the ACE, the AAU, the Land-Grant Association, the Ivy League, and others, but if so, I failed to record it. Not from neglect but rather from the knowledge that the business of admissions examinations was happily in other hands.

The same is true of pensions, insurance, and the TIAA. Although commercial insurance companies provide the bulk of the nation's insurance programs, the TIAA has developed a hand-tailored relationship with the higher education community that has reduced institutional responsibility to that of a calculating machine operation. Furthermore, the fact that payments to TIAA remain fully vested in the individual promotes mobility for faculty members and makes transfer an administratively simple process. The mind boggles at the supercoordination agency that would be required if each university had maintained its own retirement program and these programs now had to be given uniformity.

Clearly, one way to coordinate institutional practice is to take the activity out of the institution entirely and establish a functional organization to handle it. Of course, ETS and TIAA are not the only examples of such solutions to institutional and interinstitutional problems. It is not out of order to suggest that other areas could be explored for similar treatment. Scholarships and fellowships are increasingly financed and administered by independent groups—notably the National Merit Scholarship Corporation and Woodrow Wilson National Fellowship Foundation. Will the trend continue so that eventually all scholarships will be in noninstitutional hands? Housing and dining are in many places contracted for with commercial or nonprofit organizations. Will all housing and feeding of students be off the agenda of presidential staff meetings? Will any president really resist? Will computers be handled like telephones? The possibilities are endless, exciting, and not thoroughly examined.

Professional connections

One of the most neglected areas for the student of coordination is that embraced by professionals and their institutions. The professional, by definition, is one who is a member of a society with interests and standards of performance not confined to the institution of which he is a member. To the institutional administrator, this double loyalty can be a problem. To the professional, it is the door to freedom and advancement. To the intellectual community as a whole, it is the nervous system that ties it all together. And for purposes of this discussion, it is a set of connections that can and frequently does provide the means for developing and monitoring important relations between federal, state, and academic institutions. As I expand on this statement, it will become clear why the simple term *coordination of decisions* is an imprecise description of how a consensus of thought and action is actually achieved.

As examples, agriculture, physics, and economics are three areas of study where professionals are active in every walk of life. To these could be added political science, engineering, and, now, the creative arts.

Agricultural development has been made possible by the continuous chain of professional connections between the laboratory and the farm, on the one hand, and the university, the trade association, the county agent, the state capital, and the U.S. Department of Agriculture, on the other. In every place there are those who consider themselves part of the agricultural professions. Their interest, wherever located, was and is in maximizing the production and distribution of food. In the best sense of the word, they used (or worked with) every government agency at all levels. They gave direction and purpose to government actions, not by coordinating them, but by becoming part of them while maintaining their own professional connection. Some believe we would long since have starved to death had the coordination of federal, state, and university policies for food production been left to Cabinet officers, state governors, and university presidents.

No nefarious plot brought this professional group to exercise its influence and leadership. The process was essentially one of unselfconscious activity of tens of thousands of people working toward the same end but working at their own competence in their own institutional bailiwicks. It was the professional connection that kept the enterprise dynamic and productive by successfully cross-fertilizing the activity of the academy and the farm, the laboratory and the government, the researcher and the practitioner.

In other fields, such as physics and economics, the employment of Ph.D.'s is no longer—if it ever was—the exclusive prerogative of the academy. It has been said that the Air Force employs more Ph.D.'s in physics than do the combined Ivy League institutions, that a majority of the members of the Society for Public Administration are employed outside educational institutions, and that university, government, and industry jobs are, for an increasing number of professionals, quite interchangeable.

Policies and programs, strategies and tactics flow from the ferment of professional connections, and institutions increasingly receive their impulse for action and organization from this source. No one who has been waited on by biologists concerned with protein diet, astrophysicists concerned with telescopes, sociologists concerned with demography, or engineers concerned with road safety can ever doubt that he is faced with *fons et origo* of social development and that his institution's job is, as far as possible, to react sympathetically to these recommendations.

Automatic Decisions

Finally, the belief is growing that both decision making and coordination processes can be made both easier and more rational by the use of human and mechanical systems. At its extreme it sounds as if the individual human mind and judgment could be bypassed entirely: a miscellany of information would be fed into the system, and the system would not only digest it but also, under expert milking, would deliver the answers. These answers would then be reprogrammed, and individuals and societies would learn to accept these new answers and could presumably be trained to act on them.

This is, of course, an extreme view. But the idea that policy making can become more scientific has engaged the attention of bright minds. The availability of high-speed computers has whetted the administrative appetite. And the rise of debate and disagreement about policies and programs has made scientific decision making very attractive indeed.

I must register my reserve about the process of reaching agreement either through institutional coordination bodies or through automatic or automated systems that would make the decision. Both structures and systems are only tools to help those who can embrace in their thinking all the elements necessary to evolving agreement or developing a consensus. No large-scale coordinating institution can function properly if populated with parochial minds. No PPBS system can assist those incapable of institutionwide points of view. The very interest in the words "decision making" and "coordination" suggests a formal interest that can too easily represent an escape from reality. This result is no solution and must not be allowed to happen.

Where does all this leave us? Perhaps, as usual, with a few simple propositions which, if artfully stated, can lead to productive debate.

First, institutions, be they governments or universities, rarely make conscious and visible decisions.

Second, therefore, the coordination of institutional decisions is a process more romantic than scientific.

Third, real coordination is tentative and results in a process of continuous change.

Fourth, consensus or agreement is most successfully achieved through functional organization (CEEB-ETS) and through professional association (agriculture), rather than through institutional coordination.

New Imperatives in Institutional Decision Making

ERNEST BOYER

DR. PERKINS DEVELOPS PERSUASIVELY the thesis that it is difficult to coordinate decisions between the university and the government because no effective decision-making process exists within either. His analysis also bespeaks lack of coordination and lack of leadership as well: he describes colleges and universities as "anarchic" places of "silent acquiescence" dominated by people who "avoid making decisions." In that case, institutional and organizational arrangements are determined not by leadership but by drift, for failure to make decisions is itself a decision. The central problem, therefore, rather than being, How can we coordinate? becomes Is anybody in charge?

Despite the dark description, it should not be assumed that the situation is irreversible and that better coordination among the institutions, the states, and the federal government is forever beyond reach. Certainly, the pride, independence, and variety of the campus—or of the political process—cannot be made beautifully harmonious easily or soon. (Dr. Perkins is justified in a hint of pessimism.) Yet it would be equally risky to assume that the only successful path to better consensus is through vigorous outside professional organizations—such as the Educational Testing Service or the TIAA—rather than through smoother internal coordination among colleges, universities, and governments themselves. I continue to hope that we will become more than ignorant yeomen, shooting longbows blindly in the night with only some professional knight errant as a hope for greater purposes, progress, and peace.

Coordination may of necessity increase under the new internal and external realities to be faced, for social forces at work in our society press inexorably for a change in the structure and relationships of higher education. As these forces press in, the need for greater coordination will become compelling, in part for the sake of preservation. Christopher Jencks and David Riesman wrote in the 1969 preface to the second edition of *The Academic Revolution* with respect to the sheer speed of change in American attitudes toward higher education since they started studying it around 1960:

> The only widespread complaints about higher education were that Americans needed more of it. . . . Almost all educators accepted the legitimacy and authority of the academic profession a few years ago, even when they criticized specific aspects of its operation. . . . Today all this has changed. . . . the public is becoming more skeptical about educators' claims. . . . educators are far less sure than they were that their traditions . . . are worth defending. . . . A small but growing minority seems convinced that the academic system . . . is not just blemished but fundamentally rotten.[1]

To this uncertainty of purpose must be added the new austerity of budget strictures and declining enrollment, and the result is pressures that make coordination and, above all, leadership imperative.

When affluence suffused the campus, the luxury of splendid isolation was possible. Now increasingly hard choices must be made. After a period that has somewhat unfairly been described as "fatty growth" and "management by addition," there are few, if any, states where student applications continue to increase dramatically. The need to look into the future is becoming ever more a necessity. Also the new austerity has forced those in higher education to reexamine haphazard growth and to make big decisions about priorities that previously could be avoided. I feel it is significant, for example, that two years ago it was the faculty who urged our university to undertake a broad-based review of all graduate programs and recommend a careful pruning to preserve fully justified essential services.

In short, the lack of significant decision making in our institutions may be changing somewhat because of the new exigencies produced by the shift in enrollment and decreased funding. The luxury of nondecision

1. Garden City, N.Y.: Doubleday, Anchor Books, 1969. Pp. viii–ix.

was itself a reflection of affluence. Leaner times inevitably bring a new support for leadership, and the need for interaction can no longer be ignored.

Also we may see greater coordination—it might be called standardization—compelled by requirements imposed on institutions legislatively or administratively from without. I agree with Dr. Perkins that there has been no comprehensive policy *about* higher education at the federal level. And, as he said, it is tough to coordinate a "nonpolicy." But he is also correct in commenting that the Education Amendments of 1972 was a sharp exception to the rule. That act shifted federal policy toward more aid to students, it created a commission to develop an overall plan for the funding of federal postsecondary education assistance, and it also urged the consideration of uniform costing standards. Most important, it was in this legislation that the much debated 1202 commissions appeared. These moves do reflect an emerging policy at the federal level, with elements of cohesion and overall direction.

Such trends seem certain to increase and, as they do, both public and private institutions will, for better or worse, have to begin "falling in line." To put it pointedly, I foresee deep and growing frustration at the highest levels over the conditions of noncoordinating and "anarchy" that Dr. Perkins deplores. This frustration—at high levels—is leading, I believe, to increased impatience that, in turn, will take the form of enforced coordination that will significantly alter the conditions that have prevailed in the past.

Furthermore, the trend toward greater regularization is being accelerated simply because college and university operations are increasingly woven into the fabric of broader social policy. Two examples: All institutions are now completely familiar with the way their personnel procedures link into state and federal equal employment regulations. Increased legal and regulatory requirements have destroyed forever the free-wheeling independence of the past. Institutions are, in short, being held accountable. Decisions must be visible, capable of being defended, and they must be consistent with—or in the terms of this discussion, well coordinated with—state and federal policies. Out-of-state tuition fees again illustrate how federal and state intentions will interact with an area of institutional decision, and the current trends indicate that this area too will be removed forever from the independent decision previously assumed.

The list goes on and on. As institutions grow increasingly complex and broader in their impact, the social policies determined at governmental levels will increasingly limit and dictate institutional decisions. Coordination will, perforce, become increasingly a fact of life.

If my analysis is even half true, I see reasons both for alarm and for hope. But this brings me again to the issue of leadership, for the absence of self-generated goals and strategies may be at the root of the symptoms we have deplored. Thus, as I have suggested, we may be *forced* to coordinate either because of conditions *within* or even more urgently because of pressures from *without*.

Every man has two reasons for what he does, as J. P. Morgan said, a good reason and the real one. Certainly these internal and external pressures provide real reasons for greater unity and leadership in action. There is a good reason also for us to generate our own moves because we know them to be right.

Are there not still men and women in the higher education community who have the vision and the vigor to establish a more rational structure, to sharpen the issues, and to clarify the framework for more collaborative effort? Can we understand that as our purposes are blurred, as our resources are more constrained, and as the pull of students diminishes—do not these very conditions provide an ideal climate in which new purposes can be defined, new priorities established, and a new sense of shared relations explored? The issue is not whether there will be more coordination but rather who will call the shots.

The people in higher education *can* help formulate national, state, and institutional policy in such a way as to maintain their integrity and demonstrate that their contributions can indeed be bigger than the institutions they invent, and that the whole can become greater than the sum of its parts.

Decisions *Will* Be Made

S. V. MARTORANA

DR. PERKINS' PAPER RAISES MANY POINTS that deserve comment and study in depth, among them the concept of a double helix for accommodating the academic and institutional modes of administration; the proposition that the federal government has not made decisions which touch meaningfully on higher education's policy and practices; the suggestion that publicly controlled colleges and universities seek assurance of support from the state even "before making recommendations, let alone preliminary decisions."

I focus on two points. The first makes explicit a conclusion that is implicit in Perkins' presentation but which he appears to play down lest a more forthright recognition of the conclusion would produce complexities and difficulties. The second point elaborates on a cue in his paper to handling the very difficulties and complexities he envisions. More specifically, the two points are: First, decisions bearing significantly on higher education's policies, programs, and practices are indeed determined—*made* in one way or another. Second, cooperative *planning* can be a means for coordinating these decisions as they are in the process of formulation.

Neither of these points challenges the propositions and observations he advances that higher educational institutions have complicated, often vague, and unstructured ways of reaching decisions and that the decision process in academe does have a special nature. But these circumstances should not permit a conclusion that the decisions reached can be treated as isolated actions simply because the process is hard to describe analytically and precisely.

In one way or another institutional decisions *are* made. Positions are established, policies formulated, and plans for action projected. The City University of New York in 1969 announced a decision to adopt an open admissions program; that announcement was followed shortly by a proclamation by the governor of New York that special help would be provided to the State University of New York to implement an open enrollment program. And both statements appeared several years after most public community colleges in the state had been operating on a declared open-door policy. The Minnesota State Commission on Higher Education in 1971 supported legislative action to establish Minnesota Metropolitan State College, a new upper-level college in the twin-cities area where the University of Minnesota is based. The Pennsylvania State Department of Education recently announced a decision to launch a new "open university" and simultaneously declared a policy of nonsupport for establishing more off-campus branches of existing four-year colleges and universities or new community colleges. The Virginia Community Colleges not long ago abolished tenure. The federal government last year "decided" to promote action in each of the states to establish statewide commissions to carry on "comprehensive planning" of postsecondary education, and in March 1973 announced a new "decision" that the earlier one should be "tabled" (or at least not funded).

This listing could go on and on; the ones chosen are not cited to suggest any special lack *or presence* of coordination in the particular circumstances, institutions, governments, or agencies involved. The listing is presented only to illustrate one point basic to another and equally important one: decisions *are* made, and, in today's situation in higher education, a proposition that such decisions (particularly ones arrived at by institutions) can be viewed as isolated actions, much less defended as meriting such consideration, is indefensible. Whether this development is good or bad for the general health and true service of the academic community is beside the point; the fact is that unilateral, essentially autonomous decision making among postsecondary educational institutions and agencies is no longer possible. This proposition holds for community colleges and for large complex universities, for local agencies and for state and even federal agencies as well.

The many reasons that the decisions cannot be regarded as isolated actions can be reduced basically to two. First, virtually no institution or major postsecondary educational agency today can take a truly major step in a new direction *without having an impact on others*. Second, in one way or another, public support is being expected in return for the public services provided by *all types* of postsecondary institutions. To expect such public support and to expect simultaneously that any significant unilateral action that could affect many others will be permitted to pass unnoticed or unexamined by the others is highly unrealistic. It will be interesting, in this regard, to continue to watch at the state level the evolving approaches and structures for statewide coordination and planning in relation to the eventual action at the federal level on the 1202 Comprehensive Planning Commissions proposed by Public Law 92-318.

Now, if in fact decisions are made and must be taken into account, how can this best be done? Dr. Perkins' paper advances two points that merit closer examination in considering a reply. In discussing decision making, he points out, quite correctly, that at the institutional level decisions seem to be the result more of "an expression of the *operative forces* than a decision by any individual or group of individuals." This insight prompts a host of questions that ought to attract the attention of researchers in organizational behavior in an effort to gain a clear understanding of how decisions in higher education are reached. Given that there are "operative forces" and that fundamentally these are what decide at least the larger issues, should we not be asking: Who and what are they? How do they manifest their influence? What are their patterns of interaction and resolution? When is the process at critical points of functioning, and how are these crossed? Hard inquiry into such questions may well provide some answers that can themselves be a first step toward a better coordination of the decisions reached. Actually, several thrusts of research and analysis are already under way to probe questions like these, but still more are needed.[1]

Another point which Dr. Perkins makes takes up a second large step forward in handling the challenge that federal-state-institutional coordination poses. He touches briefly on "long-range plans (five years of more)" and their relation to the "total-systems approach." He notes, moreover, that these considerations have "led to the creation of some kind of planning and coordinating instrument in almost every state."

Could not these instrumentalities be improved, extended, and better applied to help face up to and resolve the challenges of coordinating the many decisions in postsecondary education? To be sure, as currently structured and defined, and on the basis of the knowledge of the "science and art" of planning and coordination as it is now understood, the "organizational solutions to organizational problems" show up at times as immature, clumsy, and ineffective and at other times as dangerous because they could evolve into monsters of a stultifying control and direction by a centralized agency. If planning and coordination were more carefully defined and refined in their functions and were buttressed by a sounder knowledge base on their philosophies as well as their techniques, however, the evils that now seem inherent in the coordinating organizations can perhaps be avoided at the same time that the promises they also seem to hold could be enhanced. The task is to find ways to preserve the creativity and diversity of services in postsecondary education which flow from institutional autonomy and freedom while assuring that these advantages do not generate a wasteful and vicious competition among the institutions and systems involved. It seems that, to do the task fully, a design is needed that not only views postsecondary education in the several states from a statewide perspective, but also permits some examination from a national vantage.

One thing is clear: There will be coordination of decisions in post-

1. For example, James S. Coleman, *Policy Research in the Social Sciences* (Morristown, N.J.: General Learning Corporation, 1972).

secondary education, whether accomplished through the voluntary types of mechanisms that Dr. Perkins suggests toward the end of his paper or by more officially structured ones. Perhaps we will have to settle for a conclusion that the answer lies only ultimately in the legislatures and the Congress; that is, we must leave traditional views of education and partisan politics and "go political." Such a conclusion may be repulsive to many in the higher education enterprise. But those in higher education who are concerned about decision making should examine the possibility carefully, for the matter is really in *their* hands.

Coordination, A Necessity

RICHARD M. MILLARD

MR. PERKINS HAS ANALYZED what might be called the dynamics of nondecision making and noncoordination in certain segments of the postsecondary educational community. He is concerned that we not escape reality through formal interest in "decision making" and "coordination" reinforced by new organizations and data-processing equipment. There is indeed a danger of becoming so enamored with the formal aspects of structures and machines that the substantive problems will get lost. Management systems are indeed "tools to help those who can embrace in their thinking all the necessary elements"; I suggest further, for example, that "coordination" simply for the sake of coordination is likely to be a waste of time or a bureaucratic boondoggle.

As Mr. Perkins points out, institutions, states, and the federal government do not make decisions. However, decisions are made by people in the name of institutions, states, and even the federal government. These are the decisions that cause problems. Mr. Perkins' description of policy formulation through systematic nondecision making in some institutions is widely familiar.

On closer examination, the horizons of Mr. Perkins' world appear to be peculiarly eastern and Ivy League with perhaps a glance toward West Coast colonization. I am not sure that it is the world of the Mankato and Fitchburg State Colleges or Memphis State University or the Miami-Dade Community College system or the Bell and Howell schools, or the University System of Florida. I am fairly sure it is not the world of the Illinois, New Jersey, Connecticut, or Washington state boards or commissions of higher education nor even, I suspect, of the University of the State of New York. I find it difficult to identify a state, governor, or legislature that would consider itself responsible only for "establishing healthy institutions and thereafter for encouraging programs that can be identified with the state and its people." I could not characterize "accommodation" to state government as the "name of the game" for the Universities of Missouri, Illinois, Michigan, or even California.

I think the game has changed in a number of respects. First, the range of institutions to be taken into account has considerably expanded beyond traditional colleges and universities to include community colleges, vocational-technical schools, proprietary schools, and various other institutions concerned with postsecondary education.

Second, the traditional college-age population—18–21-year-olds—has about reached its peak and will soon decline. The percentage of males in this group going to college has already begun to drop, and the percentage among females is not perceptibly increasing. To the extent that appropriations for public institutions are related to enrollments and direct income in private institutions is dependent upon tuition, unless new student populations are encouraged and planned for, the likelihood appears to be a period of increasing competition and decreasing funding. If the federal government follows the administration's urging and moves to a free market concept of support for postsecondary education primarily or exclusively through students, the situation will be further aggravated. These factors alone will call for some hard decisions in many institutions.

Third, at least at the state level, the legislative and public demands for accountability and more effective use of funds—in part to protect quality, in part to ensure diversity in postsecondary educational opportunity, and in part to increase efficiency—have made statewide planning for postsecondary education critical. Such planning involves not only institutions but also state higher or postsecondary education agencies. It calls for far clearer decisions with respect to institutional goals and to the development of role and scope determinations than have been characteristic in the past, such decisions to be made by or for institutions, but preferably by institutions in cooperation with state agencies. To the extent that private institutions receive public funding or to the extent that their officials and faculties consider themselves an integral part of the postsecondary educational community, they either will or should also be integrally involved in the planning and implementation process. It is notable in this context that in 1960 sixteen states had created higher or postsecondary education agencies, and by 1970 the number had increased to forty-seven. The trend over the last three years has been to strengthen rather than weaken or abolish these agencies; two states have moved from coordination to consolidated governing boards, one will do so in 1974, and such moves are under consideration in at least two additional states.

Fourth, to the extent that cooperation and coordination among institutions and state agencies have been less than effective for whatever reasons, legislatures, governors, and state budget officers have not been hesitant to see directly into institutional affairs—witness legislation respecting faculty work load, tenure, and transfer policies. As much as such moves into institutional affairs are regrettable, given present conditions and trends, they are likely to increase if institutional representatives refuse to make decisions complementary to and in cooperation with each other and with appropriate state higher or postsecondary educational agencies. The real danger is that responsibility for planning and coordination of postsecondary education will pass out of the hands of state agencies created for this purpose and move into the hands of general state planning agencies, for whom education does not constitute the first priority, or directly into executive and legislative control.

It may be true that Yale, Harvard, Princeton, Cornell, and Stanford will continue to have the luxury of nondecision making. They are indeed national universities and, it is to be hoped, will remain so. But they represent a very small proportion of institutions and students in the nation. At this juncture in postsecondary education, I suggest, the kind of functional autonomy commensurate with experimentation, free inquiry, and institutional integrity depends as never before on the willingness of institutions or institutional decision-makers to work cooperatively and with the appropriate state agencies in coordinated decision making, including decisions about appropriate levels for decision making. Laissez faire in higher education today, in my opinion, can only spell financial and academic disaster.

One final note about the federal situation. Mr. Perkins quite correctly notes that thus far the federal government has made no decisions. It came close to it in the Education Amendments of 1972, but large parts of the amendments were in effect negated by the administration's action and lack of action. What effect the report of the National Commission on the Financing of Postsecondary Education[1] will have cannot be forecast. Mr. Newman and others are issuing an additional statement on federal postsecondary education policy.[2] If one accepts a Jeffersonian approach, one thing appears clear: Institutions and states, including interstate combinations, have the opportunity (an opportunity that may be of limited duration) to develop and strengthen postsecondary educational systems to ensure diversity and complementariness among the institutions and to provide opportunities to citizens of all ages. If this effort fails, the alternative may well be national control in spite of the rhetoric about the "free market."

1. *Financing Postsecondary Education in the United States* (Washington: Government Printing Office, 1973), 442 pp.
2. *The Second Newman Report: National Policy and Higher Education: Report of a Special Task Force to the Secretary of Health, Education, and Welfare* (Cambridge, Mass.: MIT Press, 1973), 227 pp.

EDUCATIONAL REFORM
AND INNOVATION

The Faculty and the Government

KENNETH S. TOLLETT

AN UNDERCURRENT OF TENSION, mutual suspicion, and even hostility has plagued the relationship between institutions of higher education, particularly their faculties, and the government. This undercurrent flows in part from faculties because of what Lionel Trilling has called "the adversary culture" of intellectuals and from a frequently misguided intellectual arrogance and a contempt for government and its bureaucracies in general and for its politicians in particular. The government's contribution to the undercurrent is a natural resentment of the disparagement, compounded by a perception (bordering on conviction) that academics and their institutions are impractical squanderers of the public treasury in useless, theoretical, and esoteric research and in fatuously highfalutin dialogues and professorial posturing.

Because the development of higher education in the United States in the seventeenth, eighteenth, and the first half of the nineteenth centuries was marked by only a tenuous connection between government and academe, the undercurrent of distrust was not a great force. However, with the coming of the land-grant college movement through the Morrill Acts of 1862 and 1890, federal government expenditures for, and involvement in, higher education increased, spurting during and after World War II and peaking with research funds, contracts for services, and student and categorical aids in the 1960s, following Russia's launching of Sputnik. Throughout these periods a roughly parallel increase in state support also took place.

Because the federal government is a significant force for change and development in tenure, unionization, and affirmative action—the three major topics here dealt with—its thrust will be given primary consideration. (It should be noted that the historic undercurrent has probably been more intense between academe and state governments than

The research assistance of Madelyn S. Gibson, a third-year law student at Howard University, which was made possible by Howard University Sponsored Research Grant No. OA-SRP 377, is gratefully acknowledged.

between academe and the federal government.) Before I explore the growing interface of faculty and government in the issues of tenure, unionization, and affirmative action programs, a comment is needed on a trend that creates problems. From my perspective, that trend is the secularization of higher education.

In order to define "secularization," my own concept—definition—of higher education must be given. *Higher education* is essentially an intellectual process that creates and transmits knowledge, develops and structures critical cognitive powers, enhances and reinforces sensitivity and sensibility, and combines the dominant urges of self-conscious humankind to explain, control, and revere or reunite with nature in a purposeful pursuit of understanding human relationships and the relationships between humans and nature. This concept of higher education is entirely compatible with the philosophical view that the university is a community of scholars pursuing knowledge, searching for values, and envisioning a perfected social order for human community—all done freely. Its dominant assumption is that a university is a quasi enclave for the nurturance of learning and is therefore committed to, and concerned with, the belief that humans are learning beings. Thus, the organization, operation, and functions of a university should serve and support learning; indeed, the university is a sanctuary of learning.

In this context, *secularization* means that the college or university as an institution is becoming less distinguishable from other institutions in the society such as businesses, government, deliberative bodies, or the Pentagon. As it becomes more like a business, then PPBS (program-planning-budgeting systems), cost-benefit analyses, and unionization naturally follow. As it becomes more like government, then politics, the public good, and social programs become an operative concern and an activity of the university. If "deliberative body" is a part of its trend model, then preoccupation with parliamentary procedure, political maneuver, and constituency formation develops. If the Pentagon is the trend model, then the university will develop proliferating bureaucracies and mindlessly escalating budgets.

The significance of the secularizaton trend is both expressed and compounded by a parallel growth in government and higher education. As higher education has expanded in importance and scale, the public—through the government—has expanded its interest, concern, and involvement in higher education. From Sputnik until recently, the expansion in higher education was accompanied by an increase in the power of faculties—what Jencks and Riesman have labeled the "academic revolution." However, growth has abated and, in so doing, has undercut the preeminent position of faculties. Moreover, the educational enterprise has become increasingly subject to the regimen of law and the surveillance of government, in part because of internal disruptions and external intervention, interest, and concern.

Finally, the functions of higher education have proliferated. One of the functions, or goals, has been the fostering of social justice, as evidenced in the trend toward universal access, in affirmative action programs, and in social reform through services to society. These interrelated elements sharpen the issues in tenure, unionization, and affirmative action programs. In short, may a university properly carry out functions and operations not primarily motivated by, and directed toward, *learning*?

Secularization, by this analysis, implies that tenure as traditionally understood has a strong basis for modified continuation, unionization as it is developing is propelled by forces uncongenial, if not antithetical, to learning, and affirmative action programs combine some of the internal logical conditions of learning with the external pressures of law and politics, which result in an ambiguous and mixed argument for such programs.

TENURE

The Carnegie Commission on Higher Education, in its report on governance, quite properly says, "Tenure, in its derivation from land tenure, means not the ownership of a position but the right to hold it under certain conditions." The report sees two historical sources of tenure. One has been the concept of academic freedom, and the other has been "seniority practices in ... high schools." In my view, the raison d'être of tenure is academic freedom. The report sets forth additional reasons for tenure: "Greater assurance of academic freedom for faculty members to express unpopular opinions, greater protection for the public in its access to the full and free views of faculty members, greater opportunity for a more serious review of the quality of faculty members, and a fuller feeling of partnership in the campus enterprise by senior faculty members are the basic reasons for tenure."[1]

Although the Carnegie Commission strongly supports tenure, like

---

1. Carnegie Commission, *Governance of Higher Education: Six Priority Problems* (New York: McGraw-Hill, 1973), pp. 60, 53, 56.

the Commission on Academic Tenure in Higher Education, chaired by William R. Keast,[2] it recognizes problems posed by it. Because the growth in higher education is predicted to level off in the 1970s and 1980s, in the near future a high proportion of present faculty members will be tenured. A predominantly tenured faculty may prove to be unresponsive to the interests of their students and the changing times. Finally, the "new depression" in higher education forces some financial adjustments. The Carnegie Commission makes the following recommendation to deal with these and other problems:

> Tenure systems should be so administered in practice (1) that advancements to tenure and after tenure are based on merit, (2) that the criteria to be used in tenure decisions are made clear at the time of employment, (3) that codes of conduct specify the obligations of tenured faculty members, (4) that adjustments in the size and in the assignments of staff in accord with institutional welfare be possible when there is a fully justifiable case for them, (5) that fair internal procedures be available to hear any cases that may arise, and (6) that the percentage of faculty members with tenure does not become excessive.[3]

The Keast Commission goes so far as to recommend "tenure quotas."[4] Yet its support for tenure is based primarily on the belief that the Constitution and courts will not adequately protect academic freedom.

Although the Constitution and courts do protect academic freedom to a degree, there are some arguments against tenure. For example, Professor Robert Nisbet has written, "It is a guarantee by the institution to the individual, irrespective of his age, of appointment until the time of retirement comes. Mental deterioration, sloth, abandonment of professional standards, gross immorality in or outside the university, flagrant breach of academic positions, none of these on the evidence is likely to affect the permanence of appointment once tenure has been granted."[5] Apart from thinking tenure is a refuge for the lazy, incompetent, and delinquent, Nisbet believes tenure is on the way out because the status of higher education has been downgraded, the academic and the nonacademic are being blurred, training on the job is replacing university training, young faculty members may object to tenure as hampering their advancement, unions are on the rise, and there is a rage to litigate;

2. See the commission's *Faculty Tenure: A Report and Recommendations* (San Francisco: Jossey-Bass, 1973).
3. *Governance*, p. 58.
4. Robert L. Jacobson, "Retain Tenure But Ration It, Panel Advises," *Chronicle of Higher Education*, Jan. 22, 1973, pp. 1, 5.
5. "The Future of Tenure," *Change*, April 1973, p. 27.

that is, more and more faculty members are taking their grievances to court rather than to the institutional committee on privilege and tenure or the local chapter of the American Association of University Professors. Another critic, Professor Dabney Park, Jr., believes that tenure protects the academic freedom of only the tenured, that collective bargaining reaffirms tenure, and that tenured faculty members discourage experimentation and "are more equal than" other faculty members.[6]

I agree in general with both the Academic Tenure and Carnegie Commissions, but regard the preservation of academic freedom as the overriding justification for the continuation of tenure. The Constitution, the law, the courts, and perhaps even unionization do provide some protection to academic freedom.

The U.S. Supreme Court and academic freedom

The U.S. Supreme Court in 1957 gave significant recognition to academic freedom in *Sweezy v. New Hampshire,* where it held that the state attorney general, acting as investigator of subversive activities under legislative authority, could not require a faculty member to answer questions about the content of classroom instruction regarding Marxism and the like. In balancing the social interest to protect society from subversion against the intellectual interest of the university to have free discussion and dialogue unfettered by government surveillance, the Supreme Court struck the balance in favor of the intellectually free pursuit of knowledge. Chief Justice Warren, speaking for the majority of the Court, said:

> The essentiality of freedom in the community of American universities is almost self-evident. No one should underestimate the vital role in a democracy that is played by those who guide and train our youth. To impose any strait jacket upon the intellectual leaders in our colleges and universities would imperil the future of our Nation. No field of education is so thoroughly comprehended by man that new discoveries cannot yet be made. Particularly is that true in the social sciences, where few, if any, principles are accepted as absolutes. Scholarship cannot flourish in an atmosphere of suspicion and distrust. Teachers and students must always remain free to inquire, to study, and to evaluate, to gain new maturity and understanding, otherwise our civilization will stagnate and die.[7]

Although this language appears to give uncompromising support to academic freedom, the narrower ground of the decision actually was that

6. "Tenure Shock," *Chronicle of Higher Education,* June 4, 1973, p. 16.
7. 354 U.S. 234, 250 (1957).

the attorney general had been delegated so sweeping and uncertain a mandate that, in the circumstances, it could not be assured that the legislature wanted the attorney general "to gather the kind of facts comprised in the subject upon which [the] petitioner was interrogated."

However, two years later, in *Barenblatt v. United States,* the U.S. Supreme Court held questions regarding a teacher-witness's present and past membership in a Communist or Communist-related club were pertinent to the topic under inquiry—Communist infiltration into education. Mr. Justice Harlan wrote for the majority:

> When academic teaching-freedom and its corollary learning-freedom, so essential to the well-being of the Nation, are claimed, this Court will always be on the alert against intrusion by Congress into this constitutionally protected domain. But this does not mean that the Congress is precluded from interrogating a witness merely because he is a teacher. An educational institution is not a constitutional sanctuary from inquiry into matters that may otherwise be within the constitutional legislative domain merely for the reason that inquiry is made of someone within its walls.[8]

Barenblatt, which was decided during the egalitarian, civil libertarian era of the Warren Court, probably reflects more accurately than *Sweezy* the Court's attitude toward academic freedom, or at least where it will probably move under Chief Justice Burger's helmsmanship of the floating court.[9] Nevertheless, the Court has struck down teacher loyalty oath laws; Justice Frankfurter went so far in his attack on the menace of loyalty oaths to the "habits of open-mindedness" as "to regard teachers —in our entire educational system, from primary grades to the university—as the priests of our democracy."[10] In *Baggett v. Bullitt,* the Court struck down a Washington State loyalty oath and a law requiring the state not to hire subversive teachers. The Court struck down the two statutes as unconstitutionally vague. The Washington oath required promise not to alter government by "revolution" and to promote respect for the flag and the institutions of the United States and the state of Washington. The Court concluded that the vagueness of these prescriptions offended the constitutional requirements of due process.[11]

    8. 360 U.S. 109, 112 (1959).
    9. See Kenneth S. Tollett, "The Viability and Reliability of the U.S. Supreme Court as an Institution for Social Change and Progress Beneficial to Blacks," Pt. I, *Black Law Journal* 2 (1972): 197; Pt. 2, *Black Law Journal* 3 (1973): 5.
    10. Wieman v. Updergraff, 344 U.S. 183, 196 (1952).
    11. 377 U.S. 360 (1964).

The concept of due process is crucial in considering tenure. A measure of due process is secured to faculty members even if they do not have tenure; but if they do have tenure—by statute, board regulation, or private contract—elaborate procedural safeguards are secured to them against arbitrary dismissal.[12] Generally, teachers cannot be dismissed for exercising their constitutional rights, whether or not they involve First Amendment protection of free speech, association, and the like, or the Fifth Amendment privilege against self-incrimination.[13]

The U.S. Supreme Court and tenure

The Supreme Court has recently decided that even where a teacher lacked contractual or tenure rights to reemployment, a refusal to rehire him did not preclude his raising First and Fourteenth Amendments rights. The Court made clear "that even though a person has no 'right' to a valuable governmental benefit and even though the government may deny him the benefit for any number of reasons, there are some reasons upon which the government may not act. It may not deny a benefit to a person on a basis that infringes his constitutionally protected interest." This case involved a state junior college professor who had been employed for ten years under a series of one-year written contracts. The professor, as president of the Texas Junior College Teachers Association, had become involved in public disagreements with the policies of his college's board of regents. When his one-year employment contract terminated, the board of regents voted not to offer him a new contract for the next academic year. The Court held that, although the respondent's continued employment was not secured by a contract tenure provision, practice and usage constituted a de facto tenure program that entitled him to the protection of procedural due process, including notice of, and a hearing on, the grounds of his nonretention. The Court stated: "Just as this Court has found there to be a 'common law of a particular industry or of a particular plant' that may supplement a collective bargaining agreement, *United Steelworkers* v. *Warrior and Gulf Nav. Co.*, 363 U.S. 574 . . . , so there may be an unwritten 'common law' in a particular

---

12. For a review of the law with respect to academic freedom, see "Developments in the Law—Academic Freedom," *Harvard Law Review* 81 (1968): 1045.

13. Slochower v. Board of Education, 350 U.S. 551 (1956). But see Nelson v. Los Angeles, 362 U.S. 1 (1960), in which the Court held that dismissal of a social worker who refused to give testimony on subversive activities, on the ground of protection under the First and Fifth Amendments, was proper in that her refusal constituted insubordination.

university that certain employees shall have the equivalent of tenure."[14] The Court did not clearly face either the free speech or academic freedom aspect of the controversy, but it did secure to the teacher the procedural safeguards protected by tenure.

However, on the same date the Court took a less solicitous stand on the procedural rights of nontenured faculty members. In *Board of Regents* v. *Roth,* a nontenured assistant professor at a state university was unsuccessful in his demand for a hearing on a refusal to rehire him. The teacher claimed that the real reason for his nonretention was his criticism of the university administration. The Court held the teacher did not have a constitutional right to a statement of reasons for, and a hearing on, the decision not to rehire. The Court stated that the "range of interests protected by procedural due process is not infinite." The Court further argued: "To have a property interest in a benefit, a person clearly must have more than an abstract need or desire for it. He must have more than a unilateral expectation of it. He must, instead, have a legitimate claim of entitlement to it. It is a purpose of the ancient institution of property to protect those claims upon which people rely in their daily lives, reliance that must not be arbitrarily undermined. It is a purpose of the constitutional right to a hearing to provide an opportunity for a person to vindicate those claims."[15]

Justices Douglas, Brennan, and Marshall dissented in *Roth,* Justice Marshall stating that every citizen who applies for public employment is entitled to it "unless the government can establish some reason for denying the employment."[16] Justices Douglas and Brennan not only agreed with Justice Marshall but also stated concern about possible violation of First Amendment rights if dismissal or refusal to renew a contract was based upon exercise of the right of free speech, which is intimately related to academic freedom. *Roth* makes clear how uncertain and perhaps unreliable the courts are in protecting academic freedom.

The status that one assigns civil liberties in his hierarchy of values will determine the degree to which he looks favorably on the present elaborate safeguards and even rigidities of tenure. Only eternal vigilance will protect freedom of the mind and the spirit. Although the Court has been extending procedural protection of interests subsumable under

14. Perry v. Sindermann, 408 U.S. 593, 602 (1972).
15. 408 U.S. 564, 570, 577 (1972).
16. Id. at 588.

property,[17] civil liberties generally and privacy particularly are under attack, which means academic freedom needs the added protection provided by the tenure system. Those interested in preserving and improving a learning community should resist resolutely all efforts to abolish tenure.

UNIONIZATION

Some might contend that everything the tenure system has been able to secure can also be secured by unionization and the attendant collective bargaining. As already noted, I perceive unionization in higher education as a product of the secularization of higher education. Thus unionization and collective bargaining are concerned primarily with working conditions and high salaries. Job security as well is a major concern. However, job security is promoted, not for the sake of academic freedom and the uininhibited pursuit of knowledge, but, rather, for the sake of personal and collective economic well-being. Economic well-being is a desirable but not a necessary condition for the pursuit of knowledge, the search for values, and the envisionment of a perfected social order. Unionization may be the wave of the future, but it is submitted here that the forces driving it forward are uncongenial and antithetical to the learning enterprise.

Causes and effects

The Carnegie Commission, in its report on governance, has enumerated the concerns of faculties which have given rise to unionization and collective bargaining:

- Salaries are rising more slowly; real income, in some instances, has actually been reduced.
- Budgetary support for faculty interests is much harder to obtain.
- More efforts are being made to control conditions of employment, such as workload.
- Students have intruded into what were once faculty preserves for decision making, and these intrusions and their possible extension are a source of worry for many faculty members.
- External authorities, outside the reach of faculty influence, are making more of the decisions that affect the campus and the faculty.
- Policies on promotion and tenure are more of an issue both as the rate

---

17. See Lynch v. Household Finance Corp., 405 U.S. 538 (1972), enjoining summary state garnishment action against petitioner's fund where garnishment was not preceded by notice and hearing.

of growth of higher education slows down, thus making fewer opportunities available, and as women and members of minority groups compete more actively for such opportunities as exist.[18]

Furthermore, the commission notes, not only are more nonfaculty employees becoming organized on campuses, but also "the most rapidly growing segment of higher education—the community colleges—is the segment most closely tied to secondary education where collective bargaining is already quite extensive." Unionization is a response not to educational but to economic forces. The commission report quite properly says: "Unionization for [faculty members] is more a protective than an aggressive act, more an effort to preserve the status quo than to achieve a new position of influence and affluence as has so often been the goal of unionization for other groups in earlier times."[19]

Of course this observation has more validity for so-called prestigious schools than for other institutions. Thus from the governance perspective of prestigious schools, the main motive of unionization may be the preservation of authority; for other schools, the main motive may be the redistribution of authority. Among the prestigious institutions, faculties have the authority recommended by the American Association of University Professors: faculty members participate significantly in the governance or decision-making process. The commission report recommends: "Faculties should be granted, where they do not already have it, the general level of authority as recommended by the American Association of University Professors."[20] This recommendation represents a sound argument for expanding faculty participation in the governance of many institutions, but is not necessarily an argument for unionization and collective bargaining.

The motive of unionization and collective bargaining is related, not to governance, but to economic security and well-being. The effect of collective bargaining on faculty economic returns has "been less significant than many observers predicted,"[21] and has been greatest in community colleges and in four-year institutions like those in New York which are tied to or influenced by the economic gains of collective bargaining won by public school and community college teachers "in the

18. *Governance*, p. 39.
19. Ibid., pp. 39–40.
20. Ibid., p. 41.
21. This paragraph draws heavily on Robert K. Carr and Daniel K. VanEyck, *Collective Bargaining Comes to the Campus* (Washington: American Council on Education, 1973), pp. 242–46.

same community." Carr and VanEyck have observed: "It is difficult to put dollar values on the various fringe benefits provided for in faculty contracts. Contract language does not usually distinguish new fringe benefits from those that carry over from prebargaining days, nor does the language always reveal dollar or percentage increases where an improvement in an existing benefit is provided for." However, Central Michigan University is one of the few four-year institutions where a strong case may be made that significant faculty compensation gains have been obtained through collective bargaining. The administration at Central Michigan pointed out that the high percentage gains claimed by the faculty were obtained by measuring annual increases in total compensation against salary, rather than compensation, for the base year.[22] Carr and VanEyck further observe:

> To obtain meaningful figures [in measuring the economic gains of faculties through collective bargaining], account must be taken of yearly fluctuations in the size of a faculty, the number of individuals in each faculty rank, and the number at each level of the salary schedule within a rank. The number of promotions . . . , of faculty members retiring or resigning . . . or going on leave, and the nature and cost of their replacements, . . . additional appointments . . . or new programs are all variables that enter into any measurement of annual increases.[23]

The "new depression," mentioned earlier, will probably cause boards of private institutions and legislatures, through their budget responsibilities, to require "productivity gains" as trade-offs against increased faculty compensation. Indeed, Phillip W. Semas reports, "College administrations are taking tougher stances as they face their faculties across the collective bargaining table."[24]

My own preoccupation with civil liberties prevents me from opposing laws that permit faculty members in public institutions to engage in collective bargaining; however, as a matter of educational philosophy and pedagogical principle, I am less than happy with the trend toward unionization and collective bargaining. Unionization probably will affect

---

22. At Central Michigan, under two contracts covering four years, "each faculty member received an across-the-board increase in his salary over the previous year: for the first year . . . 7.1 percent and for each of the next three years . . . 6.5–6.6 percent." Bargaining unit officers claimed that "the increases in total compensation (salaries plus fringe benefits) . . . were 8.2 percent for 1971–72, 9.25 percent for 1972–73, and 10.5 percent for 1973–74" (ibid., p. 245).
23. Ibid., p. 246.
24. Semas, "Administrations Get Tougher in Bargaining with Faculty: Some Negotiations Slowed," *Chronicle of Higher Education*, July 2, 1973, p. 1.

adversely several matters which the Carnegie Commission suggests faculty members should consider: "de facto comanagement rights of faculties in academic affairs such as courses, research projects, selection and promotion of colleagues, determination of grades and degrees, admissions, academic freedom, and selection of academic administrators." The commission has observed, "It is interesting that while faculty unionization carries the connotation of a progressive alliance with the workers, it has the conservative reality of excluding students."[25] Everett C. Ladd and Seymour Lipset see the emergence of unionism among college professors as a response to their "conditions of dependence," and they also seem to make an overall positive judgment regarding unionism in higher education.[26]

Unionization probably will strengthen managerial authority, reduce campus autonomy, and increase interdepartmental and intercampus uniformity. University administrations are already making claims to "management rights" that are taken for granted in industrial labor contracts; usually management rights clauses say simply "that management retains the right to decide the policies of the business."[27] The role and influence of governing boards will increase, because the administration of negotiated contracts inevitably will project governing boards further into "the day-to-day business of the academic community."[28] These observations apply to both public and private institutions.

Academe and labor law

Two particularly difficult questions are raised by collective bargaining: "First, should they favor a narrow or a broad unit of representation —faculty members only or also other or even all employees? And, second, should they favor narrow or broad contracts in terms of coverage—

---

25. *Governance*, p. 43. But also see: "Students have a right to participate in collective bargaining between university officials and faculty unions. . . . Thus, it is important to remember that the college exists primarily to teach its students, and not to set the terms and conditions for employment of teachers. . . . Better teaching conditions do not necessarily mean better learning conditions. In fact, teaching conditions are often improved at the expense of learning conditions" (Frederic M. Brandes, "Students Should Take Part in Collective Bargaining between Faculty and University," *Chronicle of Higher Education*, April 16, 1973, p. 12).

26. "Unionizing the Professoriate," *Change*, Summer 1973, pp. 38–44. For a comprehensive presentation of historical materials and a careful weighing of the effects of faculty bargaining on institutions and on the academic profession, see Carr and VanEyck, *Collective Bargaining*, especially chap. 8.

27. Semas, "Administrations Get Tougher," p. 6.

28. Carr and VanEyck, *Collective Bargaining*, p. 251.

salaries and other economic benefits only, or also academic and financial and governance policies?"[29] These two questions require a more legalistic consideration of collective bargaining. Before entering upon the discussion, it may be noted that as of January 1973 about 250 institutions were involved in unionization and, of these, 170 had bargaining units containing faculty members.

Unionization of faculties, as Shulman notes, "has been facilitated by changes in state laws favoring public employee collective bargaining and the National Labor Relations Board's recent assertion of jurisdiction over most private institutions." She also reports that in March 1972, "19 states have laws under which public institutions have been accorded or may be assumed to have negotiation rights."[30] Inasmuch as most of these laws were passed after 1967, there appears to be a trend toward state regulation of public employee organizations. Since about two-thirds of all faculty members in higher education are at public institutions, this trend should have a significant effect upon faculty unionization. Furthermore, bargaining under state laws may well inject state legislatures more intimately into campus budgetary matters, for example, in an increased incidence of line item appropriations.

With respect to labor law, state laws regulating unionization and bargaining are, as the Carnegie Commission notes, "based on the special nature of the civil service," whereas federal labor laws are "based on industrial experience." Thus, "the sharp industrial delineation between management and labor does not fit the more collegial approach taken on a campus." Therefore, the commission recommended, regarding federal and state laws regulating higher education unions, that: "A separate federal law and separate state law should be enacted governing collective bargaining by faculty members in both private and public institutions and should be responsible to the special circumstances that surround their employment. If this is not possible, then separate provisions should be made in more general laws, or leeway should be provided for special administrative interpretations."[31]

As already suggested, a most difficult legal issue in faculty collective bargaining is that of determining the composition of a bargaining unit. How should the various categories of professional employees be classified

29. *Governance*, p. 48.
30. Carol H. Shulman, *Collective Bargaining on Campus* (Washington: American Association for Higher Education, 1972), p. 5.
31. *Governance*, p. 50.

for negotiating purposes? As Rosen put one question: Should department chairpersons be treated as part of management or as members of the bargaining unit? The NLRB generally pays greatest attention to "the authority to hire or fire employees or to effectively recommend hiring or firing."[32]

How may governance issues be affected by the mix of tenured senior faculty members, nontenured junior faculty members, part-time faculty members, and nonteaching professionals (such as librarians)? In statewide systems, should all faculty members of a state's institutions be in one unit, or should units be defined by campus or permutations or combinations of campuses? State public employee relations boards and the NLRB hearing examiners, according to Shulman, usually determine bargaining unit composition by "the criterion of 'community of interest,'" i.e., will the different groups included in the unit have the same interests and positions on the subjects to be negotiated. Do part-time faculty members have a community of interest with full-time faculty members? How about professional school faculty members vis-à-vis liberal arts faculty members? The NLRB recognized Fordham University's law school faculty as a separate bargaining unit.[33] Should not faculty professionals be placed in same unit as faculty members? What about secretaries, clerks, and buildings and grounds staff?

Once the bargaining unit is determined, elections must be held for a bargaining agent, or there will be no bargaining. And the bargaining agent once elected—whether affiliated with the American Federation of Teachers or the American Association of University Professors or the National Education Association—must impartially represent all groups within the unit.

After bargaining unit and agent are determined, the next difficult question concerns what matters are to be covered in the collective bargaining agreement, that is, the subjects that can and should be included in a negotiated contract. Should negotiations focus only on wages, hours, and fringe benefits? Or should they focus also on faculty rights and working conditions, such as faculty participation in governance, tenure, academic freedom, and appointments, promotions, and evaluations of faculty members? These questions present complex problems to which bargain-

32. See Lawrence Rosen, "The Bargaining Unit Status of Academic Department Chairmen," *University of Chicago Law Review* 40 (1973): 445.
33. Shulman, *Collective Bargaining*, pp. 10, 12.

ing agents tend to give simplified answers. For example, as Wollett has noted, "bargaining agents tend to favor policies that treat all employees alike" and promote uniformity in performance and equality in rewards. Under contract terms, both peer evaluation and administrative evaluation are likely to increase resort to grievance procedures which may ultimately lead to binding arbitration. Grievance procedures automatically channel governance away from faculty into administrative channels and, in the later steps, into legal channels. Wollett surmises, "If the vehicle for faculty participation in decision making [i.e., operation of institutions, determining the raw materials to come in, etc.] is formalized and politicized by a collective negotiations structure, rigidities and inflexibilities may develop which inhibit institutional ability to respond to changed demands and needs."[34]

The secularization of higher education as expressed by the movement toward collective bargaining seems to lead almost inevitably to the deprofessionalization of teaching. Professor Mayer has observed that the single remaining obstacle to unionization of the university "is the crumbling conviction of some professors that theirs is a profession and not a trade."[35] However, if campuses are to be torn constantly by conflict and inner tension, then, according to the Carnegie Commission report, "It may be better to institutionalize this conflict through collective bargaining than to have it manifest itself with less restraint." In other words, the secularization trend on campus has also given rise to the legalization of the campus. It is in this latter term that the Carnegie Commission makes a strong case for unionization: "Collective bargaining does provide agreed upon rules of behavior, contractual understandings, and mechanisms for dispute settlement and grievance handling that help to manage conflict. Collective bargaining also provides a means through which the public interest in the conduct and the performance of the campus can be brought to bear upon decision making within the campus. *Collective bargaining, thus, is one aspect of law, if and when a rule is required.*"[36]

Currently, the laws affecting collective bargaining by public em-

---

34. Donald Wollett, "The Status and Trend of Collective Negotiations for Faculty in Higher Education," *Wisconsin Law Review* 1971: 21.
35. M. Mayer, "The Union and the University: Organizing the Ruins," *Center Magazine*, May–June 1972, p. 4.
36. *Governance*, p. 51; emphasis added.

ployees are diverse and directed to civil servants rather than teaching professionals. Bargaining in private colleges and universities, under NLRB jurisdiction, receives more uniform regulation. The most important point, however, is that, as the Carnegie Commission recommended, state and federal laws regulating collective bargaining in institutions of higher education should be made more sensitive to the peculiar problems, needs, and conditions of academe.

AFFIRMATIVE ACTION PROGRAMS

Whereas all humankind are learning beings, none should be denied access to, or participation in, the learning enterprise because of race, color, religion, sex, or national origin. Open admissions, universal access programs, and affirmative action programs foster social justice and support learning. Nevertheless, the social justice aspects of these programs may obscure or override their learning component and, in so doing, create some disjunction in the proper functioning of the "sanctuary of learning." I must confess a categorical commitment to open admissions, universal access, and affirmative action programs, although I place the needs of middle-class white women below those of Blacks, Chicanos, and Indians.

For some time, I have viewed gravely what I call a "reactivist, ad hoc, faddist, crisis-oriented outlook of American problem solving."[37] If women's rights is an example of this faddism, it will pass from the scene and, in so doing, reduce the potentially destructive conflict between minority rights and women's rights. Minority groups, particularly Blacks, deserve better than hostility or aggressive competition from other segments of society—especially indefatigably persistent and outraged middle-class white women. Yet the ground-swell interest in discrimination against women in higher education is deflecting attention and effort away from steps to correct the more virulent form of discrimination— that against Blacks, Chicanos, and Indians. The nation has witnessed movements from the civil rights struggle to ecophilism, to feminism, to consumerism (to a lesser extent), and so on. Jonathan Kozol sees "each cause imposing claims upon us in unceasing sequence, but always with shorter and still shorter periods of concentration and perseverance. Each of these movements is legitimate. . . . We move forward, not from com-

37. *Center Report*, October 1971, p. 29.

pletion to completion, but from one incompletion to the next."[38] Having stated my perspective, I will turn to affirmative action programs.

The underrepresentation of minority groups and women throughout higher education is incontestable. At the undergraduate level, if women and minority groups are calculated as a proportion of their representation in the population, the rate for women is more than double the rates for such groups as Blacks, Chicanos, and Indians. In graduate and professional school, the underrepresentation of women and minority groups progressively coincide. Among faculty members, the proportion of women is only about half that among undergraduates; the comparable proportion for Black faculty staff is about 25 percent, and is much lower for Chicanos and Indians. Thus, under affirmative action, the needs of minority groups are twice those of women. In general, the large state institutions and many private institutions, particularly the most prestigious ones, have been remiss in treating women equitably.

Instruments of enforcement

According to *Higher Education Guidelines, Executive Order 11246*:

> *Affirmative action* requires the contractor [with the federal government] to do more than ensure employment neutrality with regard to race, color, religion, sex, and national origin. As the phrase implies, affirmative action requires the employer to make additional efforts to recruit, employ and promote qualified members of groups formerly excluded, even if that exclusion cannot be traced to particular discriminatory actions on the part of the employer. The premise of the affirmative

---

38. "Moving On—To Nowhere," *Saturday Review of Education*, January 1973, p. 10. Kozol also writes: "The forward motion from one surrender to the next is characterized by a dizzying progression of concerns, each of which is tried, consumed, and traded in: civil rights, peace, ecology, pollution, women's liberation, welfare rights, the pathos of the white and unrespected middle-class, the American Indian, the Mexican-Americans in the Southwest, the Puerto Ricans in Manhattan, the overworked pupils at upper-class prep schools in New England and so forth and so on, ... The discovery by the intelligent wife of a Manhattan millionaire that she, too, is oppressed—first because she went to an oppressive prep school that was not like Summerhill, second because she is a woman and cannot go down to Wall Street like her husband—leads her to the final step of equating her oppression with that of the victim of the slum. The problem is not only that this is a *vicious and dishonorable equation* (she is not starving; her children are not born brain-injured in unsterile delivery rooms; they do not chew lead-infested paint; her sickness—cancer, epilepsy, heart disease—does not go unexamined and untreated) but also that by such an equation neither form of oppression will ever be dealt with in a perseverant way. Each will produce literature, controversy, talk shows, a new-thing-to-be-into. Nobody who is now in pain will be in less pain when it is all over."

action concept of the Executive Order is that unless positive action is undertaken to overcome the effects of systemic institutional forms of exclusion and discrimination, a benign neutrality in employment practices will tend to perpetuate the *status quo ante* indefinitely.[39]

The laws and regulations to enforce the prohibition of discrimination are several. The chief instruments are the following:

The Equal Pay Act of 1963 was amended in 1972 to extend coverage to executive, administrative, and professional employees, and prohibits discrimination in salaries, including fringe benefits, on the basis of sex. The legislation is administered by the Wage and Hour Division of the U.S. Department of Labor. No formal complaint procedure is specified; the law simply requires that the aggrieved individual contact the nearest office of the Wage and Hour Division of the U.S. Department of Labor. The only corrective actions required under this provision are salary equalization and back pay. Of all aspects of the feminist movement, none is contested less than the proposition of equal pay for equal work.[40]

The Civil Rights Act of 1964, title vii, prohibits discrimination in employment; it also provided for the establishment of the Equal Employment Opportunity Commission (EEOC) to enforce the provisions. The Equal Employment Opportunity Act of 1972 extended the jurisdiction of the EEOC to include all employees of educational institutions. Affirmative action is not required under this provision unless a court so orders or unless affirmative action is included in a conciliation agreement.

The Education Amendments of 1972, title ix, prohibits discrimination against students and others on the basis of sex. As with title vii of the 1964 Civil Rights Act, in certain instances religious institutions may be exempted from the application of title ix. The Office for Civil Rights in the U.S. Department of Health, Education, and Welfare is responsible for enforcement in colleges and universities. After discrimination has been found, affirmative action may be required.

The Comprehensive Health Manpower Training Act and the Nurse Training Act of 1972 bar sex discrimination in admissions in certain

---

39. Washington: U.S. Department of Health, Education, and Welfare, Office for Civil Rights, October 1972. P. 3.

40. But see George Gilder, "The Suicide of the Sexes: Are Feminism, Gay Liberation, and the Playboy Philosophy Really All the Same?", *Harper's*, July 1973, p. 42. Gilder argues that males will suffer serious damage to their sense of self-worth and usefulness unless they are permitted to earn more than women in order to inflate their importance to the family. Without this pay differentiation, Gilder sees males as rather dispensable creatures.

health schools. The HEW Office for Civil Rights is responsible for administering both laws.

Executive Order 11246 as amended by E.O. 11375 is the primary instrument affecting higher education institutions. All colleges and universities with federal contracts of $10,000 or more are covered in the prohibitions against discriminations in employment—including hiring, upgrading, salaries, fringe benefits, training, and other conditions of employment—on account of race, color, religion, national origin, or sex. Every institution which employs more than fifty persons and which holds federal contracts or subcontracts totaling $50,000 must have on file with HEW a written affirmative action program. "Contract" is interpreted broadly so that even grants are considered as contracts. With any contract in excess of $1 million with the federal government, preaward reviews of the institution are conducted by HEW. The Office of Federal Contract Compliance of the U.S. Department of Labor has policy responsibility and has designated HEW as the agency responsible for enforcing compliance in educational institutions. Individuals or organizations may make complaint by letter to OFCC or the Secretary of Health, Education, and Welfare; in addition, as in preaward reviews, investigations may also be made without complaint.[41]

Effects of implementation

Under the executive orders, currently approximately one thousand institutions are required to prepare affirmative action plans. Those filed with HEW are required to contain numerical goals and timetables. When a compliance review becomes necessary, an HEW regional office notifies the institution in writing that it is to be subject to review, and the institution is given three to four weeks for preparation. Two matters in the investigation process have given rise to conflict: due process, and the great reluctance of institutions to give HEW full access to personnel records. After the HEW investigation has been completed, its regional office presents the institution with a letter of findings. The institution has thirty days to prepare a written plan—affirmative action plan—to correct "deficiencies," and the plan must then be approved by the regional OCR.

In preparing the affirmative action plan, the institution is required

41. The description of federal laws and regulations concerning sex discrimination in higher education is based on materials obtained from the Project on the Status and Education of Women, Association of American Colleges. See also Carol H. Shulman, *Affirmative Action: Women's Rights on Campus* (Washington: American Association for Higher Education, 1972), p. 7.

to set forth "goals and timetables," not quotas, aimed at correcting discrimination. J. Stanley Pottinger, former director of HEW's OCR, distinguished goals from quotas: "Quotas . . . are numerical levels of employment that must be met if the employer is not to be found in violation of the law. . . . Goals are projected levels of hiring that say what an employer can do if he really tries. By establishing goals, the employer commits himself to a good faith effort that is most likely to produce results."[42] As part of the goals and timetables requirements, institutions are required to include a "utilization analysis" in its affirmative action plan—an analysis in terms of race and sex of its current staff and of "the available employment pool for each group."[43] It is from this analysis that the goals and timetables are developed to correct discrimination.

The implementation of affirmative action plans has caused charges of discrimination in reverse and other criticisms. None of the laws or regulations discussed imposes reverse discrimination, and I have little patience with such charges. Indeed, when it comes to correcting past discrimination perpetuated against Blacks, I construe the Thirteenth, Fourteenth, and Fifteenth Amendments as requiring special protection of the interests and rights of Blacks. I contend: "In applying any doctrine which is a gloss on the equal protection clause it must be determined what values are served by that application. If it impairs the fulfillment of Black interests and rights, then it does violence to the spirit, purpose, and meaning of the equal protection clause."[44] In terms of national legislative and executive policy and perhaps, to a lesser extent, social justice, a comparable argument can be made on behalf of women.

Other criticisms of affirmative action programs are that federal regulations and policies threaten institutional autonomy, that grave financial hardship is imposed on institutions through the withdrawal of federal funds, that the burden of proof to establish innocence rests with the institution, and that the confidentiality of personnel records and thus the right to privacy of individuals are invaded. The general answer to these criticisms is that higher education institutions are not above legal reform, particularly where they have a record of discrimination, misfeasance, nonfeasance, and malfeasance. They are afforded opportunity to take

---

42. Quoted in *Higher Education and National Affairs*, April 14, 1972, p. 4.
43. Shulman, *Affirmative Action*, p. 14.
44. Kenneth S. Tollett, "Blacks, Higher Education and Integration," *Notre Dame Lawyer* 48 (1972): 202.

the initiative in designing their own affirmative action plans. They are not entitled to federal largesse while they are in violation of constitutionally sound federal law or regulation. The common law system has long recognized that where a defendant has inflicted injury on a plaintiff in circumstances under the special control and knowledge of the defendant, the defendant may have the burden of coming forward with evidence or proof that the injury was not caused by his own misconduct. Institutions that have undergone extensive contract compliance reviews have considered as insufficient the requirement that the Office for Civil Rights respect the confidentiality of files by not disclosing information obtained through investigation in pursuance of enforcing affirmative action plans. The confidentiality of personnel files is the basis for modifying the usual rules concerning burden of proof.

ACADEME IN TODAY'S WORLD

Great public interest, concern, and involvement with academe have come as a result of the expansion in institutions of higher education—in numbers of institutions, students, and faculties and in an increase in activities and services. The public interest is reflected on the part of government by public support and by a degree of regulation of, and intervention in, the higher education enterprise. These various kinds of growth have caused a secularization and legalization, if not also politization, of the campus. Notwithstanding these developments, tenure must be preserved to protect the academic freedom that is absolutely essential to the learning community. Unionization is a capitulation to the secularizing, legalizing, and politicizing forces within and outside the campus. It should be resisted if possible. However, if conflict and tension become overriding influences in the academic community, then the capitulation may be not only inevitable but also desirable. Affirmative action programs are not inconsistent with the learning enterprise, although the recent feminist emphasis in the programs may be detrimental to the more seriously oppressed groups such as Blacks, Chicanos, and Indians. Government and law may play a constructive role in all three areas. They should preserve tenure with appropriate modification, sensitize the legal process by permitting faculty collective bargaining to take into consideration the peculiarities of academe that differentiate it from industry and the civil service, and complete the civil rights revolution of the 1960s before going overboard with relieving the almost "benign" oppression of middle-class white women.

Affirmative Action for Excellence

CYRENA N. PONDROM

THE WORKING DEFINITIONS of higher education offered by Mr. Tollett serve usefully for me as well, with perhaps an inevitable few revisions. I would expect thus to be sympathetic to his conclusions. As I examine the definitions and the implications which I feel they have, however, I find that these definitions lead me into approximate agreement with his views on tenure and collective bargaining, but into substantial disagreement in the area of affirmative action. Because I feel Mr. Tollett's own views—and not simply a difference in our perspectives—lead rigorously to a different position on affirmative action, I think it useful first to elaborate on some of his essential points, noting, as I do, both their implications and our areas of agreement. Approximately following his lead, I would be willing to define higher education as *a social institution* in which individuals join together to create and transmit knowledge, develop and teach cognitive processes and capabilities, and expand and intensify human aesthetic and ethical sensibilities—with the goal of giving man ever-growing ability *wisely* to control his own circumstances and destiny and gain ever clearer and more profound understanding of what wisdom is. I would agree that institutions meeting this definition of higher education are "quasi enclaves for the nurturance of learning," and further—that "the organization, operation, and functions of a university should serve and support learning."

Implicit in these statements is the assumption that the value placed on learning is or should be dominant within higher education. And they contain the further assumption that achieving the highest possible standard of learning has (or should have) priority over less effective, lower quality attempts at learning. Making these assumptions about quality explicit will be crucial to the further analysis, for they bear directly upon how much latitude higher education should permit itself to exercise in compromising the fundamental commitment to learning.

"Secularization"—to use Mr. Tollett's words—thus means that the organization, operation, and functions of the university are coming to be more nearly congruent with "secular" models (those of other social institutions, such as the civil service, industry, or labor unions) rather than being refined to advance the specific needs of an institution which is a "quasi enclave for the nurturance of learning."

One principal reason that the university's organization, operation, and functions are becoming more secular is quite simply that significant fractions of the population as a whole, government and civic leaders, and members of the university community have *rejected* the idea that the university is a quasi enclave in which other values are usually accommodated to the primary value placed on the nurturance of learning. The rejection is addressed explicitly to the idea of the university as an enclave and more covertly to the dominance of the value placed on the nurturance of learning. The rejection of the primacy of learning as a value shows itself, as Mr. Tollett suggests, by the advancing of other goals (such as the economic well-being of the faculty) as matters of equivalent or even greater importance.

And it is this rejection of these assumptions about the nature of higher education—rather than the surveillance or largesse of government per se—that leads to deep conflicts in the relationship between government and universities.

GOVERNMENT IN THE ENCLAVE OF LEARNING

In analyzing the relationship between faculty and the government, it is important to distinguish *who* in the equation (if anyone) is seeking to expand the role of government in higher education, and who is rejecting the idea of the university as a partial enclave in which learning is treated as a dominant value. Is it the government itself? Is it the public, seeking laws from the government which reflect that rejection? Is it administration? Or faculties, seeking to import into the university legal remedies previously not applied to academe?

I would submit that the primary locus of rejection of this value differs, depending upon whether one is discussing the role of government in the maintenance or dismantling of tenure, in the development of collective bargaining, or in the rise of affirmative action programs. In the area of collective bargaining, for example, the role of government seems to me to be secondary to the role played by contending groups within higher education itself. (It may be argued, of course, that legislative power to appropriate funds places government first in this area as well and that faculty claims for unionization to win economic gains arise from the scarcity of resources available to the institution. Indeed, it may also be argued that any large-scale administrative challenges to tenure most often also arise out of economic necessity.)

But in the third area—that of affirmative action—it seems to me the role of government has been far more active than in either of the other two and has been far more provoked by problems within the society than within higher education itself. Perhaps because of this, I suspect that it is within the area of affirmative action that confrontation between government and universities over what shall be the dominant values in higher education is, and will continue to be, the sharpest.

Tenure cases, such as *Roth v. Board of Regents of State Colleges,* require a plaintiff within the university who challenges university procedures in the courts. Collective bargaining is normally initiated by groups of university employees who seek representation. Affirmative action programs, however, are required by Executive order for all public and private universities holding federal contracts of $50,000 or more and employing more than fifty persons. Thus government assumes regulatory power in the employment practices of higher education without regard to the presence or absence of complaint and without a finding of violation of antidiscrimination laws. Drafts of guidelines for enforcement of title ix of the Higher Education Amendments Act of 1972 suggest that somewhat similar supervision of practices regarding students may also be in preparation.

Affirmative action plans required by the Department of Health, Education, and Welfare under Revised Order No. 4 call for a complete analysis of the work force by job category and the establishing of goals and timetables for achieving a representation of women and minorities in all categories equivalent to the representation of qualified women and minorities in the recruitment area. The proposed revision of EEOC *Guidelines on Employee Selection Procedures* calls for a complete analysis of the duties of every position in the university work force—from president to janitor—and validation of all "tests," qualification requirements, or selection procedures in terms of the described duties of each position. No guidelines have appeared from the Wage and Hour Division of the Department of Labor concerning the recent extension of the Equal Pay Act to professional employees. Thus higher education still needs assurances from the Labor Department—as yet not forthcoming—that review of quality by departmental peers is an appropriate means of determining salaries, that salary equity will be determined within departments and not across departmental lines, and that the general practice in salary setting (rather than a single high salary) will be used to establish appropriate salary levels in an equity review.

All three of these agencies—HEW, EEOC, and the Wage and Hour

Division—have a mandate to review university employment practices and to withhold contracts or initiate court procedures to ensure compliance with agency requirements. Thus it becomes of crucial importance that these agencies recognize the special function of the university as an enclave in which excellence in learning is the paramount value.

There is ample evidence that government recognition of this special function is sporadic. Let me enumerate some of the consequent dangers:

• Efforts to assimilate the university to an industrial model or to treat it as an educational assembly line in which the product is the student and the "job" is meeting a specified number of hours of classes. (What one holding this view would regard as "validation" of the requirements for a teaching position might differ significantly from what a professor in a fine small liberal arts college would regard as valid requirements.)

• Bureaucratization of higher education. (As occupants of an "enclave," professors have been largely freed from administrative documentation to devote time to research and teaching. Wholesale data requirements collected routinely rather than in response to specific needs could threaten professors with a choice between abandoning governance responsibilities and devoting increasing amounts of time to documentation of practices.)

• Insistence upon centralized personnel procedures that remove hiring authority from departments and academic deans best qualified to make judgments on qualifications within the academic field.

• Introduction of inflexible salary schedules which place more emphasis on seniority than excellence, as a guard against charges of salary inequity.

• Intensification of emphasis on quantity rather than evaluation of quality in research.

THE COMPATIBILITY OF AFFIRMATIVE ACTION IN ACADEME

It is at this point that our opening examination of the definition of higher education becomes critical. The real goals of affirmative action are completely compatible with the goals of higher education. More: a commitment to learning and to selection on the basis of excellence in learning positively requires that the university community actively root out those stereotyped expectations and limitations on opportunity which stifle the achievements and contributions of women and minority members of the community. The bitter fact is that the mountains of statistical documentation tell some truths. We have failed to hire as professors in proportionate numbers the women to whom we have awarded highest honors in doctoral study. We have failed to provide minority students and women with the minority and female professors whose presence, studies show, is directly correlated with the decision of students to enter professional fields. We have failed to bring the recruitment message to women and minorities necessary to counteract the years of disincentives to professional aspirations. And in these failures we have refused to acknowledge the responsibility of our function: to seek the highest degree of excellence in learning and the most effective means of bringing about the highest achievement in learning among those the university community serves.

Higher education should not pass to government officials, whose principal values may be social justice or political expediency, the task of assuring that higher education provides equal opportunity in employment and education to all. What we in higher education must do is ensure that we apply our own standards of achieving excellence in learning—whether at the level of freshman physics or advanced research in the biochemistry of the cell. This means that we strip away unrelated expectations about the nature of the person we select and that we place an accurate value on the training and experience of persons whose vitae are not identical with that conventional for white males, for example, whose careers have been interrupted by childbearing or whose training may have included work in developing institutions.

Achieving a clearer focus on genuine qualifications and seeking persons from all backgrounds who have those qualifications is precisely what affirmative action means. And it is here that it becomes evident that Mr. Tollett's own allegiance to the learning value requires him to exhibit equal commitment to affirmative action for women and for minorities. Indeed, his lamentable unconcern for the need for affirmative action for women would have the most serious consequences for black women. The professional and economic disability of being minority or being female is very real. Minority females experience a double disadvantage. According to Department of Labor Statistics, in 1972 unemployment for adults was lowest for white males (4 percent) and highest for minority women (8.7 percent). All teenagers are disadvantaged in seeking employment, but the same pattern obtains: white boys have the lowest unemployment rate (15.1 percent) and minority teenage girls the highest (35.5 percent). In average salaries now white men are first, black men second, white women third, and black women last. A large portion of the discrepancy is attributable to sex, not race. The average woman worker has completed 12.5 years of school as compared to 12.4 for men. But in 1970 the median earnings of women workers ($5,323) was only 59.4 percent of that for men ($8,966). This problem is particularly acute on American faculties. Among the doctorates awarded in the last four years by the largest and highest rated American graduate schools, 22 percent in bacteriology and 21 percent in biochemistry went to women. There is a similarly high rate of availability in many other disciplines, for example, 23 percent in anatomy, 29 percent in classics, 8.5 percent in chemistry, 17 percent in communication arts, 13 percent in history, 28 percent in English, 41 percent in French, 5.5 percent in mathematics. Yet few major departments show anything similar to this representation on their faculties.

If we are committed to furthering the learning enterprise by selecting on the basis of quality, we *must* be committed to using the full resources of qualified women (nonminority *and* minority) as well as to increasing the utilization of black males. What is more, the alleged competition between white women and minority males (with, too often, little attention directed to minority females) is more perception than reality. Discrimination affecting minorities has soaked so deeply into the social structure that—relative to need—few minorities have been able to obtain the credentials for faculty appointment. We must seek out those who exist, but we must go far beyond this step to train the minority graduate students who will become the faculty members in the next decade.

There is already in many disciplines an abundant (and increasingly restive) supply of women doctorates eagerly seeking appointment to the faculty. Conversely, in some fields (although not in others) less remains to be done in the way of opening graduate opportunities for women. As a practical reality, white women and minorities are rarely actually in direct competition. But what is more, such competition is alien to what affirmative action must be: there are no "special slots" set aside to be fought over by white women and minority males. Rather there must be a careful and equitable review of the genuine and relevant credentials of available persons for all positions, with the goal that white women, minority women, and minority males will all be selected in numbers approximately equal to their availability.

In achieving this goal, the higher education university will make more real its commitment to excellence in learning. More: higher education will begin to be able to avert the danger of a governmental review which brings inappropriate values to an assessment of its hiring practices. The best foundation for resisting governmental prescription in affirmative action is a record of achievement in equal opportunity. It is time—and past time—to take up the challenge.

Effects of Collective Bargaining Laws on Institutional Processes

DEXTER L. HANLEY, S.J.

MY COMMENTS WILL BE LIMITED to faculty-government relations in collective bargaining and will highlight a few specifics of the general thrust of Professor Tollett's paper.

First, it is important to distinguish between the public and the private sectors while recognizing how issues and trends in one sector make ripples in the other. The laws governing collective bargaining in the two sectors are quite different in many specifics. The bargaining in private colleges and universities is subject to the National Labor Relations Act, whereas in public institutions it is subject to differing state laws. Into the higher education sector, the NLRA introduces many concepts from industrial unionization, whereas most of the applicable state laws have grown out of the legitimation of collective bargaining for public employees. But higher education is really a different creature and, as such, may find it hard simultaneously to digest the variant principles designed for other institutions. I emphatically concur in the suggestion that legislation should be made sensitive to the peculiar conditions of academe.

There are some special pressures that have led to the unionization of faculties in public institutions. Chief among these, in my judgment, is a perceived need to compete for available funds in the legislative budgets. A certain round-robin effect develops as each college feels that funds which might go elsewhere will not be available for its own salaries and programs. A concomitant is the injection of legislative and executive state authority into the bargaining process, a situation quite different from that found in the private institutions. To some extent, faculty and administrative positions merge vis-à-vis the governmental agencies. The growth of unions in the public sector is not without outside repercussions.

The belief increases that the unions are capable of gaining large economic benefits—a belief that is not yet substantiated but that, in the private sector, may step up the trend toward unionization.

Arbitration also has different effects in each sector. Based on laws governing public employees, the right to strike may be limited and may be compensated for by the introduction of one or another form of *interest* arbitration. In the public sector, the legislature which strikes this balance is also the forum which can appropriate funds from the public treasury. In the private sector, however, such interest arbitration could serve to equalize salaries but not afford a means by which salary increases could be paid. I commend Robert G. Howlett's article "Contract Negotiation Arbitration in the Public Sector."[1] He argues persuasively that legislated interest arbitration in the public sector may serve the public interest although it might damage the usual process of collective bargaining. He does not deal with the specific issues of higher education, but inasmuch as many state laws affecting education are modeled on the more general public employee statutes, interest arbitration may become a commonplace. If so, it will have effects on faculty demands, the process of bargaining, and the relationships of administration and faculty. Likewise, there will be a growing demand for such arbitration in the private sector, even though the underlying rationale may be absent. Contrariwise, it is possible that the ability of faculty at private schools to strike will create pressure in the public sector to grant the same right to faculty members under the state laws.

One 1973 case[2] points out dramatically the possible differences that varying laws may have on the collective bargaining process. Under the federal law, an employer and a certified union must bargain with respect to "wages, hours and other terms and conditions of employment." Although there are mandatory and permissive subjects for bargaining, the mandatory subjects involve a broad and ever-widening spectrum. The applicable Pennsylvania statute, after affirming in similar language the obligation to bargain, says that public employers shall not be required to bargain over matters of inherent managerial policy, which shall include but not be limited to such areas of discretion or policy as the functions and programs of the public employer, standards of services, its overall budget, utilization of technology, the organizational structure, and selec-

---

1. *University of Cincinnati Law Review* 42 (1973): 47.
2. State College Education Ass'n v. Pennsylvania Labor Relations Board, 306 A.2d 404 (Commonwealth Ct., June 6, 1973).

tion and direction of personnel. The recent case dealt with the interpretation of these sections, and the court held that many issues which were proposed by the union were not the subject of collective bargaining between the public school teachers and the school board. Among the issues not so subject were the availability of adequate classroom instructional printed materials, timely notice of teaching assignment for the coming year, elimination of the requirement that teachers chaperone athletic activities, and provision for maximum class sizes. Of course, in other jurisdictions these might well be matters for bargaining, and I would hazard that they are under the NLRA. If the case is upheld by higher courts, the effect in Pennsylvania will be to cause a different alignment of faculty and governmental forces than exists elsewhere. Of particular interest in this regard will be the formation of faculty agencies which can deal with the matters not on the bargaining table.

One agency that has dealt with these matters in the past has been the faculty or university senate. Collective bargaining has had and will have its effects in governance and on the senates. The final report of the Carnegie Commission on Higher Education indicates "that the structures of governance for higher education in the United States are adequate as they now exist, with the need for improvements rather than for basic reform."[3] Nevertheless, if collective bargaining becomes a norm, some, if not all, of the issues usually referred to a senate will be subject to negotiations between the administration and the union. Where, as in Pennsylvania, the subjects of bargaining are limited to nonmanagerial areas, these may be the subject of continuing collegial discussion. Under the broader mandates of other legislation, the union powers will be correspondingly greater. It will be difficult to determine which areas of decision making should be the prerogatives of the governing board, the administration, and established governance systems, such as faculty senates, and which should be subjects for negotiation.[4] There are differing opinions about the future role of senates under the impact of legislation and collective bargaining. There are those who feel that a faculty union will be willing to limit negotiations to economic issues and that on other matters it may conveniently sit on both sides of the bargaining

---

3. *Priorities for Action: Final Report of the Carnegie Commission on Higher Education* (New York: McGraw-Hill, 1973), p. 57.

4. See Alan C. Coe, "A Study of the Procedures Used in Collective Bargaining with Faculty Unions in Public Universities," *Journal of the College and University Personnel Association,* September 1972, pp. 1–25.

table. Others insist that no bargaining model can successfully give the faculty two bites at the apple and that the need for stability and a minimal level of controversy will work against such bifurcation.[5] Although this brief paper does not permit these questions to be analyzed here, they are among the most important arising out of a consideration of the faculty and the government.

At this point it is appropriate to consider the *Seton Hill College* case, decided by the National Labor Relations Board.[6] Although the decision affects only a portion of the faculties in church-related institutions, it dramatizes the effect of governmental regulation in academe. The effect of this case was to separate the religious teachers at Seton Hill College from the rest of the faculty and to exclude them from the definition of the appropriate unit for an election. The basic reason for the exclusion of the religious teachers from the defined unit was that, by reason of their vows and commitments, they returned some of their salaries to the college for college use. This practice was deemed by the Board to constitute such divergent interest as to make it inappropriate that they be in the same union as their lay colleagues. My conclusion is that the decision is constitutionally untenable and educationally unsound. However, I shall not argue the merits of the case here. What I stress is that, under the color of the NLRA, the Board has created a situation where a substantial number of the teaching faculty can be excluded from a bargaining unit. Their professional interests will not be heard by the union. As a matter of fact, it is possible that the union could bargain so as to exclude a nonunion group of religious from performing the teaching tasks which are the subject of bargaining between the college and the union. The possibility of this kind of division of faculty interests is, to me, frightening. Clearly in this instance, if collegial arrangements cede to negotiations under law, divisions will be created that could be reminiscent of other interunion rivalries.

In closing, I step outside of the field of collective bargaining to make a brief observation. One area that needs further study and evaluation is the effect of funding legislation on the true autonomy of the faculty in selecting curricula and on the functions of a university in offering education. The power of the purse string is well known, and

---

5. A perceptive discussion of these issues is Bernard Jay Williams, "Faculty Bargaining: Exclusive Representation and the Faculty Senate," *Journal of the College and University Personnel Association*, September 1973, pp. 45–56.

6. 201 NLRB No. 155 (1973); 82 LRRM 1434.

there is at least a possibility that more real faculty power is eroded by the need to seek government funding than has ever occurred in faculty-student-administrative confrontations.

The Hazards of Legal Perspectives

WILLIAM W. VAN ALSTYNE

MY IMPULSE HAS BEEN TO COMMENT on one of Professor Tollett's topics in greater detail. Each topic is obviously related to particular *legal* developments of the past several years, and it appears appropriate to draw on my professional familiarity with those developments in order to clarify Tollett's more general review. I readily acknowledge that the legal questions involved are legitimate objects of concern, but I doubt that any significant elaboration of the law of tenure, collective bargaining, or affirmative action can be compressed into a brief comment. The law journals are available and full of information on these subjects, and nearly all colleges and universities have recourse to retained counsel and the resources of several agencies in coming to terms with the legal requirements.

I have become concerned by what strikes me as a common error in the uses made by the intrinsic partisanship of purely legal perspectives in addressing problems in higher education. It may, therefore, be helpful to emphasize the limitations of those perspectives. The difficulty is implicit in a cultural feature common to the subjects Tollett has reviewed in light of legal processes, exogenous to each university, which seem to divide academic communities into adversary interests. Professor Tollett emphasized this tendency particularly with respect to collective bargaining, but it surely applies as well to emerging conflicts over tenure systems and affirmative action plans.

A certain amount of partisanship based on legalisms may be unavoidable in light of the leveling-off of college enrollments, straitened financial circumstances, and a consequential concern dividing faculties from administrations in rival anxieties over professional security and institutional solvency. However, I believe that an unnecessary degree of estrangement and adversary realignment, separating faculties from administrations more than either honestly desires, stems from a misperception by administrations that whatever the law permits an institution to do, especially as advised by legal counsel, it virtually must do as a matter of strict prudence and self-defense. Yet such prudence may well turn out to be terribly mistaken and likely to encourage the adversary relations we would all hope otherwise to avoid. What I have in mind is how some institutions have seized the advantage of a seemingly important and favorable decision in the Supreme Court on the constitutional helplessness of untenured faculty members (to which Professor Tollett adverts). The following parable will illustrate. Exactly as it may appear offensive and overdrawn, it may seem so because there are those who have encountered no tendency in their own institution to substitute whatever arrangement the law will tolerate for a more thoughtful determination of what is independently defensible in an academic community.

Once upon a time, about 1894, a student was expelled from a college for "unbecoming conduct." Upon asking what she had done that was unbecoming, she was referred to a catalogue containing a clause which provided that the college need not explain what it might mean nor, indeed, provide any means to determine whether what the college had heard the student might have done had actually occurred.

Finding herself barred as well from other colleges (none wanted to admit anyone elsewhere expelled for "unbecoming conduct"), and being from a family with money to spend in such an effort, the student brought an action at law to see whether the law would permit a college to treat her so rudely. After hearing argument by respective counsel retained in the case, and after considering and pondering each precedent the attorneys pressed upon his honor, the court decided that the law did indeed permit a college so to conduct itself. Whether it should—whether the court might personally wonder at a college which would want to treat its students in this fashion—was not of course necessary for it to say. It was enough for the law that the student was denied nothing the college had promised, and, accordingly, whatever the justice of the matter, the law could itself require nothing more.

What became of this student is not recorded. It is recorded, however, that learned counsel for other colleges, well pleased to hear of this case as it might also be of benefit to their clients, were quick to demonstrate the value of their services by bringing it to the attention of their own administrations. Desiring not to be less well off or less secure than the first college which had had the foresight of including such a clause in its catalogue, all the other colleges quickly produced similar clauses of their own.

Years went by, until several decades later when a different student was expelled from a different college under circumstances much the same as in the case of the first student. Being unaware of the "precedent" of the law, however, and similarly distressed in wanting to know what the law would say about such a college, this student also went to court. To the chagrin of lawyers who had helped the college "protect" itself by placing the same sort of clause in its catalogue, the court was unimpressed, swept the clause aside, and ordered that the student be reinstated at once: a contract of adhesion, containing an unconscionable term imitated by a veritable oligopoly of colleges acting in conscious parallelism to deny students any reason or consideration before turning them out at the gates, was contrary to enlightened public policy and would no longer be recognized by the law.

It is also recorded that other colleges, which had similarly attempted to secure every advantage they thought the law might possibly allow, had meantime come to regret the alacrity with which they had incorporated that advantage. For many of these were ravaged by disruptions and demonstrations, embarrassed by unflattering publicity generated by embittered students, and given for many months on end to ceaseless meetings, conferences, and time-consuming confrontations in efforts to explain why they felt it appropriate to have such clauses and why they thought it fair to treat students in this peremptory way.

In 1969, an untenured faculty member was given peremptory notice that he was not to be "reemployed" by his college for the next year (or any other year, for that matter). Upon asking what it was that accounted for the college's disappointment with his work, the faculty member was referred to a catalogue that the college need not explain what it might have had in mind nor, indeed, provide any means to determine whether what it had heard about the faculty member might not actually be true.

Finding himself hard pressed to secure an opening elsewhere (it was a time of a "buyer's market," and other colleges were reluctant to take a chance on a person summarily dropped from a relatively undistinguished college after only the first year of teaching), the faculty member brought an action at law to see whether the law would permit a college to treat him in this fashion. After hearing lengthy argument by respective counsel retained in the case and pondering each precedent the attorneys pressed upon them, in 1972 the justices of the Supreme Court decided (by a vote of five to three) that the law did indeed permit the college so to conduct itself. Whether it should—whether it was in the best interests of higher education for a public institution so to treat the careers of untenured faculty—the Court explicitly went out of its way to disclaim. Indeed, in a closing paragraph it went out of its way to cite the specific recommendations of the American Association of University Professors as a source of procedures which institutions of higher learning were invited to consider in their treatment of untenured faculty members. On the narrow question of law, however, the Court observed that as the college had conferred no "property" upon the faculty member in terms of any year beyond the first, it consequently had "deprived" him of no "property" and thus it had no duty to act with any "due process" which the Constitution would ordinarily require.

What became of this faculty member is not recorded. It is recorded, however, that learned counsel for other colleges, well pleased to hear of this case as it might also be of benefit to their clients, were quick to demonstrate the value of their services by bringing it to the attention of their own administrations.

Legislating Attitudes

THEODORE M. HESBURGH, C.S.C.

HIGHER EDUCATION CAME INTO THE 1970s with a certain number of built-in inequities. One often hears the question, "Can we really legislate attitudes on the part of institutions and individuals, especially to remove inequities?" To me, this is an old and familiar question. We heard precisely the same question at the beginning of the 1960s, when American society was still characterized by built-in structural inequities for most minorities. I can remember even a President of the United States saying, "What this really needs is a change of heart and that can't be legislated."

We did, in fact, remove many inequities in the 1960s, maybe not in hearts, but at least through new structures. And we did it by legislation. Not just by any kind of legislation, but legislation that was effective, that had teeth in it.

Memories tend to be short, so I shall illustrate. For more than two hundred years in America, blacks had not been allowed to use the same public facilities and accommodations as whites. This was true of hotels, of trains and buses, of drinking fountains, restaurants, rest rooms, beaches, cemeteries, movie houses, and so on. These restrictions were a built-in part of the life, mores, and century-old customs of all of the Southern and border states, and there were similar practices in many of the Northern states. If we had waited for a change of heart, we would still be waiting. But despite the enormous pressures in the opposite direction, this whole cultural situation was changed in one single day by one single piece of legislation.

The legislation was not just ordinary legislation, but legislation with sanctions built into it. The federal Civil Rights Act of 1964 specified that whatever service was provided for the public had to be provided for *all* the public, not just the white public. The sanction was simple. Either facilities and accommodations that were open to the public would be open to all the public or they would be closed. Curiously enough, practically none was shut down, a notable exception being the chicken restaurant in Georgia run by the future governor of that state.

A CLIMATE FOR CHANGE

One could legitimately ask, "How did this happen so easily?" One reason, I suspect, was that the time was ripe. Everyone understood the inequities of the past situation, when a dozen times every day a black citizen had to face insult and indignity, had to be reminded that he was inferior, not a full-fledged citizen, not a real part of American society. No one person, no one institution could change that situation; no leadership—no matter how strong in the presidency or in the governor's office or in the office of the mayor of a large city—could change it. Only one thing could change it: only federal legislation would affect the whole country and would have enough built-in sanctions to make it effective. Such legislation was passed in 1964, and the situation changed overnight.

One may argue whether or not attitudes were changed along with the customs and practices. I have to admit that perhaps hearts were not really touched, but there must have been some overall consensus in the hearts of men that allowed the change to happen peacefully, effectively, and immediately once the law was passed. The very fact that the law could be passed also says something about the national state of mind of the moment and a national recognition that attitudes were ready to be changed, at least insofar as their practical applications were concerned.

Other changes of practice by legislation could be noted in regard to voting, education, housing, employment, and the administration of justice. It would take this discussion too far afield to pursue each of these areas in detail, but the simple fact is: There were widespread inequities in each of these fields. They were accepted, practiced widely, and no one individual person or locality or state had much intention of changing the inequitable situation. However, the situation in each of these areas was changed and changed quite effectively once there was legislation to the contrary. Some situations took longer than others to change and some are still in the period of transition, but the thrust of change is clear and in every case the motive for change was legislation. I should add that legislation in many cases is also educative. It not only indicates what must be changed, but also why. I believe that too often we denigrate the law and underestimate its value as an educator. Once the law is operative and effective, it also educates by proving wrong all of the previous myths that said, "It can't work." Once it does work, you have a better argument:

Contra factum non datur argumentum, "It's impossible to argue against a fact." As Senator Tower, who voted against most civil rights legislation, said: "I had some fears it might be used by government to harass people and that some of it was a marked departure from constitutionality—the rights of individuals with freedom of choice. My worst fears, I must confess, were not realized and it has really not been that bad."[1]

The Progress of Change in Higher Education

Curiously enough, it was in the field of education that change was most difficult, even after legislation had been passed. It was declared in the 1954 *Brown* case that the dual system of black and white public education in the South was unconstitutional and must be changed. Ten years went by with only 3 percent change throughout the Southern states. Again, legislation became the motive force. The Civil Rights Act of 1964 included title VI, which stated that unless action was forthcoming, federal funds would be cut off from the public educational institutions in the South that did not follow the mandate of the *Brown* decision of the Supreme Court.

Again sanctions did what a judicial decision alone could not do. And the sanctions had to be part of the legislation process. Title VI of the 1964 Civil Rights Act, after only five years of operation, was able to bring about integration in 40 percent of the formerly dual public school systems in the South and during the next year in about 70 percent. In five years, good legislation with built-in sanctions was able to do what a decision of the Supreme Court of the United States had been unable to do in ten years.

Again, one may ask whether attitudes were changed, but certainly the change took place. Those who are close to the situation perceive a great change in attitude over the ensuing years, especially when it was proved by demonstration that integration could work and did have values that were lacking in the former dual school system. It must also be noted that the South has made much more progress in this area than the North. The North, by taking refuge in a de facto situation, strives to elude the clear mandate of the 1954 *Brown* decision, which spoke primarily to a de jure situation. The distinction between the de facto and the de jure situations is dubious at best, inasmuch as actions of the federal government deeply affected the housing situation in the North that led to segregated schooling for the majority of whites and blacks. Again, I believe

1. *Washington Post,* April 15, 1973.

that legislative leadership is needed to accomplish in the North what has in larger measure been accomplished in the South.

In the field of higher education, enormous progress was made during the 1960s. In the early 1960s, many state universities in the South had not a single black student, and, in the West, I can recall a hearing of the Civil Rights Commission, in San Francisco, when we established that there were only twenty-nine Chicano students in the whole of the University of California's Berkeley student body. Everyone can remember the crises of Autherine Lucy at the University of Alabama and of James Meredith at the University of Mississippi. Somehow those episodes seem light-years away and even somewhat silly, but the fact remains: these two students were the first of their kind to integrate what were formerly all-white campuses. Again, the law made the difference. Once the law clearly threatened to withhold federal funds, massive integration took place in the institutions of higher education in the South, and today literally thousands of black students throughout the region are enrolled in institutions which formerly did not have a single black. As for the Chicano experience, at one point a few years ago the University of California, Los Angeles, enrolled more Chicano first-year law students than there were Chicano lawyers in Los Angeles County. Again, law led the way and, whether or not it changed attitudes, it certainly changed practice and performance.

ENFORCEMENT OF LEGISLATED CHANGE

Today we face an entirely new situation in higher education wherein the inequities are not so much in the student body as in the staff, and affect not so much minorities among student bodies as minorities in staff and faculty appointments. There is also one great new dimension. Although women are not a minority but, rather, a majority in the population at large, they are a small minority on the faculty and staffs of our universities, especially in the higher echelons. Once again, one may ask whether or not the law can bring some relief to the situation. In actuality, the situation is more and more covered by the civil rights laws and Executive orders. Only last year, sex discrimination was made one of the concerns of the U.S. Commission on Civil Rights, in addition to race, religion, color, and national origin. However, the biggest stick in this area at the moment is the 1965 Executive Order 11246, as amended by Executive Order 11375, which clearly prohibits discrimination in employment on account of sex.

A few short years ago, these laws and the Executive orders began to be implemented by inquiries from the Department of Health, Education, and Welfare. Initial inquiries at the University of Michigan were followed in quick order by others in Wisconsin and a whole series of Midwestern universities, including my own, Notre Dame. The East Coast did not escape either, with great concern being voiced at many universities, particularly Columbia. Once again, the question arises, Can this problem be solved by legislation? Most of the legislation already exists. The question is, Can it be enforced? Here again I must fall back on my fifteen years' experience as a member and latterly chairman of the U.S. Commission on Civil Rights. It is not enough simply to have legislation. The legislation must have teeth and the teeth must bite. Enforcement is the key to the effectiveness of legislation. Where there is effective enforcement, and especially where the means of enforcement included in the legislation are used, then action takes place and quickly.

I believe that, in the matter of assuring women and minorities an adequate place on the faculty and staffs of higher educational institutions, it will be enormously important that enforcement, as currently sanctioned in the law, actually take place. Whether it will or will not is an open question at the moment. There have been the initial movements and the countermovements by those who feel set upon by the new demands of women and minorities. However, the long-range realities, I believe, are in favor of both minorities and women and should be honored as soon as possible. I have no doubt that there will be anguished cries of "quotas" and whatever other code words are devised, but justice is on the side of women and minorities, and, in the long run, I believe they will prevail. Personally, I prefer the word "goals" to "quotas" because the latter word carries overtones of past inequities. But even goals are useless without leadership, energy, and initiative in reaching them.

Let no one believe that reaching even goals is a simple matter. In the one institution I know best, if 50 percent of the new appointments were made in favor of women over the next twenty years, we would still only have 22 percent representation of women on the faculty. The reason is, of course, that we are starting from a very low base, and although any progress is progress, even great progress from the starting position turns out to be little. This reason alone makes it even more important that we give serious attention to this matter, whether or not we are impelled by the imperatives of legislation and the sanctions the legislation includes or, more important, by the inherent demands of the simple justice that should characterize an institution of higher learning.

Honesty impels me to state that at this point it is an illusion to equate the problems of blacks and Chicanos with those of women. If and when women put their minds and efforts seriously to the solution of the inequalities that exist between themselves and men (not a one-way street), they will make rapid progress in righting the wrongs, as is now beginning to happen. Not so for the deep-rooted inequities that blacks—men and more especially women—suffer. The color problem is far more difficult of solution, far more influenced by deep-seated prejudice than the problem of gender. We must try to solve all problems of injustice in human society, but we had better recognize that while all are not now equal, neither are the problems of blacks and women equal.

Life in higher education would certainly be easier and more decent if one could always assume that justice would be the order of the day and that inequities would be done away with whether or not one were impelled by the sanctions of the law to do so. However, I think the present situation is clear evidence that: (1) a law is needed; (2) it must be accompanied by adequate sanctions; and (3) there must be adequate enforcement of the sanctions to see that the law is in fact obeyed and observed by those very institutions which civilize and, therefore, promote lawful society. Justice does indeed impel us all, but the law sees that justice is spelled out in detail and the sanctions of the law allow us no escape from justice if the law is indeed enforced by those who have the responsibility to do so. Aristotle said that law is intelligence without passion. I would add, perhaps more cynically than I would like to, that the earlier strict enforcement of civil rights laws seems now to be giving way to myriad forms of evasion which will be practiced to perfection unless administrators with a passion for justice, both in government and in higher education, see that justice prevails in our institutions.

My personal conviction is that law can indeed change attitudes if it is good law, administered by good men and women. These persons, whoever else they may be, must also and always be the chief academic and administrative officers of our institutions of higher learning. One can never be absolutely certain of leading or of leading wisely, but the path is clear today if one is determined to lead justly. One must only and simply follow the law and help it work. If it does—and it can—then attitudes too will change.

Legislating Attitudes: A Response

DAVID B. FROHNMAYER

IN THE FIELD OF CIVIL RIGHTS, Father Hesburgh is an exemplar for our society. He has spoken and acted against the grotesque injustices of racial discrimination and the waste of human resources typified by the under-utilization of the talents and brainpower of the American woman. In addressing the broad topic "Legislating Attitudes," Father Hesburgh has fulfilled a dual role of saying something important generally about the role and limits of law in our society, and something quite specific about how the revolution in attitudes and law concerning human rights has affected the American campus.

This topic is vast and intimidating. It draws one into estimating the utility of social science research in formulating public policy. It poses profound jurisprudential questions regarding the meaning and implementation of distributive and compensatory justice. And it requires the skills of a social psychologist to assess attitude formation and change in response to legislative action. In venturing to invade such varied disciplines, one necessarily risks speaking as a presumptuous dilettante rather than as a responsible scholar.

On reflection I find a troublesome ambivalence in Father Hesburgh's message. Did the civil rights laws of 1964 really change attitudes? Or rather did the enactment of those laws itself faithfully reflect an already changed national consensus: a new conscience born of court decisions, the murder of civil rights workers, the bombing of a Birmingham church, televised close-ups of Bull Connor's outrageous brand of cattle-prod justice, and the eloquent rhetoric of a young black pastor who challenged the nation to conform to its professed ideals of liberty and equality?

Such ambivalence in tracing the operations of cause and effect in the law is hardly unique. A. V. Dicey's seminal lectures on *Law and Public Opinion in England* struggled with these ambiguities two generations ago:

> Laws foster or create law-making opinion.
>
> This assertion may sound, to one who has learned that laws are the outcome of public opinion, like a paradox; when properly understood it is nothing but an undeniable though sometimes neglected truth. . . . [T]he influence of law on opinion . . . is merely one example of the way

in which the development of political ideas is influenced by their connection with political facts. Of such facts laws are among the most important; they are therefore the cause, at least, as much as the effect of legislative opinion.[1]

Can we really legislate attitudes? Does new law change reluctant hearts? The typical law professor's response must be: It depends. Sometimes legislation can and should; in other instances, the very attempt to legislate attitudes may have invidious consequences. I justify my own equivocation on this topic in a series of working hypotheses. These propositions may restate the obvious, but they nonetheless deserve explicit articulation.

My first proposition is in agreement with an important thrust of Father Hesburgh's paper. *The law unquestionably constitutes an enormously powerful educative vehicle.* The accomplished political fact of legislation itself often resolves bitterly contested social issues with official finality. Our society no longer reopens questions concerning the entitlement to social security, the right to strike, and, it is hoped, the right to be free of racial discrimination. Social change is legitimated by law. With the educative function comes a legitimating one as well: The perceived response of legislative institutions—sometimes even a symbolic response —gives aggrieved social groups a feeling that the larger society is capable of respecting their aspirations.

My second proposition is a caveat to the first, and would require volumes to elaborate properly: *The degree to which law can change attitudes is a function of at least the following variables: the extent to which legislators have grasped the complexity of a condition of genuine injustice and addressed it; the persistence, evenhandedness, and procedural fairness of the enforcement process; the precision with which appropriate sanctions are fashioned and invoked; the quality of statesmanship in the affected community; and the degree to which competing values are, or are perceived to be, threatened or compromised.*[2]

Without question there are other powerful variables which are also significant, including the presence or absence of articulate elites supporting or opposing the change; the economic bread-and-butter implications of the change; and the verbalization of the change as "alien" or already intrinsic in old ideological commitments.

---

1. 2d ed. (1914), pp. 41, 47.
2. Many of these factors are thoughtfully assessed in Harrell R. Rodgers and Charles S. Bullock, *Law and Social Change: Civil Rights Laws and Their Consequences* (New York: McGraw-Hill, 1972), chap. 8.

DIFFICULTIES OF ENFORCEMENT ON CAMPUS

To a large degree these caveats and conditions explain why civil rights enforcement on campus has caused the anguish that Father Hesburgh so accurately described.

Let me elaborate on each of the conditions. In the first place, the principal vehicles of civil rights enforcement on campus are not legislative in the traditional sense at all. We speak of legislating attitudes when often we have legislated only ambiguity. Congress far too frequently has not resolved the problem; it has simply delegated vital policy decisions to relatively faceless administrative agencies. Therefore, questions of enforcing civil rights on campus are less problems of obtaining abstract attitudinal commitment to the noble purposes of the law than of obtaining agreement on the legitimacy of specific enforcement techniques in an area of vast and relatively unconstrained administrative discretion. Colleges and universities are not "legislating attitudes": they are "administering" them; and there is a vast difference in the legitimacy that the latter process can command.

The powerful *Guidelines* of the Equal Employment Opportunity Commission were never debated or legislated in Congress through the representative process; they are internally generated and unilaterally imposed by the agency.[3] Executive Orders 11246 and 11375, the prime vehicles for federal enforcement on campus to date, have only the barest and legally most questionable authorization in congressional statute.[4] But they are the source of a powerful "affirmative action" requirement which has vastly increased the federal presence and has dramatically changed academic employment procedures on the American campus.[5] As an admittedly skeptical but nonetheless often perceptive observer recently

---

3. See generally Blumrosen, "Strangers in Paradise: *Griggs* v. *Duke Power Co.* and the Concept of Employment Discrimination," *Michigan Law Review* 71 (1972): 59.

4. See Comment, "The Philadelphia Plan: A Study in the Dynamics of Executive Power," *University of Chicago Law Review* 39 (1972): 723.

5. It is worth noting that Labor Department officials a short four years ago could elaborate no uniform definition for the requirement of "affirmative action." Two short years ago, "affirmative action" requirements were suddenly rigidly defined and numerically measured by the "result-oriented" goals and timetables concepts of the Office of Federal Contract Compliance Revised Order No. 4 (41 C.F.R. Part. 60-2 [1971]). In no manner did this enormously significant alteration of enforcement practice become the subject of legislative enactment, let alone participation. Congressional reaction, to the extent it occurred, was largely negative. See generally Nash, "Affirmative Action under Executive Order 11246," *New York University Law Review* 46 (1971): 225.

put it: "Anyone looking for examples of the growing autonomy of the executive branch of the Federal government could do worse than focus on this quite unheralded administrative regulation."[6]

The remaining conditions can be elaborated even more summarily. It should not be surprising that the Executive order enforcement process generated confusion when it lacked any semblance of uniformity from region to region, when guidelines for its implementation were not promulgated for more than two years, and when the procedural safeguards of due process were utterly lacking in many instances where federal funds were withheld or where access to confidential university personnel records was summarily demanded.

I do not underestimate the importance of enlightened leadership on campus. The law dictates respect for genuine equality of employment opportunity, and the law cannot be evaded without mocking the ideals which American higher education has attemtped for decades to foster. It should be enough, by close analogy, to contrast the courageous leadership of a Governor Linwood Holton escorting his own child to a newly integrated public school in Virginia with the tragically misguided policy of "massive resistance" to which an Orville Faubus unthinkingly subscribed two decades ago in Little Rock.

ENFORCEMENT AND THE CONFLICT OF VALUES

But how, then, do we deal with the last of the conditions I have described: the degree to which other values are, or are perceived to be, compromised in the civil rights enforcement process? We can seldom legislate with such analytical purity that other values of potential importance are not inadvertently threatened. How does one reconcile the demand for endlessly detailed and formally promulgated internal university regulations and action plans with a well-founded distrust for bureaucratic complexity and the widely shared perception that "in a company of intellectuals, precise rules of behavior are nonsense?"[7] What is to be the fate of the peer review process as a technique for ensuring the maintenance of academic excellence in employment decisions? Do not the relentless demands by federal agencies for religious or ethnic identification of employees (see, for example, *Federal Register* 38 [Jan. 19, 1973: 1932])

---

6. D. Seligman, "How 'Equal Opportunity' Turned into Employment Quotas," *Fortune*, March 1973, p. 160.
7. Harlan Cleveland, "The Muscle-Bound Academy," *College Counsel* 6 (1972): 1, 2.

hopelessly compromise principles of privacy and other civil liberties? Decisions concerning professional employment, including the lifetime commitment of indefinite tenure, are vital and inescapably evaluative. Can procedures for the solicitation of confidential evaluations, which may seem to be an essential part of that process, continue to be utilized when ultimate decisions must be justified to the federal courts on the record in minute detail?[8]

The most explosive arena of competing values concerns the debate over whether setting "goals" for affirmative action performance involves the imposition of invidious employment quotas. Father Hesburgh sees this as a battle of "code words," an apparent semantic smoke screen which is used solely to impede the progress of human rights.

If I have not misrepresented Father Hesburgh, I at least disagree with him. The debate over the setting of employment quotas by race and sex is much more than a linguistic quibble: it implicates and perhaps contradicts fundamental concepts of justice and equality in our society. It therefore deserves to be examined openly. At least one federal court has been explicit, even while permitting ratio hiring:

> There has been much controversy in this area concerning the distinction between a quota hiring remedy, and a less rigid approach involving affirmative action toward a goal. *The distinction is ultimately illusory.* As the time to achieve the required goal approaches, members of the discriminated group must be hired in preference to a majority group person as often as required to meet the goal. A quota system, then, is simply a recognition of the reality encountered in reaching the desired goal. (Emphasis added.)[9]

Let us be clear about the stakes of the argument. Civil rights compliance is to be measured numerically and more or less rigidly by "result-

---

8. Under title VII of the Civil Rights Act of 1964, at least one federal district court (Johnson v. University of Pittsburgh, 5 FEP Cas. 1182 [W.D. Pa. May 31, 1973]) has seemingly required that the employer submit a detailed justification of an individual tenure decision. By contrast, the Supreme Court of the United States declined to require these steps under the due process clause of the Fourteenth Amendment (Board of Regents v. Roth, 408 U.S. 564 [1972]).

9. "Bridgeport Guardians, Inc. v. Bridgeport Civil Service Comm'n," *United States Law Week* 41 (D. Conn. 1/29/73): 2427, 2428.

Accord: Note, "Developments in the Law" Title VII, *Harvard Law Review* 84 (1971): 1109, 1301–2; Comment, "The Philadelphia Plan: Remedial Racial Classification in Employment," *Georgetown Law Journal* 58 (1970): 1187, 1194; Comment, "The Constitutionality of 'Affirmative Action' to Integrate the Construction Trades: The Philadelphia Plan," *Temple Law Quarterly* 43 (1970): 329, 333, "To call these 'goals' but not 'quotas' appears to be semantic gymnastics"; Note, "Executive Order 11246: Anti-Discrimination Obligations in Government Contracts," *New York University Law Review* 44 (1969): 590, 599, "Judging the adequacy of a contractor's efforts at compliance by quantitative results seems effectively to impose a duty which has been rejected in theory."

oriented" underutilization analysis concepts transplanted from industrial sector employment.[10] These techniques almost invariably create strong de facto pressures for preferential hiring on the basis of race or sex, as the ombudsman of the Department of Health, Education, and Welfare has candidly acknowledged.[11] It is not enough to respond, accurately, that women and minorities have been the objects of discrimination in the past. That is conceded. The issue is the form and scope of the legal remedy.

Dangers in Legislating Attitudes

The point is that there cannot be hope for legislating appropriate attitudes if the governing regulations themselves are so fraught with camouflaged analytical confusion that they render it impossible to undertake a law-abiding response. It is not yet really clear whether in higher education we have quotas, "soft quotas," "quotas which permit a good faith defense," goals, or "targets." The rhetoric of "affirmative action" may thus mask a vital unresolved policy question concerning the moral and legal justification for a reparations policy of compensatory justice in civil rights. There are powerful arguments for such an approach. But it represents a radical departure from conventional theories of distributive justice based on nondiscrimination and equality of opportunity. For that reason it deserves to be debated openly if the legislation of attitudes is indeed to be a principal object of the law.

This agreement is fundamental. On some important points we remain unsure of what attitudes we actually mean to legislate. Are we legislating equality or compensatory preference even at the cost of other measures of social or institutional goals? The ambiguity of choice and the potential areas where values are alleged to clash are witnessed in industry in the goal of productivity, in the academic world in the asserted primacy

10. As "availability" data become more complete, it may be questioned how effectively the underutilization technique will actually encourage equal opportunity. The most complete survey to date estimates that there are only 2,500 black Ph.D.'s in the nation (*Washington Post*, Aug. 30, 1973, p. A1). Even assuming that the Ph.D. is not invariably a bona fide occupational qualification for university employment, the paucity of numbers of available persons suggests that setting goals and timetables, by discipline or subdiscipline, for each of the nation's 2,500 colleges and universities can be accomplished only in terms of fractions of a person for the immediate future. Federal enforcement agencies are apparently aware of the problems of the supply side of the employment equation with respect to minorities, but have not reflected this awareness by differential techniques for the quite distinct problems of discrimination suffered by women and by minorities.

11. *Parade*, June 3, 1973, quoting Mr. Sam Solomon of HEW. Rather clearly these practices are subject to the "reverse discrimination" proscription of §703(a) and §703(j) of title VII of the Civil Rights Act of 1964.

of professional standards, and elsewhere in the principle of advancement on the basis of individual merit rather than group membership. These goals can often be a smoke screen for noncompliance, but the genuine clash of values may also often be present.

The third and final proposition of this necessarily brief examination and response is as follows: *We cannot always legislate attitudes directly, and we should sometimes avoid the attempt.* Law *can* create the catalytic conditions for attitude shifts over a longer time period.[12] Moreover, to take the minimum position, law can at least demand the conduct-oriented response often attributed to Frederick the Great: "Think what you want, but obey the law." To paraphrase Father Hesburgh, we need not always change hearts to give tangible redress through law to the victims of discrimination. Finally, in a pluralistic society in which values differ and often clash, we should be wary of efforts, some of which verge on totalitarian attempts at thought control, to impose a monolithic attitude through the mechanism of sanctions.

I urge this caution because I see the most difficult problems in civil rights enforcement on campus as questions largely of technique rather than abstract commitment. Do we really want to fossilize instrumental means into an ideology? I urge this restraint also because at some point there is a finite limit to the functions law can perform in our society. Spinoza put it bluntly: "He who tries to determine everything by law will foment crime rather than lessen it."[13] Profound legal philosophers of the last generation, Roscoe Pound and Morris R. Cohen,[14] have explored this problem with sensitivity. In our time we have seen corroboration both in important works of theoretical scholarship[15] and in specific ex-

12. "Laws in line with one's conscience are likely to be obeyed: when obeyed they still establish an ethical norm that holds before the individual an image of what his conduct should be" (Gordon W. Allport, *The Nature of Prejudice* [Garden City, N.Y.: Doubleday & Co., 1954], chap. 29). For evidence that law frequently has created new behavior patterns in civil rights areas, see authorities cited in Rodgers and Bullock, *Law and Social Change*, chap. 8.
13. *Tractatus Theologico-Politicus*, chap. 20.
14. Pound, "The Limits of Effective Legal Action," *American Bar Association Journal* 3 (1917): 55; *International Journal of Ethics* 27 (1917): 150. Cohen, "Positivism and the Limits of Idealism in the Law," *Columbia Law Review* 27 (1927): 237. Note, however, Cohen cites the failure to secure Fourteenth and Fifteenth Amendment rights to equality for the Negro as an example of the limits of law. Certainly the passage of the Civil Rights Act of 1964 suggests a more optimistic conclusion.
15. Herbert L. Packer, *The Limits of the Criminal Sanction* (Stanford, Calif.: Stanford University Press, 1968); cf. Karl Menninger, *The Crime of Punishment* (New York: Viking Press, 1969); H. L. Hart, *Law, Liberty and Morality* (Stanford, Calif.: Stanford University Press, 1963).

plorations of the failures of law to regulate attitudes (at least regulate them appropriately) with respect, for example, to drug use and the treatment of narcotics offenders.[16] All of these considerations suggest some outer limits to the sanction-oriented Benthamite "policeman at the elbow" theory to which Father Hesburgh appears to subscribe.

A brief focus on the pitfalls of law should not cause us to ignore its undeniable contributions. Law has forced the American campus to recognize serious problems of pay inequity and to discover practices which discriminate more subtly by limiting professional opportunity and mobility. It has often forced a beneficial effort to articulate quality standards with a precision that will limit the opportunities for arbitrariness. And it has given legal remedies and visible champions to victims of exclusionary practices.

I do not agree, as Father Hesburgh concludes by suggesting, that a new "law is needed." This is not a message of pessimism. The creation of new attitudes is not beyond us if the powerful laws already on the books are obeyed. I believe that they will be obeyed. Universities have internal incentives to maintain excellence, for which true equality of opportunity is prerequisite. They have increasingly powerful internal constituencies which are sensitive to problems of discrimination. And, perhaps most important, universities cannot avoid challenges in fulfilling human rights when they have been in the forefront of those battles for centuries.

Colleges and universities treasure values of self-governance, excellence, and professionalism. Civil rights enforcement agencies can be made sensitive to these values without compromising their own commitment to the law. I am confident that, with patience, the accommodation can be made.

The Social Influence of Legislative Acts

RUBY G. MARTIN

FATHER HESBURGH HAS WRITTEN—I believe, properly so—from the point of view of a white person who sees the importance of legislation as it

---

16. John Kaplan, *Marijuana: The New Prohibition* (New York: World Pub., 1970); T. Duster, *The Legislation of Morality: Laws, Drugs and Moral Judgment* (New York: Free Press, 1970).

affects white attitudes. Clearly, white persons and institutions continue to hold the keys to entrance into the first-rate colleges and universities, jobs, decent housing, and most of the other things that take one into the so-called mainstream of American life. Thus it is important that white people accept, understand, and be willing, at a minimum, to abide by social legislation—legislation that affects their individual and group conduct. My remarks are written—I believe, properly so—from the point of view of the importance and influence of legislation on black opportunities and black attitudes.

Legislation, especially as described by Father Hesburgh (with sanctions, teeth, and strong enforcement), is perhaps the most powerful weapon available to social engineers, not alone because of its immediate impetus for change, but also because of its long-range influence on the attitudes of future generations. Legislation establishes a pattern and a routine that, with each new generation, becomes more and more an integral part of the traditions and mores of our society. Certainly the first generation of Americans who were forced to give up a fixed percentage of their hard-earned wages to pay federal income taxes were resentful and annoyed, yet today—despite the arguments about rates, loopholes, inequities, and uses to which these general welfare funds are put—few argue the principle, because paying federal income taxes has come to be as American as apple pie. Even more important, the legislation creating a federal income tax set the stage for the multiple taxes that each of us pays every year as residents of states, counties, and municipalities, and every day as consumers.

The civil rights legislation of the 1960s, opening up as it did for blacks and other racial and ethnic minorities access to institutions of education, places of public accommodations, and public offices, afforded us our very first opportunity to enter into the mainstream of American life. But it did more than that; it created a new climate and atmosphere for our children, who now view their rights to access to facilities and services as being as American as apple pie. Indeed, most black youngsters under fifteen years old are astonished almost to the point of disbelief when they hear us talk about having to sit in the back of the bus, or about all the schools in Little Rock, Arkansas, being closed for a whole year simply because nine black high school students had, through the courts, been given the right to attend all-white Central High School. Indeed, the civil rights legislation of the 1960s is directly responsible for the new attitudes that prevail among the black and minority youngsters of the

1970s, who are, in camparison with their parents, strong, searching, adventurous, unafraid, and determined to forge better lives for themselves and for their children to come.

In my opinion, there is no question that the legislation which forced school integration in the South did a great deal to shape, indeed change, the attitude of black youngsters toward whites. The myths that all whites are smart, clean, honest, righteous, and moral crumble before the very eyes of black youngsters in integrated classes. Several years ago, a black mother from Mississippi whose first-grader was the only black in his class told me that each day that her son sat next to a white child she could see less and less fear in his eyes and more and more strength and courage in his outward manifestations, and she was proud.

In a broader context, the civil rights legislation of the 1960s changed the attitudes of blacks toward almost all of the institutions in our society. The all-white colleges and universities, which were once looked upon by blacks as untouchable bastions of intellect and power, were exposed as resenting change, not only with respect to their student bodies and faculties, but also with respect to their academic programs. In the early and middle 1960s few of these institutions indicated any concern about building into their ongoing program any social consciousness. At these institutions, it was clear to a black student of city planning that the institution was not concerned about the problems created for blacks by urban renewal, mass transportation, highways, and so on. And even now, many of these institutions will readily offer a course in black studies but will not deal with the special problems of blacks in their major courses of study.

Prior to the decade of the 1960s few blacks even understood the legislative process itself. And, in our jubilation over the *Brown* decision of 1954, the Civil Rights Act of 1964, and the Voting Rights Act of 1965, we failed to understand the need to keep a watchful eye not simply on the law alone, but on the regulations, guidelines, and policies to implement those historic pieces of legislation, and the result of this failure was devastating. That experience was an educational one for us, and we now are beginning to understand that laws are not self-operative and that we must protect our legislated rights all along the line from the legislator to the lowest bureaucrat. We are also beginning to understand the need to monitor and involve ourselves in legislation that does not have a civil rights tag on it, for often it is the non-civil-rights legislation that locks us in or out for years to come—the Higher Education Amendments of 1972 being a prime example. We also are beginning to have a healthy appreciation for the appropriations process because we have learned from experience that laws unfunded or underfunded are meaningless.

It is my belief that the revolution of the 1960s had its roots in the federal social legislation of the decade and that it radically changed the attitude of blacks toward white America. I believe that change is healthy because it laid the groundwork for the new black self-respect that we see all around us.

As a lawyer it is easy for me to say that laws are not intended to change the hearts and minds of the people they affect, that they are designed to govern conduct and behavior. But as a person who was an activist in the social struggle of the 1960s, and who continues to be concerned about the activities of the 1970s, I believe that attitudes are changing; I know that black attitudes are being reshaped. Administrators and policy-makers of institutions of higher learning who are grappling with minority recruitment programs, affirmative action plans, open enrollment, and the like must understand that the Charlayne Hunters and the James Merediths were the blacks of the 1960s, the heroes who withstood the abuses to implement the Civil Rights Act of 1964. The blacks of the 1970s frequently have no historical perspective (should they?) of gross racism, and thus their concerns are with their generation of racism or racism as they see it. They are building upon the social changes fought out during the last decade, although, perhaps, they do not realize it.

It is my hope that the white youngsters of the 1970s are going through similar attitudinal changes because of the legislation of the 1960s. For if they are, respect for individual differences and human rights in America will, like income tax and apple pie, be accepted as a long-standing American tradition.

The Time Is Now for Women's Equity

ANITA HUGHES

MY TASK IS TO REOPEN the matter of discrimination and to develop a case and plan for women's equity now.

We live in a period when it is no longer popular or respectable to articulate crude and primitive prejudices. Almost everyone has learned to talk inoffensively; too few have learned to think differently or to act positively; most people have simply adopted a new system of rationalization. Because good people do little or nothing, inequalities for all groups continue to hold sway. For this reason, laws alone will never be the ultimate solution; rather, the effects must be felt in the dark places of people's minds and hearts.

The purpose of legislation then is not to alter the attitudes of people initially but to influence their behavior. Laws are the manifest of the national purpose, and when government is unwilling or unable to provide them, there is no standard to which the wise and just may repair. Laws will prevent one person from acting out disrespect and hate by denying or withholding another's basic rights. Legislation adds the full force of law and of support to the many people who have wanted to do the right thing but have never felt strong enough to risk either the real or imagined consequences. Legislation allows the blame for changes to be placed impersonally on government or its representatives. Legislation provides the condition through which opposed persons come into contact with one another, causing some to lose their stereotypes and eventually change their attitudes, minds, and hearts.

SOME ASSESSMENTS

The women's equity movement faces two major problems, the first of which deals with a state of mind. Most decent persons understandably feel guilty about the problems of sex discrimination; they want to believe that they live in a truly open and free society where sex is no barrier. Therefore, there is at present a great danger that people will read into the new laws and regulations and into the removal of signs and symbols which so disturb them the conclusion that the problem is solved and all is well. The second major barrier has been created by generations of discrimination against women. The woman who fails to recognize sex discrimination or acts as though it does not exist is guilty of stupid chauvinism. And the man who ignores this reality or acts as though it does not exist is guilty of dishonesty.

As Americans, we find ourselves, even with our resources and prosperity, unable to understand chronic unemployment, the need for better education, health, and welfare systems, and the fact of islands of poverty in our sea of affluence. Though Americans assert a stated goal of freedom for human beings everywhere, it is still obvious that America is not proof of our intent. Women professionals are on trial and are being challenged to show that all of the freedoms that have been written into the Bill of Rights, all the freedoms that have been guaranteed in the Constitution, yes, and all of the slogans that we toss around, in fact, have life and meaning in our society.

Americans are suspect to the world, and our claim as world leaders may be based on false standards. We are learned in the art of war; we are ignorant in the art of peace. We are proficient in the art of killing; we are unskilled in the art of living. We probe and grapple with the mystery of life on other planets; we reject the Golden Rule and the Sermon on the Mount. And because of the developments in our capital, we are once again confronted with an American truism and way of life, "Thou shalt not get caught." America is an environment where it is all right to hate, to steal, to cheat, and to lie if we dress it up with symbols of respectability, dignity, and love. This unhealthy gap between what we preach in America and what we often practice has created a moral dry rot that eats at the very foundation of equity.

To Advance Women's Equity

The current women's equity revolution has the objective to broaden the application of the American dream to women citizens. This is a revolution against those who maintain that the measure of a person's achievement is determined by and related to sex. This is a revolution peculiarly characterized by a heroic drive and a courageous fight to gain the rights and respect that should be synonymous with the word "American." It is a revolution by people who are right against those who are wrong. This revolution is unlike others in that, after a lifetime of deprivation, the deprived seek redress for their grievances in an expression of faith in a nation that has done little to deserve and nurture such faith. Our demands are simple and elemental, and those who would describe them as difficult and complicated do a disservice to America and Americans.

Women's equity is long overdue. Equity is the presence of justness. Nothing is more immoral than the suggestion that women adjust to injustice or that we make a god of "timing." The time is always ripe to do right. Women's equity is no longer a hobby for the well-intentioned, the idle, or the status-seekers. The challenge must be met by professionals and practitioners and must be backed up by every thoughtful volunteer.

At this point when the scales of justness are so grossly unbalanced, they cannot be brought to balance simply by applying equal weight. We are talking about correcting the injustices of the past. We have to develop the law and affirmative action plans to silence those people who rationalize and say that they are against any form of preference. These same people have never said anything about zero percent quotas of women and 100 percent quotas of men. Laws and affirmative action plans are also necessary for those persons who say, "We don't discriminate; we have some women," for these same people will cite the use of quotas as an excuse for maintaining the status quo.

Out of years of suffering and deprivation, women have developed certain qualities—humanness, compassion, patience, and endurance—and certain values that can be useful to men. It was these qualities of perseverance, patience, resilience, of ability to adjust and adapt that were the sustaining pillars of all people, women in particular and men in general.

Women's equity is an opportunity for men to show to the whole world—for the first time—their maturity and their security. It is time for men consciously to proclaim the creative possibilities in that diversity from which they have consciously benefited.

What can be done to hasten fairness and justness for women?

1. Face the fact that your community does discriminate and view this not as a problem but as an opportunity for making great strides toward equality.
2. Make right, justice, and democratic process your objectives. Do not take a monolithic approach to the problem.
3. Understand what women want, but—even more important—realize that, as American citizens, our rights are both God-given and constitutionally guaranteed.
4. Do not use the tragic results of inequality to justify continuing inequity. Adopt criteria that are valid.
5. Understand that words like "gradualism" and "moderation" are results from, not methods of, working. Are your practices permitting each person to advance at as rapid a pace as abilities allow?
6. Do not become patronizing or condescending. Discuss sexism among staff, and acquaint staff with subtle and overt forms of sexism.
7. Work for the adoption of legislation and affirmative action plans so that with equal opportunity will go the opportunity to be equal. This step calls for adequate finances and staffing of the enforcement machinery.

The drive to be equal is a crusade for justice, for decency, for morality, honesty, and frankness. We in higher education are at a time when the alternatives to facing ourselves frankly and seeing our roles are clearly so tragic, so dangerous, so foolish, so irresponsible that even the most insensitive, the most blasé, or the most adept at rationalizing among us must stop and analyze both their attitudes and their actions or inactions and give battle to an overdue cause—women's equity.

The Moods of Academia

CLARK KERR

HIGHER EDUCATION in recent decades has gone through a series of cycles of development, each lasting about five to seven years. Each cycle has had one or two dominant themes. During World War II the theme was one of "standby" for the duration. Then came the GI rush with efforts to accommodate vast numbers of returning soldiers and to respond to their attitudes and aspirations. This was followed by a "return to normalcy," and by the "apathetic generation" of students. Then came the period of advance planning and of great growth to meet the "tidal wave" of students and adjust to the accent on science after Sputnik— the theme was "full speed ahead." This was followed by an abrupt change into a period of political protest and financial depression—it came like a bolt of thunder out of an almost cloudless sky. Now we are in a cycle of recovery and austerity, a time for looking inward and more at the immediate concerns of the present. What may the next turn of history bring? Most probably, it now seems, a period of change and transition. Such a period offers both opportunities and dangers, and thus requires careful consideration and wise judgments; it is a time to look outward as well as inward, at the future as well as the present. I should like to discuss how we may wish to approach this time of transformations, in what kind of a mood.

We probably all have on our shelves, read or unread, books with titles or subtitles like these staring out at us:

Academia in Anarchy (1970)
Academics in Retreat (1971)
Academy in Turmoil (1970)
American Universities in Crisis (1968)
Anarchy in the Groves of Academe (1970)

So much for some of those starting with *A*. Among the *B*'s, including one reprint:

Back to the Middle Ages (1969)
Bankruptcy of Academic Policy (1972)

> *Blow It Up* (1971)
> *Blind Man on a Freeway* (1971)

And among the *C*'s:

> *Chaos in Our Colleges* (1963)
> *Confrontation and Counterattack* (1971)

And among the *D*'s:

> *Death of the American University* (1973)
> *Destruction of a College President* (1972)
> *Degradation of the Academic Dogma* (1971)
> *Down and Out in Academia* (1972)

And among the *E*'s and *F*'s:

> *Embattled University* (1970)
> *Exploding University* (1971)
> *Fall of the American University* (1972)

And so on down the alphabet. They leave in the mind associated ideas like Academic—Anarchy; College—Chaos; Dogma—Degradation.

People in the past also were critical but they did not seem to strive so hard to display their criticism on their jacket covers, as though negativism would sell books in competition with sex. Veblen had his grave doubts but he called his book *The Higher Learning in America;* and Hutchins chose the same title for his attack; and Flexner used the neutral *Universities: American, English, German* for his aspersive comments.

One supposition might be that these titles were put on the books by their publishers in order to get wide distribution for them. Academic books, however, are mostly read—if at all—by academic people, and it gives one cause for thought as to why smart publishers think that smart academic people are more likely to read books if they have negative titles. Why?

But it is not just the promises held out by the titles—behind the scary titles lie some scary contents. Look inside:

> Indignation in some, passivity in others conspired to establish as a universal truth that the American university was an engine of oppression, rotten to the core, a stinking anachronism [from a former academic provost].[1]

> we sense acutely the tragedy that is occurring before our very eyes.... as if Nemesis had once again struck . . . [two university professors].[2]

---

1. Jacques Barzun, "Tomorrow's University—Back to the Middle Ages?", *Saturday Review*, Nov. 15, 1969, p. 25.

2. James M. Buchanan and Nicos E. Devletoglou, *Academia in Anarchy: An Economic Diagnosis* (New York: Basic Books, 1970), pp. xi, 168.

> Most of us . . . are beyond the point of mere rebelliousness and mere paralyzed dismay. The academy is already a shambles: we need devote no further energy to bringing it down [a former college professor].[3]

> Today's colleges are not worth the price. In fact, they are probably doing more harm than good . . . [a college professor].[4]

> there has arisen a despair that transcends simple description [a college professor].[5]

This is what some of our "best" and our "brightest" in higher education—defined as those who get books published—think about us. But not only they, so also some of those in power and close to power, some of those who have sold in Peoria and seem to have known what sells in Peoria. Some seem to have believed that higher education badly needed to be saved, was itself solely responsible for the fact that it needed to be saved, and that nobody outside could or would come to its rescue:

> And it is time for the responsible university and college administrators, faculty and student leaders to stand up and be counted, because we must remember, only they can save higher education in America. It cannot be saved by government . . . . Listen to this: If the war ended tomorrow, if the environment were cleaned up tomorrow morning, and if all the other problems for which government has responsibility were solved tomorrow afternoon—the moral and spiritual crisis in the universities would still exist [Speech, Kansas State University, September 16, 1970].[6]

Another high official, in an attack on the Scranton Commission report, said:

> responsibility . . . does not belong on the steps of the White House . . . [but] on the steps of the university administration building and at the door of the faculty lounge [Statement, September 29, 1970].[7]

And the wife of a then highly influential Cabinet member locked herself in her bathroom, called up a reporter, and had this to say:

> The academic society is responsible for all of our troubles in this country . . . . The whole academic society is to blame . . . . the profes-

---

3. Judson Jerome, *Culture Out of Anarchy: The Reconstruction of American Higher Learning* (New York: Herder & Herder, 1970), p. xviii.
4. Lawrence E. Langdon, *Can Colleges Be Saved? A Critique of Higher Education* (New York: Vintage Press, 1969), p. vii.
5. L. G. Heller, *The Death of the American University* (New Rochelle, N.Y.: Arlington House, 1973), p. 11.
6. Richard M. Nixon, speech reported in *New York Times*, Sept. 17, 1970, p. 28.
7. Spiro Agnew, as reported in *New York Times*, Sept. 30, 1970, p. 1.

sors in every institution of learning . . . . They are totally responsible for the sins of our children [September 20, 1970].[8]

Some of us say it about ourselves. Some of our elected leaders and those close to them say it about us. Is it true?

Yes, in part:

• Responsibility for the recent turmoil in the academy did lie at the doors of college presidents and faculty members, but at many other doors as well. Higher education is responsible for some of the unrest of youth, but so are many other elements of society. We should neither ourselves insist upon nor should we accept all of the blame.

• We did have the greatest series of episodes of campus unrest in American history; but not "anarchy"; and that period is now in the past —at least for the time being. Ending the draft and the war in Vietnam actually did help. The campuses, as institutions, have shown remarkable long-run organizational endurance; and their "moral and spiritual crisis" no longer seems to be so great, or at least so visible.

• We have entered a "new depression" financially—but not "bankruptcy"—at least not in many places; a "fragile stability" has been restored; and, throughout most of the history of higher education in the United States, it has been subject to genteel and sometimes to not so genteel poverty; "down" yes but not "out."

• We have fallen in the esteem of the American public, fallen badly for a time; but not "degradation" in the sense of public disgrace; and other institutions have lost favor as much or more, and the level of esteem for higher education may now be rising. A recent California Poll report, in a state where higher education has known its recent disappointments, starts out this way: "The California public today has a very high opinion of the value of a college education." Only 25 percent of those surveyed disagreed with the statement that "Colleges and universities are being blamed for a lot of things these days that aren't really their responsibility." And 80 percent disagreed with the statement that "The way colleges and universities are being run nowadays, a person is better off not going to one." These opinions, in what has been a bellwether state, are all the more surprising since the public learns about the campus largely from the news. And bad news—and there has been a lot of it—makes news more than does good news.

• We have our current problems, even crises—how to adjust to collective bargaining, how to handle tenure, how to absorb into our facul-

8. Martha Mitchell, as reported in *New York Times*, Sept. 21, 1970, p. 23.

ties more women and more members of minority groups, and many others; but we do not have "chaos"; and all these problems, given time and good judgment, are potentially subject to reasonable solutions.

• We do now experience a decline in the rising rate of student enrollments and the prospect of a decline in absolute numbers during the 1980s; and this will mean modest overall curtailment for a few years in the numbers to be taught, affecting some institutions much more than others, but not "retreat" for the system of higher education as a whole —not for its research, not for its service activities, not for its essential contributions to society in their totality.

• We are now faced with a less favorable job market for our graduates; but this does not mean "death" for our efforts at the higher education of youth. It does, however, mean many adjustments by many people.

Now I fully realize that I have used several of these terms in a different sense and context than employed by the authors themselves in their books; but I have been responding to the general tone of these many treatments of higher education, to their themes of derogation and even denigration rather than to their specific arguments.

Another set of words could have been employed in the titles of recent books on the state of higher education, and I think more accurately—words such as "The Campus Muddles Through" or "Modest Successes in Academia." Higher education has been and is going through a time of troubles, but it is more likely that it will survive and surmount the challenges it now faces than that it will decline and fall—those with visions of the Apocalypse to the contrary. There are some favorable signs as well as unfavorable:

• Students are generally satisfied or even very satisfied with their colleges and with the education they receive.

• Alumni also show general satisfaction with their college experiences.

• Faculty members nearly universally like their profession and their institutions, and would choose each again if they had the chance.

• State legislators, even at the height of student disturbances, showed considerable understanding of the problems of higher education and a desire to continue their support.

• The states have kept on appropriating funds for higher education in an almost unbroken rise in the burden placed on per capita personal income. It is remarkable what aid most states have given.

- Private contributions are at an all-time high.
- The federal government has, for the first time in history, committed itself to remove financial barriers to access to college, although the appropriations as yet are woefully inadequate.
- High school graduates who are blacks, for the first time in history, are entering college at the same rate as whites.
- Deficits in health manpower are being overcome quite rapidly with the full cooperation of higher education.
- The truly historic transition from the more selective arrangements of the past into a system of higher education where access is guaranteed for all high school graduates into some institution of advanced education, as is now the case in several major political jurisdictions, has been taking place with remarkably few difficulties considering the magnitude of the change.
- Enrollment rates are disappointing to many, but most of this is due to demographic changes that cannot and should not be reversed; and some quite temporary forces have also been at work, such as (1) the decline of military inductions which has added more to the civilian labor force than to college enrollments and thus has reduced the percentage of civilians in the age group who are in college, (2) lifting of the recession which has drawn more young persons into gainful employment, and (3) the significant rise in the "stop-out" rate (now apparently about 10 percent) with a temporary impact on enrollments. These short-run factors should not be cause for alarm. And the colleges can offset some of the longer-range demographic impacts by more consideration for community college transfers and for part-time enrollees and for adults. Also, the reduction of enrollment pressures will make it easier for the federal and state governments to finance equality of opportunity than would otherwise be the case.

I cite these facts not to argue that all is well, for it is not, but to note that there are grounds for hope as well as for despair, and that there are accomplishments as well as failures. I find myself much more in sympathy with the following evaluation by Alan Pifer than with that by the doom-sayers: "In view of the formidable burden the nation has placed on its higher educational system, the astounding fact is how well it has succeeded, not how badly it has failed . . ."[9]

9. Alan Pifer, "The Responsibility for Reform in Higher Education," *Educational Digest,* September 1972, p. 29.

Why then have so many within the groves of academe been so subject to the "doomsday syndrome"? Roger Heyns, last year in speaking to the American Council, ascribed it to "the masochistic need that is perhaps our [meaning the academics] most prominent common personality trait." Perhaps so; but perhaps we are just given to moods. Not so long ago we were euphoric—science would have the world and the campus was the "home of science"; growth would go on forever; there was an almost endless need for more Ph.D.'s; faculty salaries would keep on transporting us into a standard of living to which we would like to become accustomed; the university was the center of the postindustrial society—not the farm, not the factory, not the government bureau; and so on. There were few—hardly any—"Chicken Littles" then, when we needed some words of caution, and the sky subsequently did, for a time, seem to be falling down.

This swing in moods does raise some questions about the quality of our collective judgments, particularly since we are supposed to be, as academics, in a better position to view the long run more analytically and to see basic forces at work more objectively than almost any one else. It may turn out, however, that we are just as likely to project short-run circumstances into long-run laws of development as are nonacademics, perhaps even more so. To project the present unchanged into the future ignores the lessons of history; to do so in a crescendo fashion, like Ravel's "Bolero," does so to an even greater extent. As an example, we once overdid student apathy; then we overdid the students on the march to revolution; and now we may be overdoing the apathy theme again.

Some elementary truths we all know: (1) There are always adjustments that are made to any major development. (2) Nearly always there are countervailing forces at work. (3) Also, positive trends have their negative aspects, and negative trends have their positive aspects. (4) And there are surprises. Rothblatt, in writing about the University of Cambridge a century ago, noted:

> In a plural society, ... it is entirely possible that the university and society will be in subtle and complex states of disagreement as well as agreement with one another, that the direction of university change may not be completely obvious, that surprises will occur. It is entirely possible that disagreement and agreement together constitute the peculiar quality of the modern university.... A university which is being asked

to reform, but is still allowed a high degree of internal freedom, may restructure itself to acquire an identity which few expected.[10]

So also today.

The mood of the times on campus, and not just of the authors whose titles I have listed above but of many others as well, may have recently carried us too far along a one-track concentration on despondency. A. P. Herbert, during World War II, wrote a take-off on a strategic services training center under the title "Number Nine." One section was concerned with psychological testing. The participants were asked to show how their minds worked by starting in with a word given to them and then filling words into three subsequent blank spaces; to show how they associated ideas. One young lady had the same fourth word, for example:

| Shell | Fish | Oyster | Bed |
| Class | First | Sleeper | Bed |

For many in higher education today the sequence might start with "collective bargaining" and end up with "despair"; or with "tenure" and end up with "despair"; or with "budgets"; or with any one of a number of other key words and end up with "despair."

Should we just note this moodiness, if moodiness it is, as a possibly interesting but minor social phenomenon and then forget it? Or should it be a matter of concern? I believe it should be a matter for concern. First, because it has external impacts that can be harmful. If we do not believe in ourselves, how much should others believe in us, when we provide so many of our own self-chosen gravediggers and they are in such unseemly haste? Second, because it has internal impacts. The current mood of so many administrators is one of survivalism—to survive one more year, to keep, as Roger Heyns described it last year, a "low profile." The current mood of so many faculty members is to doubt the future, to hang onto past gains as best they can. There has been, as the Carnegie Commission states in its final report, "too much excessive, almost paralyzing, criticism."[11]

It takes social energy to carry out functions effectively, to undertake reforms, to prepare the way for a better future. An attitude of "back to the Middle Ages" or even, as I heard one academic person

10. Sheldon Rothblatt, *The Revolution of the Dons: Cambridge and Society in Victorian England* (London: Faber & Faber, 1968), p. 26.
11. *Priorities for Action: Final Report of the Carnegie Commission on Higher Education* (New York: McGraw-Hill, 1973), p. 83.

suggest recently, "back to the catacombs" for the sake of protection is less supportive of that necessary social energy than one of "ahead to the twenty-first century." It is, in any event, the twenty-first century, and not the Middle Ages, that lies ahead.

We always start from where we are. We cannot, even though we might like to, start from any place else. The course of the journey and the nature of the future destination are always uncertain; but both the journey and the destination are affected by how we approach them—in despair or in guarded expectation. We need less euphoria than we once had, and less despondency than we now have, and more realism than we have heretofore displayed.

These are historic times particularly with the transition—the first in the world—into universal-access higher education; with the end of the much more rapid growth for higher education than for American society as a whole that has marked our past history; and with the possible birth of new mentalities, challenging the traditional "work ethic" both in youth and in the general population. Higher education does continue to require many constructive changes; but it does not really need to be "saved." In fact, we now have more time, with the "tidal wave" of students and the wave of political dissent currently behind us, to think more about purposes, to concentrate more on constructive change, to emphasize quality rather than quantity, to bring equality of opportunity closer to reality, to improve governance, to give more attention to the effective use of resources, and to do much else.

To those who see only gloom and doom, we can say that much that is good is also occurring. To those who say that everything fails, we can say that much is, in fact, succeeding. To those who see only problems, we can say there are possibilities available for their alleviation.

Higher education is too vital a force in any modern society for us to be in despair about it; it provides too much in the way of skills and of research, and responds too much to the human desire to understand. These are sound bases on which to move forward with a sense of cautious confidence.

AMERICAN COUNCIL ON EDUCATION

Roger W. Heyns, *President*

The American Council on Education, founded in 1918 and composed of institutions of higher education and national and regional associations, is the nation's major coordinating body for postsecondary education. Through voluntary and cooperative action, the Council provides comprehensive leadership for improving educational standards, policies, and procedures.